What others are saying about this book:

Our criminal justice system often malfunctions when addressing the needs and rights of sexual abuse survivors. As a result, more and more survivors are turning to the civil courts in their search for justice. This wonderful new book—the first of its kind—outlines in readable, straight-forward language the many issues and procedures involved in suing one's sexual abuse perpetrator. I heartily recommend it to survivors, therapists, and attorneys.

John Briere, Ph.D.
Assistant Professor, USC School of Medicine
Author of *Therapy for Adults Molested as Children: Beyond Survival*

Shifting the Burden of Truth is an essential, empowering guide for any survivor who is considering or pursuing legal recourse for childhood sexual victimization. In a concrete, yet friendly manner, this book translates complex legal language into understandable terms, provides a realistic picture of legal processes, traditions and strategies, and offers many suggestions to help survivors make informed decisions, handle the stress of a lawsuit and increase the likelihood of a favorable outcome.

Wendy Maltz, M.S.W.
Author of *The Sexual Healing Journey*
Co-Author of *Incest and Sexuality*

This book, *Shifting the Burden of Truth*, comes at a perfect time for survivors, and for the therapists who want to be fully present for them. It speaks clearly and concisely not only to survivors' rights, but also to the intricacies and often inequities of the law. With respect, and always mindful of possible repercussions, the reader is led through a careful exploration of exactly what suing may entail. There is a real sense of empowerment for the survivor no matter what decision s/he makes. For professionals, this book forces us to look at our own fears and biases regarding taking legal actions. Through such exploration we are less likely to instill our own issues in our clients and more likely to be clear in our role with them.

Sharon L. Tobin, LCSW
Founder, *Safe Harbors Workshops*
Senior Staff, *Elisabeth Kubler-Ross Center*

To Kim, for never giving up in a fight she never asked for.

To Joe, for believing in me, sticking by me, and having the idea for this book and the determination to follow through.

**Suing Child Sexual Abusers—
A Legal Guide for Survivors
and Their Supporters**

Joseph E. Crnich, J.D.
Kimberly A. Crnich, J.D.

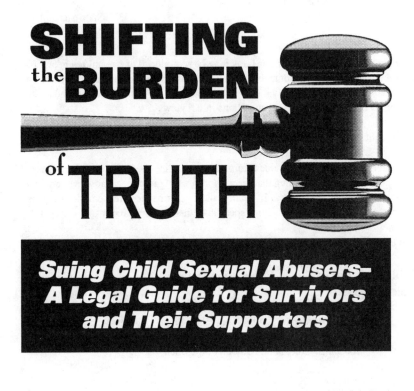

Shifting The Burden of Truth

Suing Child Sexual Abusers—
A Legal Guide for Survivors and Their Supporters

By Joseph E. Crnich and Kimberly A. Crnich

Published by:

333 S. State St., Suite 326
Lake Oswego, OR 97035, USA

Cover design by: Joseph E. Crnich

Publisher's Cataloging in Publication Data

Crnich, Joseph E.
Crnich, Kimberly A.
Shifting the Burden of Truth: Suing Child Sexual Abusers—
A Legal Guide for Survivors and Their Supporters /
Joseph E. Crnich and Kimberly A. Crnich
p. cm.
Includes index.
ISBN 0–9631608–3–4

1. Child Molesting—Law and legislation. I. Title.
2. Adult Child Sexual Abuse Victims—United States.
3. Incest Victims—United States.
4. Child Abuse—Case studies.

362.76 91–91468

COLOPHON

This book was created using Apple Macintosh® SE/30 and IIfx computers, Aldus PageMaker® 4.01 and Adobe Illustrator® 3.01 software, and a NEC Silentwriter 2 90®. The body style is Times 11 point on 14.1 point leading. Final text output was to a NewGen TurboPS 480®. The cover design was produced with Adobe Illustrator® 3.01.

Foreword

Child sexual abuse is, by its nature, an unjust act. Children are fondled, raped, humiliated, used and silenced by adults who can easily overpower and manipulate them. The fact that one in three girls and one in seven boys are sexually abused by the time they reach eighteen is a situation that cries out for justice. Yet for most survivors, there is little justice—not only do they have to bear the pain and anguish of the abuse, they must shoulder the burden of healing, too. Abusers, on the other hand, are rarely held accountable or forced to compensate for their crimes.

This is beginning to change. As the movement of adults healing from child sexual abuse continues to grow, more and more survivors are choosing to confront their abusers. Confrontations can be a powerful way to face the abuser and lay blame and responsibility where it belongs: "This is what you did to me. Here's how it's affected my life. Your selfishness and cruelty are at the root of my suffering. I remember. It was *you* who hurt me. I was a child. I was innocent. I did nothing wrong. *You did this to me and I hold you responsible.*"

Survivors have confronted their perpetrators in a variety of creative ways—in person, in a telegram, through an emissary, via Federal Express. One survivor recently told me she taped a picture of the abuser to the soles of her shoes, so she could have the pleasure of walking on his face. Another sent his father a videotape in which he outlined each incident of abuse, including the time, date and location.

Confronting the abuser can be a powerful, life-affirming experience, but it can also be terrifying. It is devastating to realize that the abuser (or your family, as the case might be) is probably not going to rally around you and support you in resolving your pain. There is little chance that the abuser will get down on his knees and say, "Oh honey, I'm so sorry. And can I pay for your therapy?"

The rewards from a confrontation are rarely gleaned from the abuser's response—which is usually one of denial, rationalization, silence or counterattack—but rather in the fact that you stand up as an adult, face the person you fear most, and speak the truth. The impact of breaking that silence is legendary. It changes lives. And as confrontations begin to take place in the public arena—in court, for instance—that change moves beyond the personal to the political arena.

Child sexual abuse does not exist in a vacuum—one abuser, one child, one troubled family, one individual survivor struggling to recover her sense of worth or his dignity. Child sexual abuse is not about each of us; it is about all of us. There are millions of us. Our pain is an epidemic. The solutions to epidemics are rarely personal—they are political—and radical—and must cut to the root of a society that allows these horrors to continue.

The legal system, as imperfect and unfair as it is, is still at the core of the American sense of justice. People look to the courts to determine innocence or guilt, to seek restitution, to right wrongs. It was only a matter of time before adult survivors sought redress through the courts for abuse they suffered as children. Laws governing the statute of limitations have been (and are being) challenged and changed nationwide. It is becoming increasingly possible for adult survivors to sue their perpetrators in civil suits, even if their abuse took place decades previously.

Adult survivors sue their abusers for a myriad of reasons. They want to publicly confront the abuse, force the perpetrator into treatment, stop abuse of children at risk today, get money to pay for therapy, "have their day in court," be vindicated, "make her pay for what she did to me," or raise public awareness about abuse. Depending on the laws of the state in question, the specifics of the abuse, the skill and knowledge of the survivor's attorneys, the response of the perpetrator, and the particular judge assigned to the case, some or all of these outcomes are possible.

If you are considering filing suit against your perpetrator, however, it is crucial to remember that our court system is not designed to sensitively and efficiently handle crimes perpetrated against children, particularly those that take place in the family. Survivors who've tried to take cases to court have been told they didn't have enough proof, that their state wouldn't allow such suits, "there's not enough chance of winning money to make your case worthwhile," that they'd waited too long, that no one would take their case, or that their abuse was "too bizarre to be believed in court." Others have gone to court and been subjected to brutal cross-examination, interminable delays, insensitive attorneys, abusers who could afford expensive lawyers and expert witnesses, or legal loopholes and technicalities that invalidated their claim.

I've personally spoken to dozens of adult survivors who've filed claims against their perpetrators in civil court. Some say it was the most empowering thing they could have done; that they felt vindicated in a unique and public way; that they felt good knowing they'd done something powerful to change the legal system and the society. Others said the court experience was devastating and definitely not worth the pain, exposure, and emotional trauma involved. Many others have considered suing, but felt the time constraints imposed by the statute of limitations (even when extended) didn't afford them enough time to wait to bring suit until they were emotionally stable enough to handle it.

The decision to sue your abuser, just like any decision to confront, should be made carefully with forethought and planning. Entering the legal system as a victim of sexual abuse is not something to be done lightly or naively. It is important to be informed about the possible pitfalls and problems inherent in bringing a challenge through the courts. Fortunately, you are holding in your hands an excellent guidebook to the process. *Shifting the Burden of Truth* is a clear source of guidance and information for adult survivors who are considering legal action against their perpetrator. Written in language a layperson can understand, *Shifting the Burden of Truth* offers a step-by-step analysis of the court process, demystifies legal terminology, and helps you explore the pros and cons of suing the abuser. It is a supportive and clarifying guide for making an informed decision about taking legal action. Once you've decided to sue, *Shifting the Burden of Truth* will help you each step along the way.

Fighting back against abuse in the larger world is an empowering and necessary choice. There are many ways to embrace activism and say no to abuse. Going to court is one. If your healing and activism lead you to take action through the courts, Joe and Kim Crnich's guide will prove an invaluable and welcome resource.

Laura Davis
Santa Cruz, California
November 1991

Preface

The beginnings of this book started many years ago, although I had no idea at the time. The memories of my own abuse surfaced years after I graduated from law school. During law school I had plans of pursuing an advanced law degree in taxation and had anticipated a professional career as a corporate lawyer. If told by a fortune teller five years ago that I would be writing a book on the rights of survivors of childhood sexual abuse and acting as a victims' advocate, I would have vehemently rejected any such prophesy.

All that changed dramatically when I experienced my first flashback of childhood sexual abuse several years ago. My ordered, structured world was turned upside down, inside out, backside front. I struggled to maintain my professional competence as flashbacks tumbled nightly to my forefront, causing me to question everything—my past, my future, myself. Out of that distraught, traumatic period came a change in direction for me. I had to find a way to help, a way to make a difference. My prior career interests faded and a new future started to shape. I left a commercial law position to teach in a law school clinic for domestic violence victims.

During that year I began considering the possibility of suing my abuser in civil court. Although both my husband and I are lawyers, I was paralyzed in my decision-making process. When I tried to think rationally about the choice, fear would overwhelm me and I would shake, cry, and feel like running away. My thoughts would become confused and I'd have a feeling of being in a trance. My years of legal training apparently were useless to me. I struggled with difficult questions like: "Can I withstand the emotional upheavals of a law suit?," "Can my marriage survive such a process?," "Can I put my siblings through the publicity?," "Can I live with myself if I did nothing, especially because I'm a lawyer?," "Will I prevent any chance my family could heal?," "Will my abuser follow through with the threats of harm for telling that he made to me as a child?," "Will my friends and supportive relatives stick by me?," "Will this destroy my career?," and the biggest question, "Will suing help or hurt my own healing?"

I began searching for attorneys who had represented survivors in civil court so I'd have first-hand information about these cases. To deflect my personal terrors about the issue, I conducted the research as an "objective" law professor writing a professional legal article. I interviewed numerous attorneys who were representing or had represented survivors in civil suits. Sometimes I disclosed that I was a survivor, and sometimes I didn't. I always asked how the attorney began taking adult survivor cases, and in many cases the attorney would disclose that he or she was a survivor and wanted to help other survivors. From that project I wrote a law review article for attorneys representing adult survivors of childhood sexual abuse.

My husband (this book's co-author) suggested getting my research findings to a broader audience than a legal journal would reach. I had toiled desperately with my own decision-making process without the benefit of any books on the topic. In particular, I would have greatly appreciated accounts by survivors who had sued their abusers that disclosed information such as: how they perceived the legal process, the likelihood that they would file suit again if they'd known at the beginning what it would be like, the value they perceived of suing, and any advice they might have about the process. We began another study, this time directed nationwide to both attorneys and survivors, and out of that work comes this book.

A year ago I contacted an attorney to represent me in a civil suit. The legal process is slow, and I have no resolution at this point. At the request of my abuser, I have been evaluated by an objective psychiatrist and psychologist and taken numerous psychiatric and psychological tests, from the "ink blot" test to I.Q. tests. The evaluations have all stated that I have the symptoms of being abused from well before the age of five up through adolescence.

For me the legal system means power and empowerment. I now believe that my interest in attending law school was to a large degree derived from my own childhood abuse. A hidden, terrified inner part believed that a law degree would somehow make her safe. That part believed that the abuse was her fault, that she would have to legally defend herself some day, and that a doctorate of law would restore the power stripped from her by her abusers. A law degree did not restore all my self-worth or heal my memories, but a law degree does allow me to analyze legal problems and to write books like this.

I can control neither what my attorneys will recommend that I do nor what witnesses, judges, and juries will think or decide. But I do have control over my writing and can offer this book to the healing movement. My hope is to help other survivors, and their supporters, who are struggling with the decision of whether or not to sue. I envision a future world in which children are safe enough that our book will no longer be needed. Let's make it so.

Please take good care.

Kim Crnich
December 22, 1991

WARNING—DISCLAIMER

This book was written to provide information about the subject matter covered. It is sold with the explicit understanding that the publisher and the authors are not engaged in rendering legal or other professional advice or services. If legal or other professional assistance is required, the services of a competent professional should be sought.

This book does not contain all information available to the publisher and authors, but is written merely to give a basic understanding about the topic. You are urged to research other materials for additional information that may be helpful or necessary for your individual circumstances.

As stated throughout the book, if you are a survivor reading this book it is imperative that you contact an attorney as soon as possible if you are considering filing a civil suit. Statutes of limitations impose deadlines covering when you must bring a civil suit and vary by state. Do not assume that your time periods for filing such a suit have expired, even if, after reading this book, it appears that your time periods have expired, because individual courts and judges may construe statutes of limitations liberally. A competent professional should be consulted to review your particular facts.

The purpose of this book is to give general information to help survivors and their supporters in assessing whether legal means will aid healing from childhood sexual abuse. The authors and Recollex Publishing shall have neither liability nor responsibility to any person or entity with respect to any loss or damage caused, or alleged to be caused, directly or indirectly, by the information contained in this book.

If you do not wish to be bound by this disclaimer,
you may return this book to the publisher for a full refund.

Acknowledgments

Joe and Kim:

First, we would like to acknowledge and thank all the attorneys and survivors who responded to our questionnaire or talked to us. To the survivors, we are honored that you chose to share such a personal part of your life, and we thank you for helping give the book a more human face through the survivors' stories section and general comments throughout the book. To the attorneys, our thanks for taking the time to donate your comments, and our respect for being willing to take cases that cause much emotional strain. We would also like to acknowledge the attorneys and supporters who were unable to be a part of the research, for whatever reason. None of this is easy for any of us.

To Jan Lindeman, Mary Rex, Betty Button and Allen Dietz, who provided couple support during the healing process and allowed us to recognize and honor commitment in marriage.

To J. Martin Burke, Dean of the University of Montana School of Law, who respected our career paths, encouraged us to write, and helped us to imagine more opportunities than we dared dream.

To Bard Michaels, for professional input into the role of attorneys and therapists in litigation, and for his wonderful sense of humor, of play, and of zest for life.

To Deeta Lonergan and Marcia Shannon, who helped us explore career options, see a broader range of possibilities, and consider becoming writers.

To the peers, colleagues, and supporters who offered manuscript commentary, critiques, or encouragement, including Frank Carrington, Rick Drummond, Gloria Steinem, Elizabeth Morgan, Jill Otey, Mickey Morey, Katherine O'Neil, Lee Atterbury, William Barton, Sally Goldfarb, Mary Beth Williams, Mark Panitch, Christine Courtois, Claudia Black, E. Sue Blume, John Briere, Wendy Maltz, Kelly and Patti Barton, Laura Davis, Carol Stephens, Mary Allman, Judith Armatta, Diana Craine, Shelby DePriest, Scott Sorensen-Jolink, Nancy Walseth, Pat Mickiewicz, and Shari Clark.

To Pat Myers, who provided a space for a writing retreat in Montana, encouraged us to proceed, reminded us of the special love of animals, and nudged us to start writing each morning.

To Mary Paige Rose, who came into our lives during a period in which we were overwhelmed, surrounded by disorganized paperwork, behind schedule, and frazzled, for reminding us that we can't do it all.

To Larry and Lisa Crnich, for opening their hearts and their home to us and for encouraging Kim that she could survive.

To Brad, for his wonderful drawings of dogs and tap-dancers to cheer Kim up, and to Joey, for reminding Kim to look at the colors of the rainbow, and to both of them, for providing us with insights into child-play without trauma.

To Therese Gustin and Lisa Crnich, who, despite jobs, toddlers, and newborns, found time to proofread the final copy of this book.

Kim:

I have so many people to acknowledge for help in writing this book and for help in getting me to this point in one piece. I'm sure to forget some, and I want them to know that I thank them, too.

To my therapists, without whom I would not be here. To

Rosemary, who began this journey with me and, by providing a safe, believing place, allowed the first child part to speak. To Bonnie Wickes, with whom I recovered extensive abuse and who started my healing work through art. To Carol Lambert, who helped me continue my healing through art work and understood my deep grief at the loss of a pet. To Mary Beth Williams, who helped me through a transition phase of healing. To Antonia Rathbun, who has a special insight into recovery paths and the role of artistic expression.

To Sharon Tobin of Safe Harbors Workshops and all the staff who helped me survive critical periods, including Shannon, Connie, Phyllida, Nancy(s), Dave, Ann, Larry, Kay, Sheila, and Paula. Their workshops provided a space for me to be safe, go through flashbacks, and find reasons to continue living.

To my attorney, Don Harris, a "carrel mate" in law school who believed in me enough to represent me in my own legal proceedings.

To Judy Wolf, from whom I learned to dream more and to try for things I never thought I could obtain, and to the Women's Law Fellowship, which provided role modeling for advocacy work.

To Patricia, who talked me through 3 a.m. flashbacks over the telephone, helped me pack a household in Alaska and get it, a car, and two dogs to Washington, D.C., let me crash on her sofa bed for a week in a clinical depression, and who has been a cherished companion, friend, and "sister."

To Jill Hitchner, for her friendship as a roommate during college, her concern for and belief in me as I struggled with the reality of my past, and for offering technical expertise in editing the manuscript.

To other dear friends who have believed me, been concerned about me, listened to my pain, and cared that I live, including Alexis Gabay, Francine Harbour, Linda Stevens, Jeanne Danison, Bernadette Janet, Diane Smith, Betty Button, Judy Hursh, Kathryn Reid, Marjorie Black, Angela Butkus, Denise Grills, Kay Gouwens, Peter Maassen, and Lisa Lanphere.

To Jim, for encouraging me to ask why since childhood, and to Susan, who's been willing to listen objectively, offer suggestions, and not give up on me.

To Terry, for caring, and to my mother, who died too young.

To Joan Bjeletich, for finding experts to help in my physical and emotional healing, and for her joyous outlook on life, and for Pat Dixon and Pam Peterson, for keeping me a part of the family, despite my disclosures.

Joe:

To my friends at SERP, who have been very supportive and encouraging about this project, despite its demands on my time.

To Walt Garretson, my former law partner, who showed great grace and understanding when my path took me elsewhere.

To Bonnie Matlock and Debbie Maxon, old friends who have always listened and remained close, regardless of the lengthening of the years, my lack of correspondence, or geographical distance.

To Linn French, a good and true friend with a wonderfully humorous, twisted, and positive conception of the human condition.

To the group at the OAAP, for listening repeatedly to the demented rantings of a seriously stressed budding author.

To my mother, Betty Crnich, for imparting the love of absorbing thoughts on paper. I hope she would approve of this attempt to give some back.

To my father, Ed Crnich, for his unfailingly positive reinforcement and encouragement about everything I've attempted.

To all those listed before, and the many others, who have helped us through recovery and through the birth of this book.

Contents

Introduction

What Is This Book About?

What Can I Expect to Get Out of This Book?

You have been wronged, terribly wronged. Someone in whom you justifiably placed great trust betrayed this trust and hurt you in ways you didn't understand at the time of betrayal. If:

- you discovered several years after the fact, through the use of reasonable diligence, that your business partner ran off with the company funds, you could have found justice through the courts in almost any state at any time in the past 50 years and recovered for this breach of trust;

- a doctor operated on you and left surgical implements inside you, and you could not have known they were there until years later when you developed strange symptoms, you could have found justice through the courts in almost any state at any time in the past 25 years and recovered for this negligence;

but if:

- you were a victim of child sexual abuse who repressed the memories of the abuse out of psychological necessity, you would have found no justice in *any* court in the United States until the mid-1980s.

Fortunately, this inhumane incongruity in the law is rapidly becoming a thing of the past.

Societal awareness of the prevalence of child sexual abuse has recently reached an unprecedented level. Since the Women's Movement of the late 1960s first freed many women to speak out about their lives, the reality and scope of previously denied atrocities such as rape, family violence, and child sexual abuse has become disturbingly more apparent. Increasing numbers of adult survivors have publicly told their stories of child sexual abuse, and the professional therapeutic community has responded by publishing a growing number of books discussing methods of healing.

Current research has produced varied but, nonetheless, staggering results regarding the prevalence of childhood sexual abuse, ranging from 6% to 62% of females and from 3% to 30% of males. Some therapists are finding that boys are abused at a rate that approaches the rate of abuse of girls. Child sexual abusers are mostly people known to the family. Some studies show that 75-85% of child sexual abusers in this country are family members and friends. Child sexual abuse is a tremendous social problem causing severe, and often lifelong, suffering to survivors.

What You'll Find in This Book

This book addresses issues and problems that face adults who sue their childhood sexual abusers in civil court. It does not address the related topics of physical abuse of children, emotional abuse of children, abandonment, or psychological or psychiatric therapeutic treatment of victims, unless these issues are addressed in a lawsuit about childhood sexual abuse. This book covers both cases involving **incest** and cases involving sexual abuse by strangers. In using the term *incest*, we are indicating a more inclusive definition of the term than is typically understood by the general public. This book covers situations in which the perpetrator and child/victim are related in some way (the traditional definition of incest) and also those in which sexual abuse is committed by non-related parties who have an emotional bond with the child/victim.

Incest

the imposition of sexually inappropriate acts, or acts with sexual overtones, by— or any use of a minor child to meet the sexual or sexual/emotional needs of—one or more persons who derive authority through ongoing emotional bonding with that child; *See* E. Blume, *Secret Survivors: Uncovering Incest and Its Aftereffects in Women* (1990).

Incest cases differ in their particulars from cases of sexual abuse by strangers. Unless otherwise noted, however, the same principles apply to cases involving perpetrators who are complete strangers that apply to incest cases. To indicate sexual abuse that is perpetrated on any child, we have used the all-inclusive phrase *child[hood] sexual abuse.*

This book is written primarily for survivors of childhood sexual abuse, as a guide to help determine whether lawsuits against their perpetrators are possible or advisable. It should also be useful to supporters of, and advocates for, survivors, such as therapists and attorneys. It touches upon issues involved in criminal proceedings against perpetrators, but does not address these issues comprehensively.

Legal terminology is complex and full of subtle meanings. This book uses standard legal terms to ensure that an accurate legal description of each situation and legal doctrine is provided to the reader. To further aid the reader in understanding these concepts, we have provided definitions, examples, tips, and personal stories of survivors who have sued their abusers. These additional types of information are identified by the following.

Tips are useful pieces of information or actions that survivors can take to help themselves. They are found in the main body of the text, with this symbol in the outside margin.

Personal stories are found both in the main body of the text (in italics, set off by double horizontal lines at their beginnings and ends) and in Chapter 8, "Case Histories." These stories are true stories of survivors or attorneys who have gone through the civil trial process in a child sexual abuse case, and are written in the survivor's or attorney's own words, where possible.

These stories are always marked by this symbol in the outside margin.

Examples are found in the main body of the text. Examples are fictitious stories used to illustrate legal principles.

Examples are set off by thick horizontal lines at their beginnings and ends, and with this symbol in the outside margin (with the topic identified inside the symbol).

Defined legal terms

a term with a definition in the margin, like this

Defined legal terms are set out in **bold** type in the main body of text, with the term in italics, followed by its definition, in a box to the outside of the emboldened text. Defined legal terms are also included in Appendix A. The index lists the page on which each term is defined. We have provided definitions in this manner so if you understand a legal term, you can continue reading without interruption.

Please understand that different **jurisdictions** use different definitions for the legal terms defined here and use procedures that differ from those mentioned in the examples and stories. The differences can range anywhere from slight to extreme, so you should not depend on these definitions and descriptions as being legally binding in your area.

Jurisdiction

Definition

a legally recognized area governed by a specific set of laws (*e.g.*, Missouri, the Western District of Washington); *also*, authority to hear and decide a case

We use the terms *victim* and *survivor* interchangeably, to indicate those people who have been subjected to incest. Similarly, we also interchangeably use the terms *perpetrator* and *abuser* to indicate persons who subject children to incest. *Suit, case, lawsuit*, and *action* are also used as synonyms for a civil lawsuit. *Attorney* and *counsel* are also interchangeable.

Victims of childhood sexual abuse are both male and female, and perpetrators of childhood sexual abuse are both men and women, but research indicates that most victims of such acts are women, and that the perpetrators are primarily men. However, because both males and females can be either perpetrators or victims, this book does not refer to either as *he* or *she.* Unless otherwise specifically noted, references to *victims* and *perpetrators* apply equally to male victims and female perpetrators.

Statute of limitations

the time within which a particular legal *claim* must be filed in a particular jurisdiction

Members of the legal and therapeutic professions are referred to as both *he* and *she*, interchangeably, as both males and females act as both victims' and perpetrators' counsel, as judges, and as therapeutic counselors.

Attorneys who either have experience representing survivors in cases against their abusers, or want to represent survivors, are listed in Appendix B.

How This Book Is Designed to Be Used

This book is meant to give a general understanding of the issues, terms, and processes involved in a suit against a perpetrator and of your rights as a survivor. **This book is neither intended, nor should it be used, as a replacement for an attorney.** The legal principles and procedures set out in this book are defined in their most commonly understood or used meanings. However, you should not assume that any of these definitions is the law in your jurisdiction.

If you want to make or preserve a legal claim against your perpetrator, seek advice from an attorney licensed in your jurisdiction as soon as possible. Laws limit the time period in which an injured person can bring a legal action against a wrongdoer in sexual abuse cases as well as other types of cases. The time periods (**statutes of limitations**) are discussed more thoroughly in Chapter 2. Once the time period has run out you will no longer be able to sue your abuser because your **cause of action**

Cause of action

a right to bring a legal action because of some injury that was caused by another party; also known as a *claim* or *claim for relief*

will have expired. It is, therefore, very important to contact an attorney as soon as you are emotionally and financially able.

The book's chapter titles and subtitles are written as a series of questions you should ask yourself while deciding whether to take legal action. The text that follows each of the subtitle or title questions will give you more information and guidance. Commonly asked questions about the legal process in child sexual abuse cases are answered in Chapter 9.

This book covers a topic that is difficult and may evoke strong emotional responses, in particular to the survivors' stories. Please remember that you don't have to read the book straight through in one sitting. We encourage you to take whatever breaks and to get any support you may want or need.

Chapter 1

Should I Sue?

Am I Ready to Sue?

The decision of whether to sue is a very personal choice. You, and you alone, must make the ultimate decision of if and when to sue.

If you have recently remembered your abuse after years or decades of repressing your memories, you may be filled with conflicting thoughts about your abuser. Anger, resentment, hatred, and loathing may be seething inside you. You may also have financial difficulties after months or years of therapy and meager earnings caused by the abuse. You may want to sue to stop the pattern of abuse by having your abuser's actions brought to public attention. If your abuser is a close relative, you may feel the conflicting emotions of sorrow or love for your abuser, and want to shield him or her from the fallout of a public confrontation.

Because the emotions associated with the retrieval of memories of childhood sexual abuse are so conflicting, you will probably need to go through several months or years of therapy to reach emotional and psychological stability after first remembering being abused. During early therapy, public confrontation of your abuser may very well be counterproductive to your recovery.

Before you decide that filing suit is one of the first things you should do, review the steps in a lawsuit set out in Chapter 4 and the subsection titled "Emotional Needs" in this chapter so you'll have an idea of what to expect from the process, which can be fairly brutal. If it is at all possible, you and your therapist should discuss how your recovery is progressing, and use your therapist's recommendation about your emotional readiness to file suit as a guide for when to sue. For most survivors, suing their abusers should be one of the last steps in their recovery, and definitely not the first.

As noted in the Introduction and in Chapter 2, laws limit when you can sue. To be able to win your suit, you must file your suit before these limits expire, but filing suit before you are emotionally ready to sue may be far more psychologically and emotionally detrimental to you than filing no suit at all.

Why Sue?

Lawyers often say that you can sue anybody at any time for any reason. Although said somewhat in jest, this idiom is essentially true. (Of course, just because you can sue for any reason doesn't mean you'll win.) **Plaintiffs** have a variety of reasons for bringing legal actions against **defendants**, ranging from a need to recover money to the desire to advance a principle in which they believe. Your reasons necessarily will be personal, but you should understand them clearly *before* beginning your lawsuit.

Plaintiff

a person who files a lawsuit against someone else; the party who is initiating the legal action

A clear understanding of what you want to get out of a lawsuit is important, because not all goals are attainable through a lawsuit. Even if it is theoretically possible to attain one of your goals by suing, you should be aware of the likelihood of attaining that goal before you sue. You should also consider the negative consequences of filing a lawsuit, such as emotional strain.

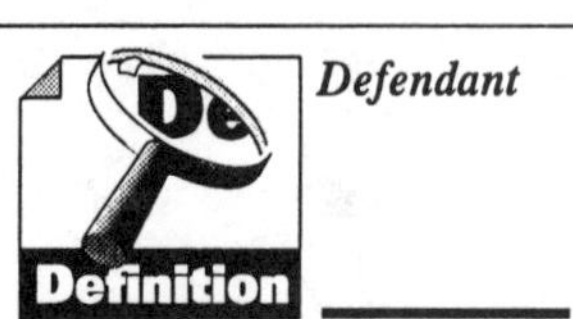

Defendant

a person against whom a lawsuit is filed; the party who is defending in the legal action

You may be seeking to recover money for damages caused by your abuse, such as money spent on therapy, time lost from work, or money you expect you'll have to spend in the future to cover therapy. You may want to sue for emotional reasons, such as a desire to publicly confront your abuser or to finally assert your autonomy from, and power over, him or her. You may be hoping to protect other children from your abuser. You may be trying to force your abuser into therapy so your family will have a chance to heal. These and other positive outcomes are sometimes possible through a civil suit against your perpetrator.

The likelihood of any of these outcomes, however, varies from state to state and case to case. None of these outcomes are guaranteed in any particular case or place. You must understand that you will probably not be able to achieve all of these goals. Therefore, it's important to ask yourself as honestly as you can, if possible with the aid of your therapist, what you really want out of your lawsuit. Your attorney will tell you, after studying the facts of your particular case, if what you want is possible, and if so, its likelihood of occurrence.

Discovery

the formal legal process of learning what the other party has or knows that will have a bearing on the case; *also*, the techniques allowed under the law to find this information, such as interrogatories, depositions, requests for production of documents, and requests for admission

Interrogatory

a question asked by one party, through his or her attorney, of another party, through his or her attorney, that relates in some way to the issues involved in a civil lawsuit; it must be answered under oath (usually administered by a notary public); generally several questions are asked in one set of interrogatories

What Do I Expect From the Legal Process?

The popular media have both glorified and overdramatized the role of law and lawyers in our society. Almost everyone can identify Perry Mason and correctly state that he was a brilliant courtroom adversary. Very few people, however, understand even in general how the legal machinery works. Fewer still could describe a single **discovery** technique, such as an **interrogatory** or a **deposition**, and tell you its importance to a

Deposition

oral questioning, under oath, by one party's attorney of another party or other witness, generally well in advance of trial, to determine the facts as the witness remembers them; similar to trial questioning, except that the questioning can be broader than what is allowed at trial; participants include attorneys for all parties, a witness (to be questioned), and a court reporter

lawsuit. The law in the real world is much more about mundane paper skirmishes involving discovery methods than glorious courtroom cross-examination battles.

One of the most profound illusions created by movies, radio, and television is that lawsuits are filed and decided within weeks or even days. Modern television trial attorneys such as those on *L.A. Law* seem to get cases before judges within the same hour that they first learn their clients' names. Unfortunately, this is pernicious Hollywood literary license. A real case takes anywhere from several months to several years to get from the filing to the ultimate decision, and the average case of any size or magnitude—which includes most child sexual abuse cases—tends toward the latter length.

Litigant

a participant in a lawsuit; a *party*

What Are My Needs?

Emotional Needs

A **litigant** in any lawsuit faces a roller coaster of emotions, from elated highs when a helpful witness is found to dismal lows when a preliminary **motion** or final verdict is lost. No matter how strong you are, the litigation process will have an emotional impact on your life.

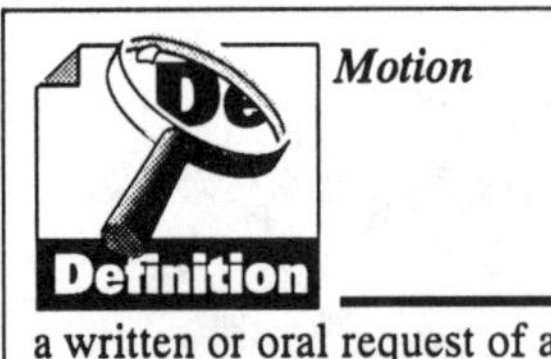

Motion

a written or oral request of a court to take some action

Trial

a public determination of one person's liability to another person (in a *civil action*), or guilt (in a *criminal action*) for a wrong committed

If you have gone through therapy or other recovery work to help heal the wounds from child sexual abuse, you undoubtedly have already gone through an upheaval of emotions. A lawsuit almost certainly will open up these emotions again. You will have to tell your attorney all the details of the abuse. Most likely you will also have to tell the facts several additional times during depositions, preparation for **trial** and, if the case does not settle, during the trial. With luck, your attorney will be supportive as you tell the facts, but at other times you will be testifying in an adversarial atmosphere. Your abuser and your abuser's attorney probably will do everything they can to discount your testimony. They may try to confuse you. They will look for inconsistencies to try to prove that you are lying, and they may attempt to blame or shame you. Unlike a supportive, nurturing therapeutic setting, the litigation process often re-victimizes the victim.

Additionally, the judge may allow the perpetrator's attorney to question you about your past conduct, especially any kind of trouble you may have had with the law, either as a child or as an adult. This information may be **discovered** if it is **relevant** to the lawsuit. Similarly, your past and present sexual conduct and relationships may also be questioned. Some states have passed victim protection laws that prevent questions about past sexual conduct, such as **rape shield statutes**. Although the job of the survivor's attorney is to act as a buffer between the survivor and the abuser/abuser's counsel, you must understand that you may have to discuss some of your life's most personal areas under grilling questioning.

You may be subjected to physical and/or mental examinations by **experts** hired by the perpetrator. If your mental or physical health is relevant to the case, which it usually is, the court has the power to order such examinations. Lawyers generally recognize that an expert can be found somewhere to say something favorable for the side hiring them. These "hired guns," although they are well educated and trained individuals, may or may not be scrupulous in their findings and could greatly confuse a jury if the *perpetrator's* expert says you're "crazy," while *your* expert identifies you as a survivor of abuse. Even if the perpetrator's expert is diligent and honest, he or she may not be aware of current research about child abuse and, therefore, incorrectly label your symptoms. Either way, your sanity or trustworthiness may be made the

Discovered

information found through the process of *discovery*

Relevant

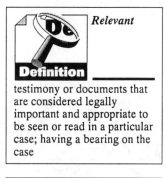

testimony or documents that are considered legally important and appropriate to be seen or read in a particular case; having a bearing on the case

Rape shield statute

law in some jurisdictions that protects rape survivors from being questioned about their sexual experience before the rape incident

Expert

a person hired because of his or her special skill, training, or experience to give guidance to an attorney and/or testify at trial

issue, which may subject you to extreme stress.

In addition to the harassment you will probably face from your abuser's attorney and experts during the case, you must also be prepared to handle society's stereotypes about child sexual abuse. Victims are often not believed. Parents and other people who care for children are often accorded more credibility than they deserve. In the process, victims are usually "bashed" to preserve peoples' ideas of what reality is, regardless of what the facts are.

Discoverable

information capable of being found through the process of *discovery*

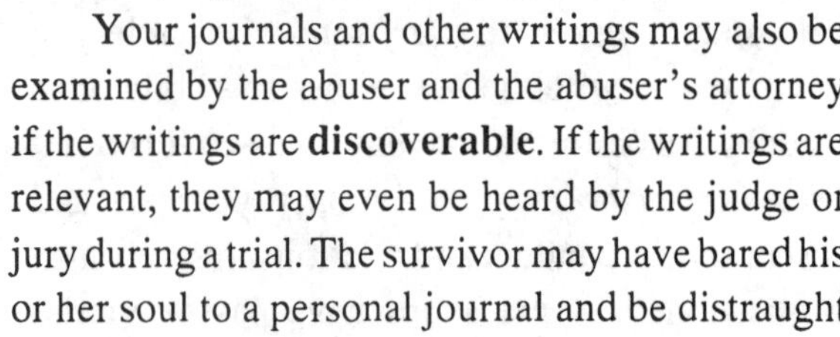

Your journals and other writings may also be examined by the abuser and the abuser's attorney if the writings are **discoverable**. If the writings are relevant, they may even be heard by the judge or jury during a trial. The survivor may have bared his or her soul to a personal journal and be distraught to have the abuser and others read it, yet in most cases a survivor must be willing and emotionally able to have such writings be seen.

Alleged

claimed; not yet proven; see *allegations*

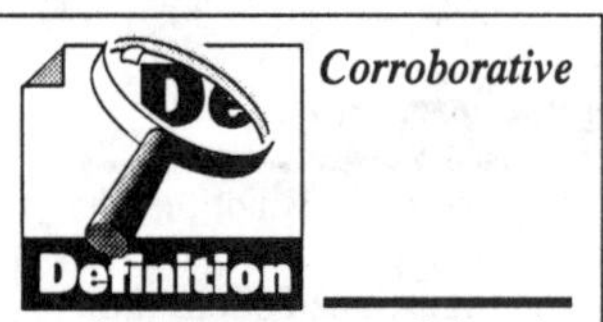

Corroborative

tending to support a claimed fact

Intimate partners of the survivor may also be drawn into the litigation if the abuser attempts to show that the survivor's emotional trauma is caused by some other source than the **alleged** abuse. Evidence of sexual difficulties or dysfunctions (which are very common with survivors) may be relevant, allowing the abuser's attorney to inquire about those topics (and possibly question sexual partners). Of course, such sexual difficulties may be used by your own attorney as **corroborative** proof that the abuse happened, but you must realize that bringing a lawsuit is a public airing of intimate areas of your life.

Some readers at this point may seriously question the value of suing. Perhaps you have finally begun to reach a peaceful point in your life after years of intense therapy. A lawsuit will result in revisiting the painful facts of the past. You will be reminded, at least intermittently, of your abuse for a lengthy period, as many courts are so overloaded that a trial cannot be heard for several years. If the suit continues for years, though, you won't often be directly involved.

During a lawsuit, the vast majority of time is spent waiting for court decisions and other deadlines, and your attorney will handle most of the face-to-face confrontational aspects of the suit.

Some survivors have reported getting stronger as the litigation process continued, making obstacles that appeared insurmountable in the beginning much more manageable later on in the process. For example, emotionally draining as questioning during the course of a case can be, one survivor was greatly empowered by witnessing her abusive father nervously fidgeting as he was asked difficult questions. If your attorney/therapist/client relationship is strong and takes care of your needs, great personal empowerment can result. Although no case's outcome is a certainty, and you may lose your case, just the chance to sue your abuser might lead to empowerment that you can find no other way. And should you win, as one survivor's attorney has noted, your victory will be like victory in no other kind of case—it is a victory of the mind, body and soul.

Financial Needs

Your financial situation also figures prominently into your decision. Lawsuits are expensive. Although many attorneys take child sexual abuse cases without requiring the payment of hourly fees, in many jurisdictions it is unethical or illegal for an attorney to pay the client's court costs. Attorneys may not pay these costs for you even if it is legal, because it is out-of-pocket money to the lawyer. Court costs include the court fee for filing the suit, the costs of taking testimony before trial, telephone charges, expert witness fees, and copying charges. Depending on your attorney's policies, you may also have to pay legal fees up front in an initial payment called a **retainer**, as well as regular hourly billings for time spent working on your case. These attorney fees and court costs can be

Retainer

a prepayment of fees to an attorney estimated by the attorney to be the cost of preliminary legal work on the case; attorneys often require additional prepayments as the initial retainer is depleted.

Contingency fee arrangement

payment schedule in which a *plaintiff* pays his or her attorney for non-court costs only after the *defendant* pays following a *settlement* or *judgment*; usually a percentage of the total amount recovered from the defendant; typical percentages are 25% for settlement before trial, 33.3% for settlement during or after trial, and 40% for settlement after an appeal following trial; percentages vary by area and law firm

Pro bono

legal work provided free of charge; literally, *for the (public) good* (short for *pro bono publico*)

substantial, ranging from several thousand to several tens of thousands of dollars.

You should understand that many lawyers will not take a case just to advance a principle. Unfortunately for those who are wronged and financially unstable, the legal profession is also the legal business. Lawyers generally must have some reassurance that they are going to be paid for their work. If you are able to go forward with a lawsuit only under a **contingency fee arrangement** and on initial examination your case looks legally shaky, most lawyers will not take your case, even if they believe in you and your cause. If you are fortunate, you may be able to find an attorney who will work on your case for free, or ***pro bono***, or find a low-income legal clinic with sliding fees.

You must also be prepared and able to absorb lost time to your job and from your family, as court proceedings and pretrial procedures occur almost entirely during normal business hours. With limited exceptions, judges do not have enough open time to schedule court proceedings at the convenience of the parties. However, court proceedings that require absence from work or other commitments likely will be sporadic, at least until your case reaches trial. Although many cases settle out of court and never reach trial, you can't count on getting such a settlement before trial.

Family Situation

You should also assess your relationship with family members before suing your abuser. Suing child sexual abuse perpetrators may cause strange and unexpected emotional and psychological responses in family members. If you have a good relationship with your family members, you should consider the effect the filing of a lawsuit will have on them. If you are suing a parent, siblings or your non-offending parent may abandon you after you file suit, even if you currently enjoy a good relationship with them and they believe your accusations. There are many reasons for this reaction, including denial because of their own psychological needs or their own abuse and protection of the family name and image. You must be prepared to 'lose' other family members, at best temporarily, after you sue.

Complaint

document that normally starts the legal process in a civil case; *plaintiff* files this document, which states the wrongful or *negligent* actions the *defendant* has committed and the injuries—financial, physical, and psychological—that have resulted, and asks for some compensation or other remedy

Remember that other family members may be extremely dysfunctional and react in an irrational manner, especially when their own denial to themselves and to the world is being threatened by the openness of a lawsuit. The media routinely check **complaints** that are filed in local courts, and the complaint is a public record open to public review. The **allegations** made in a complaint will very likely be published in local newspapers. If the suit is filed where family members currently live, the allegations in a complaint may become town gossip, especially in a small town. Family members may be confronted with questions or accusations from concerned friends or prying intruders. Although the backlash to family members is not the fault of the survivor and should properly be directed at the abuser, the unaddressed dysfunctionality of family members may result in anger directed to the survivor.

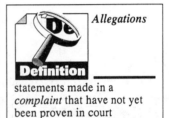

Allegations

statements made in a *complaint* that have not yet been proven in court

Similarly, you must be willing to withstand the disbelief of more distant family members, friends, and neighbors who are either unaware of the abuse or are seeking to cover it up out of psychological or guilt-based denial. On the other hand, more distant family members or friends may become strong supporters.

One survivor found that after a distant cousin she did not know well heard about the lawsuit, the cousin became a staunch supporter.

The cousin confided that the survivor's perpetrator had not allowed the cousin or other relatives to visit which, in retrospect, made sense as a method of covering up the abuse.

If your perpetrator was/is a respected professional or business leader in the community, family friends or members of the community may be unable or unwilling to see through the defenses your perpetrator employs to appear respectable. People you thought were close friends or supportive relatives may distance themselves from you by withdrawing all support or may even turn on you and support your abuser. Your lawsuit may separate your true friends from more fickle acquaintances who, for a variety of reasons, including the possibility of their own unresolved abuse, either withdraw from or reject you.

Can These Needs Be Met Through a Lawsuit?

Understand Your Personal Goals

No reason to sue is more right than another. If you are angry because of the high cost of therapy and want reimbursement, you could base your trial strategy on maximization of financial recovery, which may mean being willing to settle out of court (before trial) to reduce attorney fees. If, however, you are eager to have a public confrontation of your abuser in a trial, with a determination of **liability** by a jury, you may be unwilling to settle out of court. As noted earlier, it is important for you to understand your personal reasons for pursuing suit so that you can work with your attorney and structure the lawsuit to get the best results for you.

Liability

party's responsibility to another to pay an obligation or debt, generally monetary; assessed in a *civil* case by a judge or jury; compare *guilt* (assessment of responsibility for wrongdoing by a judge or jury in a *criminal* case)

The process of contacting a lawyer and inquiring about your rights, even if you decide not to go forward with the case, may meet your needs. Some survivors have found merely contacting a lawyer very empowering. This may be the first time that someone in a position of legal authority tells you that you have been wronged and that you have legal rights against your abuser.

Financial Situation of the Perpetrator

No assessment of a potential lawsuit is complete without an evaluation of the defendant's ability to pay a potential **judgment**. Indeed, unless you can afford to pay your attorney by the hour, most attorneys will need to be assured of the perpetrator's (or the perpetrator's insurance company's, if an insurance policy covers the actions) financial resources before they will even agree to take your case. You should determine, to the best of your ability, what financial or property resources your abuser has available for recovery. You will probably know some of the things your abuser owns from your own knowledge. If you are suing a parent, you may learn about other resources through conversations with siblings or a nonabusive parent. Your attorney will have other ideas about how to determine your abuser's financial position.

Judgment

court's final ruling in a case; usually accompanied by an order from the court demanding payment of a sum of money by one *party* to another

Insurance may be one possible financial resource. Insurance policies for home owners, renters, and automobiles (and possibly professional malpractice) usually contain a provision covering liability of the insured for **negligence**. Depending on your state's laws, acts of child sexual abuse may be considered intentional and not negligent, which would probably preclude coverage under the insurance policy for child abuse. A creative lawyer can sometimes make other claims against your perpetrator, such as deceit or defamation, to recover against the insurance company. In some cases, suing a parent who was not the direct abuser but did not stop it (often the mother) is another possible way to receive insurance coverage. Of course, you may not desire to sue the other parent for a number of reasons. If you were abused by a non-family member who was in a position of trust and who worked for a large

Negligence

wrong committed when a person injures another through acts that a reasonable person should know would lead to a foreseeable chance of harm

organization, such as a boy scout leader or clergy person, you may also be able to sue, and recover from, the organization itself. (Recovering from insurance companies and institutions and companies for their employees' sexual abuse is covered more fully in Chapter 6.)

The perpetrator's financial resources come into play in another, more indirect fashion. Your abuser, if wealthy, will probably be able to hire more skilled attorneys and more impressive experts to attempt to disprove your allegations. Your perpetrator might also encourage his or her attorneys to use every possible procedure against you, such as excessive motions, causing you to pay more attorney fees.

Chapter 2

Can I Win?

What Does the Law Allow?

The Law in General

When most people think of the law, they think of some larger-than-life, hard-to-describe set of rules that seemingly has been around forever. "The Law" is not carved in marble. It is constantly, although often glacially, evolving. Also, "The Law" is not a body of rules handed down by unknowable, omniscient mountaintop-dwelling gods. Rather, at least in the United States, it is an extension of the people themselves. People create laws.

Legislation

laws, ordinances, and regulations drafted and enacted by elected officials on the state, local, and federal levels

Laws are created in several ways in the United States. The two most common ways are through **legislation**, which is usually more general law that applies to society as a whole rather than to one person or group of persons, and through court action, which is law created in response to a particular situation and particular parties.

Statute

law enacted by the legislature that demands, regulates, or prohibits some act

Legislative laws are generally called **statutes**, and this type of law is usually called statutory law. Legislation can be created on any governmental level with legislative power. This includes the federal government (Congress, which creates federal statutes, and federal agencies, which are given power by Congress to create regulations), states (state houses of representatives, which create state statutes, and state agencies, which are given power by state legislatures to create regulations), and municipalities (city councils, which create ordinances and regulations).

Prospective

applying only after a certain time

Retroactive

applying to events in the past as well as to future events

After a legislature enacts a statute, the statute does not become effective law until a date set by the legislature (the same is true of court-made law, described below). Some statutes apply to past events, even though their effective dates are in the future. Laws can be **prospective** or **retroactive**.

If a law is passed on May 1, 1992, becomes effective on June 1, 1992, and applies only to causes of action that accrue (become available to someone) after June 1, 1992, the statute is said to have *prospective* application.

If, however, a law is passed on May 1, 1992, becomes effective on June 1, 1992, and applies to causes of action that arise at any time (or to causes of action arising or accruing after a certain date in the past), the statute is said to have *retroactive* application.

Trial court

court in which evidence is presented by the parties to a judge or jury; also called a *lower court*

Appellate court

court that reviews trial court decisions for legal errors (does not generally decide facts); also called a *higher court*

Federal and state court systems are composed of **trial courts** and **appellate courts**. Disputes between parties are first heard by trial courts. If one or more of the parties thinks a legal error was made by the trial court, an appeal can be made to an appellate court. Appellate courts create law in **decisions**, which appellate judges write after one or more parties appeal a trial court decision. Appellate courts may come to several conclusions in their decisions: follow old law; overrule old law, thus creating new law; or create entirely new law, in areas in which the court have not yet ruled. Law created by appellate courts is known as **case law** (or *common law*).

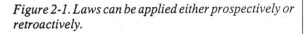

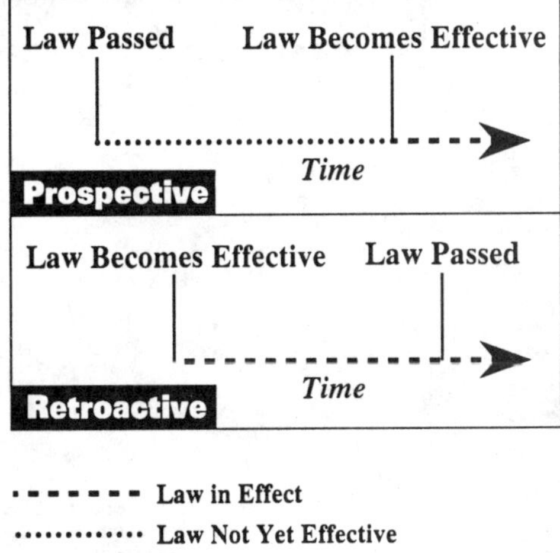

Figure 2-1. Laws can be applied either prospectively or retroactively.

Decision

written ruling by a court that states which party has prevailed on the questions put before the court by the parties; usually includes explanations for the rulings

Each of the governmental levels mentioned above is also known as a jurisdiction. Every jurisdiction (city, state, and country) has its own separate statutes, and the federal government and each state also has its own case law.

If you live in Atlanta, Georgia, you are subject to Atlanta city ordinances, Georgia state legislation, Georgia state common law, federal legislation, and federal common law.

Someone who lives in Minneapolis, Minnesota, on the other hand, is subject to the same federal laws, but to different city ordinances (Minneapolis') and state legislative law and common law (Minnesota's).

Case law

law created by various courts, state and federal, based on the facts of individual cases, that makes, overrules or extends rules of law; published in volumes known as *legal reporters*; derived from English *common law*

Fortunately, legislatures and courts in most states follow similar legal principles and procedures in most areas of the law, although they have defined them differently. As you might expect, some states are more legally progressive than others.

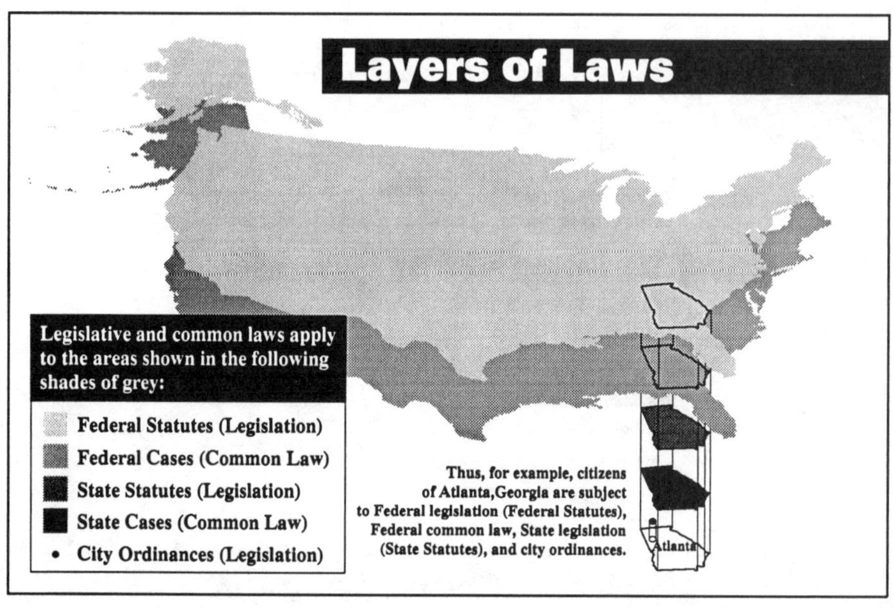

Figure 2-2. Many sets of laws apply to citizens of the United States.

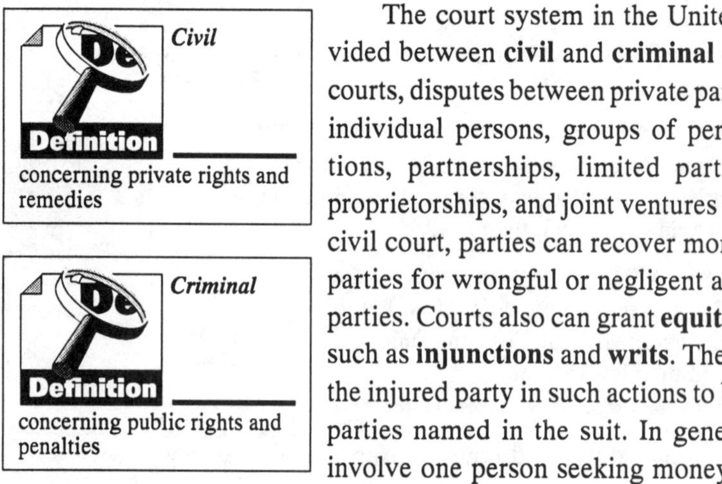

Civil
Definition
concerning private rights and remedies
Criminal
Definition
concerning public rights and penalties

The court system in the United States is divided between **civil** and **criminal** courts. In civil courts, disputes between private parties, including individual persons, groups of persons, corporations, partnerships, limited partnerships, sole proprietorships, and joint ventures are decided. In civil court, parties can recover money from other parties for wrongful or negligent actions of these parties. Courts also can grant **equitable** remedies, such as **injunctions** and **writs**. The law considers the injured party in such actions to be one or more parties named in the suit. In general, civil suits involve one person seeking money from another person for damages.

In criminal courts, the states (or other governmental entities, such as the federal government or municipalities) can bring criminal actions against persons or other entities (including those listed above) for offenses that the legislature has mandated as offensive or repugnant to society as a whole.

Types of actions considered criminal include rape, murder, burglary, and arson. Criminal courts impose fines and sentences on guilty parties. In general, criminal suits involve the government seeking to punish a person for some transgression against society.

Equitable

remedy based on fairness, rather than under traditional rules of law; derived from the old Chancery courts in England, which had only these powers, and no legal jurisdiction

If a drunk driver hits a pedestrian, and the pedestrian is injured, the pedestrian generally can sue the drunk driver for money damages for the medical costs necessary to recover from injuries and for the approximate value of pain and suffering endured, among others.

Additionally, the state generally can bring criminal charges against the driver for, among other things, driving while intoxicated, reckless driving, criminal assault, and reckless endangerment and can put the driver in jail.

Thus, the driver could be involved in both civil and criminal cases resulting from the incident and be subject to both civil damages and criminal incarceration.

The law is further subdivided between federal and state law. Both federal and state courts hear both civil and criminal cases.

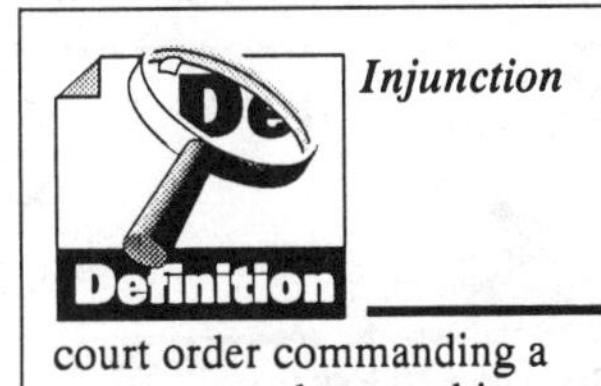

Injunction

court order commanding a party not to do something

Childhood Sexual Abuse–Criminal Law

Writ

court order commanding a party to do something

Under the law, child sexual abuse is uniformly considered a crime, punishable in criminal court by sentences up to many years. Increasingly, perpetrators of child sexual abuse are being jailed for their activities. Criminal incest laws, however, were not generally enacted to protect the child, but rather to prohibit marriage and inbreeding among kin. These statutes'

Tort

wrong committed either intentionally or negligently by one person against another that leads to damages and is recognized under common law; *e.g.*, battery, negligence, intentional infliction of emotional distress

Intentional tort

wrong committed through the act of a person desiring to cause injury

Battery

intentionally harmful or offensive contact caused by one person to another

Assault

acts intended to cause harmful or offensive contact or the apprehension of such imminent contact to another person or a third person, that cause such contact or apprehension to another person

definitions of incest are, thus, usually restricted to sexual intercourse between blood relatives. Few states include sexual conduct other than intercourse within the definition. Some states include intercourse between adoptive parent and child, and many states include intercourse between stepparent and child in their definitions.

What many people don't realize, though, is that in many jurisdictions victims of incest, as well as child sexual abuse victims in general, can also sue their perpetrators in civil court to recover monetary damages or win other remedies. Also, it is important to understand that suing your perpetrator in civil court, as opposed to criminal court, does not require that you meet the requirements listed in criminal incest statutes. As the next section demonstrates, the acts of your abuser do not have to be proven criminal for you to recover damages. Don't get hung up on how child sexual abuse is defined in the criminal statutes in your state unless you are seeking a criminal prosecution, and jailing, of your perpetrator. Be aware that statutes in virtually every state protect children from both incest and sexual contact from non-family members. Even if you don't want to try to get your perpetrator jailed, the existence of these statutes demonstrates the severity of the wrong inflicted on survivors. To put it bluntly, child sexual abuse is a crime.

What Rights Do I Have as a Child Sexual Abuse Survivor?

The American civil legal system, which in general evolved from the English model, grants to its citizens the right to demand compensation for various wrongs caused by others. These rights are set out in the language of case law and in legislation. The rights of all citizens include the right to sue for damages caused by acts done either intentionally or negligently by another person. In general, these causes of action are known as **torts**.

Torts are various actions (or, in some cases, inactions) by someone against another that result in injury, loss, or damage. Several torts are generally recognized by American courts. Torts are divided, roughly, into three groups: **intentional torts**, negligence, and strict liability torts. Among the intentional torts are **battery**, **assault**, **false imprisonment**, **defamation**, and the **intentional infliction of emotional distress** (battery and assault are also criminal offenses, with different definitions than their tort counterparts). Included within the definition of negligence are negligence (a generic cause of action) and **negligent infliction of emotional distress**. Among the strict liability torts are strict liability in keeping dangerous substances or dangerous animals.

Some tort causes of action allow recovery for injuries to people. These actions are known as *personal torts*, or *torts to the person*. Other tort causes of action are for injuries to property. These actions are known as *property torts*, or *torts to property*.

It is important to note that distinct actions, like acts of child molestation, are not generally considered individual causes of action. Causes of action are more broadly defined to include many different types of behaviors and include within them several seemingly different types of actions. Many different actions of perpetrators can be considered batteries, for example, from genital fondling to physical torture, even though they differ widely in their particulars.

False imprisonment

intentional confining by one person of another who is aware of or is harmed by the confinement, within boundaries fixed by the confiner

Defamation

statement made by one person to another that harms the reputation of a third person, when the allegations stated are known, or should be known, to be false; verbal defamatory statements are generally known as *slander*, and written defamatory statements are generally known as *libel*

Intentional infliction of emotional distress

outrageous conduct that one person hopes will, and does, cause severe emotional distress in another

Negligent infliction of emotional distress

conduct that a reasonable person should have known would cause severe emotional distress in another

A Perpetrator Can Be Held Accountable in Civil Court

Many different types of actions can be torts. Child sexual abuse is a wrong that causes both physical and psychological problems in its victims. The ways in which a perpetrator can harm a victim are numerous, including improper touching, physical and psychological torture or other abuse, physical and psychological confinement, rape, and threats of violence or death to the victim or other family members. These acts cause various types of injuries, from flashbacks to sexual dysfunction to feelings of low self-esteem. Your injuries may include any or all of the following*:

- intrusive flashbacks, nightmares, and night terrors
- repressed memory or denial
- gastrointestinal or gynecological disorders
- dissociation
- sleep disorders
- physical ailments with no organic origin
- sexual dysfunction
- escapism through alcoholism or drug dependence
- eating disorders
- suicidal thoughts or actions
- self-mutilation
- phobias
- depression
- anxiety
- swallowing and gagging sensitivity
- fear of being alone in the dark
- psychic numbing
- sexual issues (promiscuity to aversion)
- multiple personality disorder
- prostitution
- limited tolerance for happiness
- problems with intimacy
- inability to trust
- feelings of guilt, shame, low self-esteem, worthlessness
- feelings of helplessness
- clinging behavior
- repeated victimizations
- inability to recognize or express anger
- inability to care for body, poor body image
- high risk-taking or no risk taking ability
- patterns of ambivalent or intensely conflictive relationship.

---

* This list is derived from *Secret Survivors* by E. Sue Blume, © 1990, John Wiley & Sons, Inc., and *Healing the Incest Wound*, by Christine Courtois, © 1988, W.W. Norton & Co. For an excellent and more complete list of the effects of incest, *see* "The Incest Survivors' Aftereffects Checklist" in *Secret Survivors*.

Although money can't make the pain of these problems go away, your attorney will help you calculate a dollar amount to claim as the monetary value of your injuries. One of the inadequacies of our legal system is that money can't solve the harm done to you by the abuse. Unfortunately, attorneys and judges can only make some financial approximations of the cost of your abuse, such as $100 per day, $100,000 total, etc.

Your injuries can also lead to financial damages which can be directly tied to a certain dollar loss, such as lost income because of an inability to work and medical, psychological and psychiatric bills.

Confer with your therapist for a more complete list of the ways perpetrators can harm victims, and for other damages that may result, as well as for insight into the ways in which your perpetrator in particular harmed you, and what damages are a direct or indirect result of these abuses.

Because perpetrators often commit several types of wrongful acts against their victims, many or all of which lead to injuries, often several traditional tort causes of action can be successfully argued in a child sexual abuse case. Improper touching, physical torture, and rape are almost universally considered battery. Threats of violence or threats of death to the victim or other family members can fall within the definitions of either assault or intentional infliction of emotional distress. Although under the tort of assault a victim must prove that he or she suffered from apprehension of imminent harmful or offensive contact, victims can often identify certain behavior patterns of the abuser that indicate the abuser intended to engage in sexual conduct. Psychological and physical confinement is false imprisonment. Making statements that you are crazy (for example, in response to your claims that you were abused) may be slanderous (and thus be defamation, as slandering someone's reputation is considered a form of defamation).

Other abuser actions may be negligent. The most likely negligence theory, however, is that of negligent infliction of emotional distress. Unfortunately, only a few states recognize this cause of action. You might also be able to recover on the theory that a nonabusive parent's negligence contributed to your injuries (failure to protect).

These wrongful acts are only examples. Your attorney probably will have ideas about other claims you can make in your particular situation and jurisdiction.

Proving intent can be difficult. Abusers can state that they didn't know the contact was offensive to the child and may actually be unaware that it was. The jury could find that the abuser was insane (which doesn't absolve the abuser from liability in all states). Some courts may waive the intent requirement by ruling that if the abuser intended the act, because of the very nature of the sexual abuse, he or she also intended the harm.

In analyzing the merits of your case, your attorney will also be looking at how believable you are. Even if your attorney believes you, if your story is uncorroborated or if the details of your victimization are difficult for people ignorant of the prevalence of child sexual abuse to believe, your attorney may have difficulty proving your case in court. If you used coping skills in your past such as alcoholism, drug abuse, or promiscuity, a judge or jury may question your credibility. Under difficult circumstances like these, many attorneys will not represent you. In some cases, however, a skilled attorney and a good therapist/expert can conclusively show a judge or jury that your substance abuse or promiscuity was caused by the abuse and is not a sign of your lack of truthfulness or social unsuitability.

A Perpetrator Can Be Jailed

In addition to being held liable for damages to a survivor, it is possible for a perpetrator to be charged with, and convicted of, crimes for committing child sexual abuse. If convicted, a perpetrator may be jailed for a period of months or years. Under the criminal statutes of most states, a perpetrator can be convicted of rape or sexual abuse of a minor and, in some jurisdictions, a perpetrator can be convicted of a separate crime of incest when the abuse was done to a related party. Most criminal cases have a very strict definition of incest which does not include people in positions of authority, such as baby-sitters or other caretakers.

To convict an abuser of any crime, the government prosecutor must prove all elements of the crime **beyond a reasonable doubt**. This standard is difficult to meet. If the prosecutor believes that there is insufficient evidence to convince a jury of each element of the crime to this level, he or she may decide not to pursue the case. Child sexual abuse cases with adult survivors, where witnesses are often few because of the passage of time and the denial and secrecy involved and where corroborating evidence is generally slim, often present prosecutors with insufficient evidence to charge or convict perpetrators. Additionally, many jurisdictions have limits (*criminal* statutes of limitations, which have different lengths than *civil* statutes of limitations) on how long after criminal actions occur a person may be convicted of a crime.

Beyond a reasonable doubt

standard of proof that requires a fact-finder (judge or jury) to find that there can be no reasonable doubt that something happened; usually a criminal standard

If you have strong feelings about wanting or not wanting criminal charges filed against your perpetrator, you should consult with your attorney to determine the chances of the local prosecutor pressing criminal charges against your abuser, and the likelihood of conviction.

When Must I Sue?

Statutes of Limitations–General Considerations

Civil actions have limits on when they can be filed. After the actions that cause the harm or the manifestation of the damage or injury to the victim, depending on the cause of action and the jurisdiction, an injured party has a limited time within which to file a claim against a wrongdoer. This time limit is known as the statute of limitations. If the claim is not filed within this period, there can be no recovery on that claim.

Kary Kindheart is struck in the face by Billy Bully, and she suffers a broken nose. She incurs $500 in medical expenses and loses $700 in wages for time lost from work.

Kary has a cause of action against Billy for battery. She can sue him to force him to pay her costs and wages. If Kary waits too long without beginning a lawsuit, however, the statute of limitations will run and her cause of action will disappear. Kary will then lose all rights to recover any money from Billy for her injury.

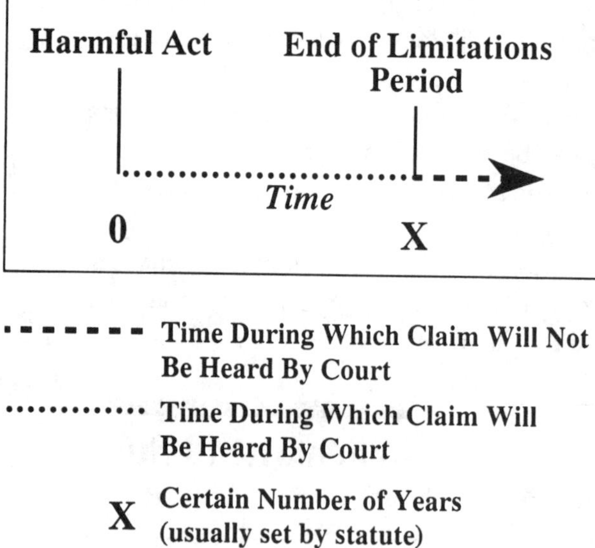

Figure 2-3. Statutes of limitations are time periods beyond which particular claims can no longer be filed.

The statutes of limitations for tort actions generally range from 1 to 6 years, with most being from 1 to 3 years. The reasons for these time limitations are practical: memories dim after several years, witnesses are hard to find, and the courts want to discourage the filing of frivolous, difficult to prove or defend lawsuits. Our judicial system also places time limits on claims to protect against an overburdened court case load and to give causes of action some degree of finality.

In some states, different tort causes of action have different limitation periods. For example, some states have different statutes of limitations for negligence than they do for some intentional torts, such as battery, and perhaps still other limitations periods for other intentional torts, such as defamation. You may have different time limits within which to file for different actions by your abuser, or against different defendants.

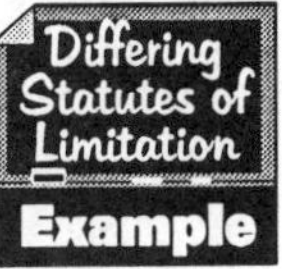

Jason, an employee of Humungous Corporation, intentionally tripped Bill, another employee, while both were on the job. Bill suffered a separated collarbone when he fell after being tripped. Dorothea, their supervisor, watched the whole episode, but did nothing to stop Jason.

If the statute of limitations for negligence in the jurisdiction is two years, the statute of limitations for battery is three years, and it is now two and a half years after Jason tripped Bill, Bill's cause of action for negligent supervision against Dorothea and the Humungous Corporation has expired. However, Bill's cause of action for battery still remains, as he still has half a year to sue.

In most cases, the act that caused the injury and the injured person's realization that he or she has been injured occur nearly simultaneously.

Prudence Perfectdriver is injured in a two-car accident by Doug Dipstick and suffers a broken leg. The act that caused the injury (the negligent driving by the second driver) occurs just before Prudence realizes that the act caused the injury (which occurs when Prudence, probably still seated in her crunched car, looks down at her broken leg).

In such a case, Prudence's statutes of limitations for whatever civil claims she could make against Dipstick start to run at the time Prudence sees the injury.

Sometimes, however, injuries do not become apparent to the injured person or the link between who or what caused the present injury or condition can't be made by an injured person until a much longer time after the damaging act.

Patrice has an operation to remove an infected appendix and the attending surgeon or operating nurse accidently leaves a sponge in the patient's abdominal area before sewing up the incision. Patrice has no way of knowing about the sponge until suffering severe stomach and chest pains several years later. Thc act that caused the injury (the negligent closing of the incision with the sponge still in Patrice's abdominal cavity) occurs several years before Patrice realizes that the act caused the injury (which doesn't occur until Patrice has abdomina! discomfort several years later and goes to [with any luck] another doctor to find out what is wrong).

In such a case, in most jurisdictions, Patrice's statutes of limitations for whatever civil claims she could make against the injuring doctor or nurse start to run at the time Patrice learns that the pain she feels is caused by the forgotten sponge.

Statutes of Limitations–Sexual Abuse Causes of Action

Traditional Laws

In child sexual abuse suits by many adult survivors, special problems exist that make traditional statutes of limitation unjustly restrictive. Child sexual abuse victims often repress their memories for several years because of the severity of the damage done to them. This repression can last from several months to several decades, with repression in many cases lasting 15–25 years. Even when the survivor has not repressed the memories, the emotional dominance perpetrators have over most survivors makes bringing suit against these perpetrators nearly impossible until after years of therapy. Many other survivors who remember the abuse are often psychologically unable to link it to later physical and psychological problems they have. Traditional statutes of limitation in most states generally make the filing of suits involving tort causes of action impossible beyond 1–3 years after the wrongful act, so survivors have until recently been without a legal remedy in such situations.

One other legal concept figures into the equation of when victims must bring suit against their abusers. Under traditional statutes of limitation, the time limit is measured from the time the wrongful act occurred or the harm was discovered, unless the victim is under a **disability**. A disability in a legal sense is not the same as what is generally thought to be a disability, like paraplegia or blindness. A legal disability is anything that the law considers as a justifiable reason why a person cannot file suit against someone else. Minority, or lack of adult status, is considered a legal disability. A traditional statute of limitations for a child-victim begins to run after the child reaches majority, or adulthood, which occurs between the ages of 18 and 21, depending on the jurisdiction. After the child-victim reaches adulthood, the full statutory period (or a shortened version, in some jurisdictions) begins to run. This leads to unfair results, because the statute of limitations runs out when the victim is a young adult, often still under the control and domination of the perpetrator and probably still repressing the memory of the experience or experiences.

Disability

legal handicap, caused by either age or infirmity, that is a justifiable reason for not suing another person for a wrong; *e.g.*, minors are considered to be under a disability

Marie is 34. Her stepfather molested her repeatedly when she was between the ages of 10 and 13. She repressed the memories until she was 32, when she suddenly began to have flashbacks. She has suffered physical symptoms such as severe headaches, bulimia, and insomnia since she was 25. She did not tie the symptoms to the sexual abuse until she was 32, when her therapist told her they may be related.

In a jurisdiction that follows traditional *statutes of limitations*, has a majority age of 18, and has a 1-year limitations period after reaching majority for intentional torts, Marie's claims for intentional torts expired when she was 19 years old. She was a minor when the abuse occurred, so the limitations period was **tolled**

Tolling

stopping of the running of the statute of limitations until a later time or occurrence

until she was considered an adult under the law and no longer under a disability. After she became an adult, she had 1 year to sue. Therefore, her cause of action expired when she was 19.

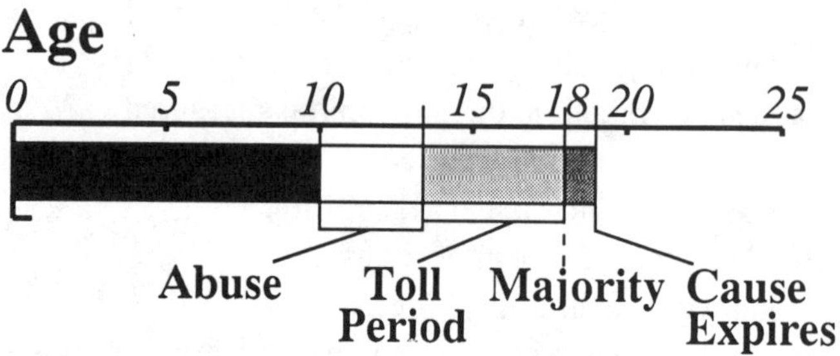

Figure 2-4. Traditional statutes of limitations have denied many survivors the right to sue.

Newer Laws

Recent legal developments in many jurisdictions have changed this outcome for child sexual abuse victims: extended periods and the **delayed discovery rule**.

Some states have legislatively extended the traditional statutes of limitations to give survivors a longer period of years after reaching adulthood to file their suit. Although this type of statute is better than a normal tolling until the age of majority, for many survivors it is practically worthless. A large proportion of survivors either do not remember their abuse, do not draw the connection between the abuse and the harm until many years after the abuse occurred, or cannot emotionally handle filing suit, any of which puts their claims beyond the lengthened period.

[Assume the same facts as the previous two examples.]

In a jurisdiction that extends the start of the statute of limitations to five years after adulthood (age 18 in this state), Marie's claims for intentional torts expired when she was 23 years old.

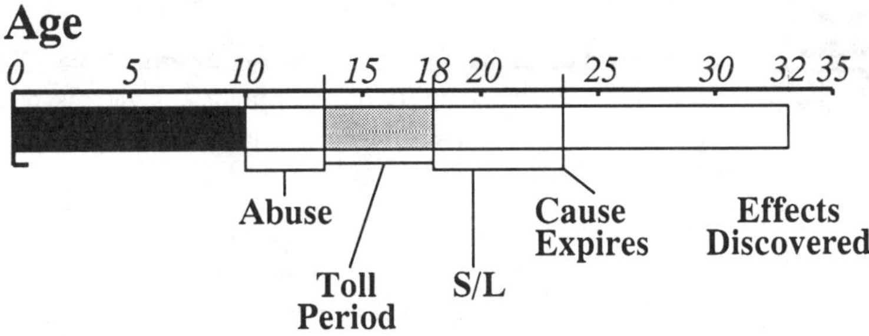

Figure 2-5. A lengthened limitations period does not help many survivors.

Delayed discovery rule

extension of the beginning of the statute of limitations to when the damage from a tortious act is discovered or, alternatively, to when the relationship between the tortious act and the damage is realized

The delayed discovery rule has been used most extensively in medical malpractice cases where patients have been harmed by physicians and could not have known that the physician's actions caused the harm, generally because it became apparent years later (as demonstrated in the "Later Realization of Injury or Link" example above). The delayed discovery rule allows the statutes of limitation to be tolled for the period during which a victim is unaware of the harm caused by a perpetrator or does not realize that the harm was caused by the perpetrator's actions. Under this rule, victims have a statutory period in which they can sue—after the injuries from their perpetrators' actions surface and the link between the damages suffered becomes apparent.

Even more recently, some courts and legislatures have further changed child sexual abuse statutes of limitations. Some state courts have created, and some state legislatures have passed, modified statutes of limitations in these cases. The modified statutes of limitations do not begin to run until the survivor remembers the abuse and draws a connection between the abuse and the physical or emotional harm, or until a reasonably prudent person in the same or similar circumstances would have discovered this connection. Some courts and legislatures even allow the recollection of separate instances of abuse as separate causes of action. In other words, a new statute of limitations begins each time the survivor remembers a different abuse memory.

[Assume the same facts as the previous example.]

In a jurisdiction that follows the more modern delayed discovery rule or the newer statutory or court-made delayed discovery rule for child sexual abuse, Marie's claims for intentional torts will expire when she is 35 years old.

Because she did not discover the injuries caused by the abuse until she began to have physical and psychological problems when she was 25, and the link was not apparent until she was told by her therapist that there may be a link, the limitations period was tolled until after both of these discoveries. After discovering the link between the abuse and the injuries, she has 3 years to sue. Her cause of action expires when she is 35.

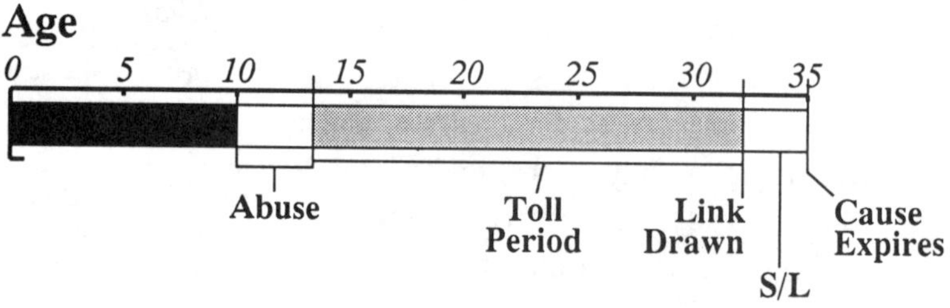

Figure 2-6. Modern delayed discovery statutes of limitations give more survivors a chance to recover from their abusers.

Courts in some jurisdictions make a distinction between cases in which survivors remembered their abuse from the time it occurred and cases in which survivors repressed the memories until some point after the abuse happened (for example, as an adult during therapy). These courts, even if the jurisdiction follows the delayed discovery rule, often hold that a survivor who remembers the abuse from the time it occurred cannot file a claim based on the abuse after the traditional statute of limitations expires. Claims by survivors who have always remembered the abuse are often referred to by the courts as *Type 1* claims. Claims by survivors who have repressed their memories are known as *Type 2* claims. Some jurisdictions (*e.g.*, Wisconsin) allow both Type 1 and Type 2 cases. Other jurisdictions allow only Type 1 cases. Check with your attorney about the current law in your state.

Jean is 39. His brother sexually abused him for two years beginning when he was 10. Jean remembered the abuse from the moment he was first abused. He had severe back problems, sexual dysfunction, and stomach and lower digestive tract problems from his early adolescence into adulthood, but he never tied the abuse to his problems until he was in his mid-30s, when he made the link after several years of therapy.

If the jurisdiction has a majority age of 18 and a 1-year limitations period on intentional torts after a person reaches majority (even if the jurisdiction has a delayed discovery rule), Jean's claims for intentional torts expired when he was 19 years old. The limitations period is tolled until he was considered an adult under the law (age 18) and no longer under a disability. After he became an adult, he had 1 year to sue. His cause of action expired when he was 19.

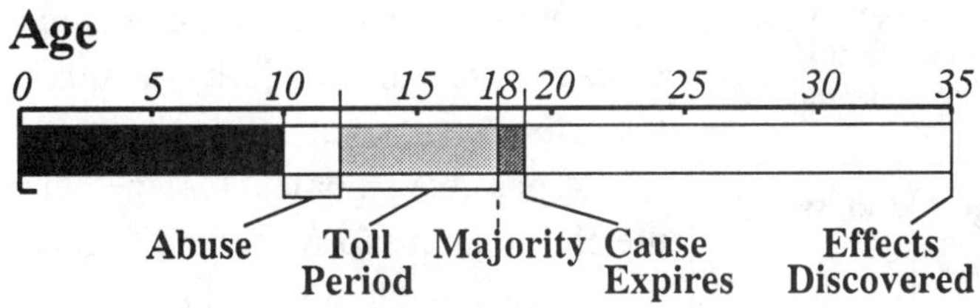

Figure 2-7. Many jurisdictions do not allow Type 1 claims.

In some cases, other theories may be successfully advanced for the lengthening of the time within which to sue. Attorneys have successfully argued that the parent-child relationship is sufficiently similar to the relationship between a **fiduciary** and another to apply the breach of fiduciary duty exception to child sexual abuse cases. In such situations, courts generally rule that a person who is in a special relation of trust (fiduciary) with someone else cannot mislead the person to whom the trust is owed about the nature of the acts the fiduciary is taking, or the limitations period does not begin to run until the person owed the duty of trust discovers the harm done. This situation closely approximates the relationship of trust and confidence between a parent and child. If a parent tells a child that his or

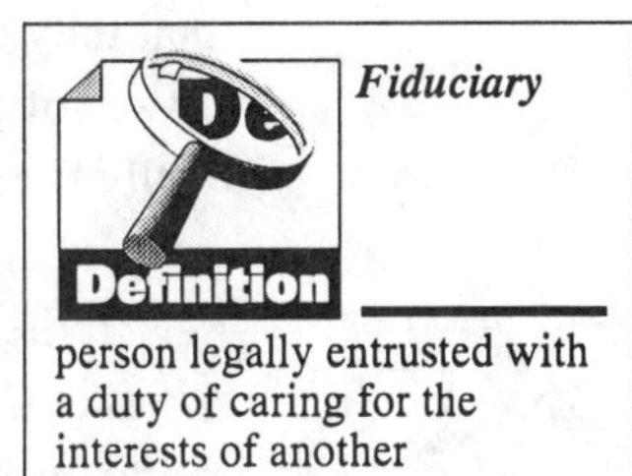

Fiduciary

person legally entrusted with a duty of caring for the interests of another

her actions are not harming the child, it's unreasonable to expect the child to identify a tortious injury. Similarly, if a court determines that a perpetrator has committed **fraud** concerning a survivor's knowledge of the injuries, it might rule that the limitations period does not begin to run until the survivor learns of the link between the perpetrator's actions and the resulting injuries. Another possible argument in some cases is that the limitations period should not begin during childhood because the power differences between a parent and child virtually ensure that there is some element of coercion, **undue influence**, or **duress**. Some survivors may also be able to argue that a victim who suffers from post-traumatic stress disorder should be allowed to bring an action within a period of years after reaching majority (adulthood) because the disorder constitutes a disability.

Fraud

false representation intended to deceive another and cheat him or her of legal rights or property

Undue influence

improper inducement or persuasion that takes advantage of or overpowers a person and causes the person to do something he or she would not ordinarily do

Duress

illegal pressuring of a person to do something that they wouldn't normally do

A possible argument for lengthening the statute of limitations for victims with sexual dysfunction caused by child sexual abuse is that because emotional maturity is a prerequisite to adult sexuality, sexual dysfunction cannot be discovered until maturity. Such a victim cannot reasonably discover the effects of the abuse, the sexual dysfunction, until becoming sexually active as an adult. This argument will not help many survivors. Many survivors repress the memories of the abuse for years after recognizing that they have sexual dysfunction. Survivors often become aware of the connection between the abuse and the injury well after the discovery of the sexual dysfunction and well beyond any extended limitations period.

If the statute of limitations is going to run out before you can face the rigors of the trial process and emotionally handle suing, or before you have fully remembered the events that constitute the wrong, sometimes it is possible to get the court to grant you an extension of time within which to go forward with the suit. To do this, however, you must file the suit, and then your attorney must file and win a motion for an extension. An extension is not required in any jurisdiction, so you cannot depend on a judge granting you one. However, in at least one jurisdiction, if the abuse has made a survivor emotionally and psychologically unable to file suit within the statute of limitations period, the period does not begin to run until the survivor is emotionally and psychologically able to file suit.

Statute of ultimate repose

law setting an absolute time limit after which an action cannot be filed; *e.g.*, a state may allow a medical malpractice claim to be filed at any time up to 3 years after the discovery of the injury, but in no event later than 10 years after the surgery occurred

Some jurisdictions also have other laws that impose absolute time limits on bringing causes of action. These laws, known as **statutes of ultimate repose**, require certain causes of action to be filed within a set number of years from when the harm happened, no matter when the link between the harm and the harmful act is discovered.

Some states have statutes of limitations on child sexual abuse claims that includes both a delayed discovery limitations period and language that imposes a period of ultimate repose.

A state allows a survivor 3 years beyond discovering the effects of child sexual abuse to bring suit, but in no event past 12 years after reaching adulthood. The state's age of majority is 18 years old.

If Sally brings a suit in this state when she is 32, the court will disallow the claim even if Sally didn't discover the until she was 31. If Sally recovers memories when she is 29, she has 1 year to file suit.

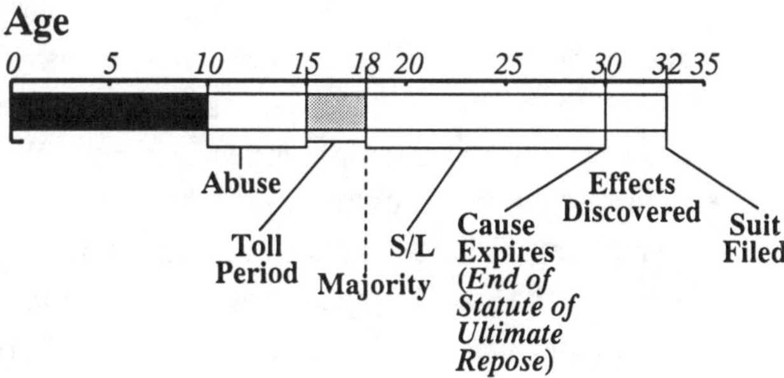

Figure 2-8. Delayed discovery rule limitations periods are sometimes shortened by statutes of ultimate repose.

Other states have no laws that directly address the issue of whether a survivor suing many years after the abuse. In these states, you may be able to recover against your abuser, but recovery will depend on a favorable trial court ruling—that the time period should be lengthened in this type of case. If the state has a law allowing delayed discovery in some cases, you will probably have a better chance of winning than if there is no prior law at all on delayed discovery in the jurisdiction. Even if the state in which you sue has a general rule allowing delayed discovery, the chances are much greater that your abuser will contest your case through trial, and probably through an appeal. Your case may be more difficult to win in this situation than if the jurisdiction had case law or a statute that specifically applied the delayed discovery rule to child sexual abuse cases.

If you are attempting to file suit many years after reaching adulthood, identification of *when* you knew of the abuse and *when* you made a link between the abuse and the injuries you have suffered is critical in most states, even if you can file in a state with a delayed discovery rule. If you repressed the memories until therapy or some other trigger made you recall them several years into adulthood (Type 2 claim), you will have a better chance of beating the applicable statutes of limitations than if you remembered the abuse all along (Type 1 claim).

The statutes of limitations are often the deciding factors in determining whether you can recover from your abuser, so the applicable statutes of limitations in your jurisdiction should be learned at the earliest possible date (*See* Chapter 6 for information on where you can sue). Recovering from a lapsed statute of limitations is nearly impossible. The statute of limitations must be among the first things you discuss with an attorney. Failure to address this question early can result, at best, in the loss of a substantial amount of attorney fees and court costs and, at worst, in the loss of all of your rights to recover from your abuser. You can find references to cases and statutes that set out statutes of limitations for civil child sexual abuse causes of action in Appendix C, "Civil Child Sexual Abuse Statutes of Limitations." Remember that these references are to the law as it existed at the time this book was written and may not accurately reflect the law at the time of reading this book. Consult your attorney to learn the current law and how the courts are construing it.

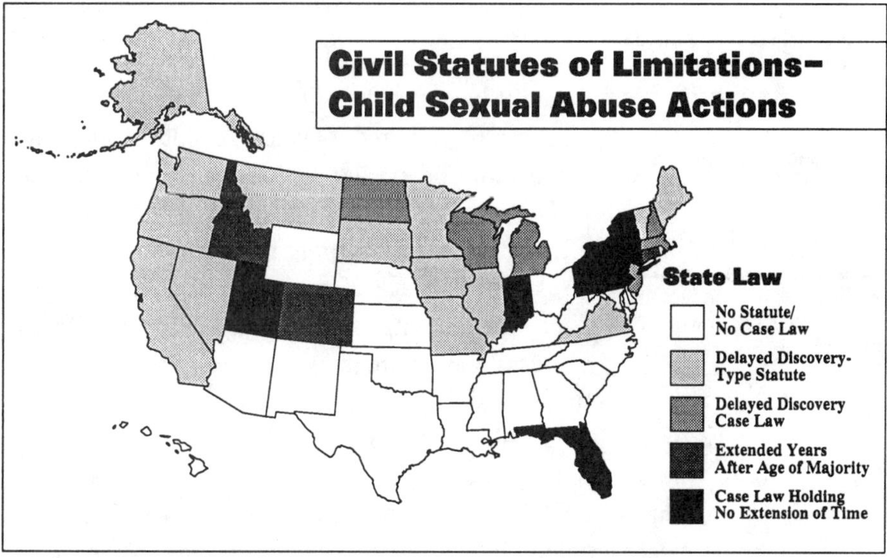

Figure 2-9. Statutes of limitations in civil child sexual abuse cases in the United States vary considerably from jurisdiction to jurisdiction.

Is the Law on My Side?

Although persons who are injured through the actions of others generally have the right to recover damages from the injurers, there are several possible exceptions to this rule in the context of a child sexual abuse case. Your abuser may be able to use these exceptions to avoid liability to you.

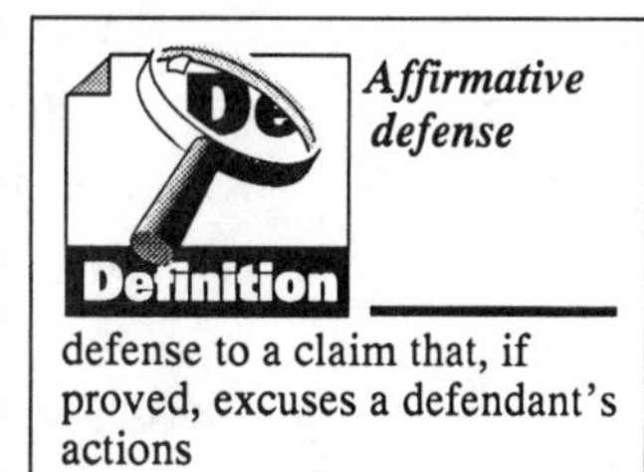

Affirmative defense

defense to a claim that, if proved, excuses a defendant's actions

Your abuser may try several different approaches to defense. For instance, if the evidence of sexual acts between you and your abuser is very compelling, your abuser may decide to defend using one or more **affirmative defenses**. The two

Parent-child immunity

legal protection of a parent from a suit by a child for negligent, reckless, or intentional acts committed by the parent

Consent

willingness for conduct to occur, given either expressly or impliedly

most likely defenses in child sexual abuse acts are **parent-child immunity** (if you are suing a parent) and **consent** (in any child sexual abuse case).

Parent-Child Immunity

Adults have had the right to sue others for tortious actions for hundreds of years. A child's right to sue a parent for similar actions, however, has not always existed, and is not, to this day, absolute, at least in some jurisdictions in the United States. The result of this lack of consensus on a child's rights may make it impossible for you to recover if your abuser was a parent.

Until a hundred years ago, there was no law that prohibited a child from suing a parent for intentional, reckless, or negligent acts. In a widely followed 1891 decision that did not follow any previous precedent, however, parents were granted blanket immunity from actions by their children for most torts (such as battery, assault, intentional infliction of emotional distress, and negligence). This doctrine became known as parent-child immunity. In the decades that followed, courts in almost every state in the United States followed the reasoning in this decision and granted parents immunity for the following reasons:

1. A family is a unit;
2. A husband and wife have a similar immunity from suit by the other spouse;
3. Allowing such suits could lead to fraud (for example, the parent could conspire with the child to recover insurance money);
4. Allowing one child to recover from a parent would use up the other children's inheritance;
5. The family finances might be adversely affected and have an impact on other children in the family;
6. The tranquility of the family might be disrupted; and
7. Parental discipline would be disrupted.

The most often-cited reason for immunity was the likelihood that such a lawsuit would disrupt the family's peace and tranquility. Most courts also construed the general rule to prevent any suit by an adult victim who was suing a parent for actions that happened when the victim was a child.

Over the decades, courts saw the inequity of such universal immunity for parents and began to make exceptions to the general rule. By the 1960s, the rule itself had become the exception because of the exclusions the courts had created to prevent injustice.

Today, many jurisdictions allow a child to sue a parent for torts to the person without limitation. All jurisdictions allow children to sue their parents for intentional torts that injure the child. The application of parent-child immunity to the tort of negligence (not an intentional tort) is less uniform, however. Some jurisdictions allow negligence suits by children only to the extent that liability insurance covers the amount of the damages (which has come up most often in automobile insurance cases). Other jurisdictions allow negligence suits by children only if the negligent acts of the parents involve neither the exercise of reasonable parental authority nor the exercise of parental discretion. One jurisdiction allows immunity only if the negligence involves parental authority or parental discretion regarding "food, clothing, housing, medical and dental services, and other care." Other jurisdictions keep the immunity only if the parent has been reasonable and prudent. Other jurisdictions, though, do not allow children to sue their parents for negligence, still blindly following the reasoning of the outdated, misguided decisions.

Even in jurisdictions that do not allow children to sue their parents for some personal torts, it is unlikely that a court today would apply parent-child immunity to an incest suit. The rationale most often cited for parent-child immunity has no application to this situation. Family harmony and peace have already been destroyed by the abuser's actions, and the need for harmony obviously diminishes as a victim leaves the abusive household to start a life of his or her own. The parent also has no right to discipline a child who lives outside

Incompetent

without the legally required qualification or capacity

Minor

person younger than the age of majority (generally 16–21 years)

the household, so this rationale is also unpersuasive. The chances of fraud are also slim, as it is extremely doubtful that a parent would agree to go through a fake incest suit (complete with public reaction to the allegations) merely to recover insurance proceeds. Also, because courts always allow suits by children for intentional torts, it would be difficult for a modern court to allow immunity for incestuous acts, which in most cases are intentional torts. Most modern courts probably would simply not allow the defense of parent-child immunity because of the outrageous nature of the conduct.

Consent

Your abuser may also outlandishly allege that you consented to the abuse. Consent, however, can be proven to be invalid, if either it was obtained under fraud or duress, based on insufficient information, or was given by a person who was **incompetent** to consent. **Minors** are among those who are considered incompetent to consent to intentional torts, except under narrow circumstances. A minor can consent if he or she is **emancipated** or is a mature minor who understands the nature and consequences of the act. However, if sexual intercourse occurred, the perpetrator may be guilty of **statutory rape**, a crime. Even if no sexual intercourse occurred, the perpetrator may be guilty of other sexual crimes. A young, unemancipated child does not have the legal capacity to consent to an illegal act, so any consent would not be legally binding against such a victim. Also, a child has neither the emotional nor the psychological capability to agree to sexual intercourse with a parent, as the inherent power discrepancies between a child and a parent makes some element of coercion inevitable.

Emancipated

no longer living under parents' or guardians' control

Statutory rape

sexual intercourse with a minor (generally a female) under a certain age (generally 16 years)

Consult with an attorney to determine how your jurisdiction has ruled on the questions of consent and parent-child immunity. Different jurisdictions have different rules, and the law is constantly evolving.

Although defenses of parent-child tort immunity and consent are possible, your abuser probably will defend by saying that no sexual abuse occurred. Your abuser may claim that you are insane or delusional or that you have some motive for bringing the suit, such as greed, revenge, or animosity brought about by difficulties in your family or interpersonal relationships. You should carefully review any other problems or disagreements you have had with your abuser and candidly tell your attorney about them. You should try to recall any instance that could be used by your abuser as evidence of motive for bringing such an action against him or her.

Be aware, though, that your abuser may make up motives or twist facts around to make them appear to be motives. Although the lawsuit may be difficult for you to handle, your abuser may face losing an occupation, important business and personal relationships, and many possessions. If the lawsuit becomes public, your abuser may also face public shame and humiliation. Just as a cornered animal may become vicious to protect itself, your abuser may lash out by making up stories about you or twisting innocuous facts to put you in a bad light. Although it would be tactically damaging for an abuser to physically attack you during the litigation process, you should take extra precautions to stay away from a known violent abuser.

What Can I Gain or Lose in a Lawsuit?

Before you decide to sue your perpetrator in a civil action, you should be fully aware of the consequences. This section highlights the potential rewards and penalties you may expect from a civil lawsuit. This section does not, however, present every benefit and detriment of such a suit, as legal remedies differ between jurisdictions. It lists the gains and

Damages

approximate amount of money necessary to compensate a person wrongfully injured by another

losses that are typical in such cases.

It is important to remember that the consequences of filing suit against a former or current abuser are much more extensive than merely winning or losing a lawsuit. Although the potential for recovery of money is a prime motivator and, perhaps, the only available means of exacting some measure of justice for an unspeakable wrong, there are many other ramifications of such a suit, several of which may be more important to a wronged survivor. Keep these consequences in mind while determining whether to sue.

Gain

You can gain many things through suing a perpetrator. The most visible to the public, and the most damaging to some perpetrators, is the recovery of money. Monetary recovery is one of only a few standard methods allowed by the law.

Money

Consortium

companionship of husband and wife, including affection, aid, and sexual relations

Compensatory damages

amount of money that most closely approximates the value of, or cost of repairing, the actual injuries or losses suffered by a person

No amount of money can compensate a child sexual abuse survivor for the months or years of endured horror. There is no way that a court can completely repair the damage that child sexual abuse causes. The legal system's only alternative, as inadequate as it may be, is to award monetary **damages**. Damages can be awarded for several losses suffered by a victim because of a perpetrator's actions. These damage categories include, but are not limited to, pain and suffering, medical and therapy bills, lost wages, loss of **consortium**, and loss of enjoyment of life. These damages are known as **compensatory damages**.

Under the laws of most states, if you are wrongfully or negligently injured and you suffer pain and suffering because of your injuries, you are entitled to damages for this pain and suffering. How the amount of damages is calculated differs widely from state to state. Some states have laws limiting the amount of damages that can be recovered for pain and suffering. You should consult your attorney for information about how much you might recover in your jurisdiction for pain and suffering damages should you win the lawsuit. It is a good idea to keep a journal or other record of your daily emotional and physical health to help prove your suffering.

You should also be able to recover damages for therapy and medical costs incurred to recover from symptoms and illnesses caused by the abuser's actions. Proving the relationship between the abuser's actions and the various symptoms, such as phobias, multiple personality disorder, post-traumatic stress disorder, and the host of other problems, both physical and psychological, from which victims often suffer will require the testimony of one or more experts trained in diagnosing and treating them, such as social workers, psychologists, psychiatrists, and physicians.

Wages or salary lost because of a victim's inability to work due to either psychological or physical impairment from the sexual abuse is also often recoverable. Testimony from an economist or other expert is often helpful to prove past or future wage losses.

In some jurisdictions, a person can sue for loss of consortium because of the loss of a spouse's affections. This type of damage may be recoverable in a child sexual abuse case in these jurisdictions.

A person can sometimes also sue for loss of enjoyment of life caused by the actions of another. The damages caused by child sexual abuse certainly fall within those allowed under this type of recovery. Loss of enjoyment of life damages should be claimed if they are available in your jurisdiction.

Punitive damages

amount of money added to actual losses and injuries to punish the defendant and deter others from committing similar egregious actions

In addition to the damages for injuries to the person harmed, many jurisdictions allow another type of damage award against defendants in certain situations. These awards, called **punitive damages**, are levied against defendants to punish them for particularly offensive behavior and to dissuade others from committing similar acts in the future. Punitive damage awards are often much larger than compensatory damages awarded in a case, but most jurisdictions require them to be related in some way to the other damages. For example, if the compensatory damages are very small, in most jurisdictions a court or jury cannot award punitive damages that are disproportionately large.

Punitive damages should be sought in a child sexual abuse case in a jurisdiction that allows punitive damages.

It is very difficult to predict the amount of money you might recover if you win your case. Attorneys representing survivors throughout the country have reported awards ranging from a few thousand to a few million dollars, depending on the facts of each particular case, most notably how severe the abuse was, how believable the parties were, and who was sued. Sometimes organizations who hired or supervised the abuser are sued. Awards are generally much higher against organizations that hire or supervise abusers than they are against abusive siblings, or even abusive parents.

Cases that go completely through trial often have higher awards than cases in which a **settlement** is reached by the parties. Even though settlements are generally lower than awards received through trial, settlements are usually much more collectable. In other words, just because a judge or jury finds in your favor and grants a large dollar amount in damages, your abuser may not be able to pay it, may hide assets, or may even file bankruptcy to avoid paying the award. In settlements, however, your attorney probably will be able to make your abuser's ability to pay one of the cornerstones of the settlement agreement.

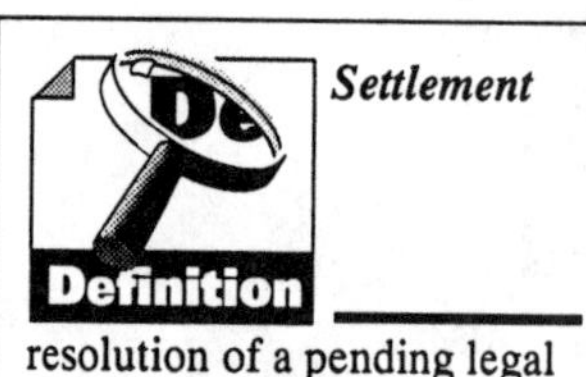

Settlement

resolution of a pending legal dispute without trial

Emotional Empowerment

Another important potential benefit of suing is the emotional empowerment you can gain through standing up to your abuser. Suing can provide a means of overcoming years or decades of emotional, psychological, and physical servitude to a manipulative, overpowering abuser. Filing suit can shift the power imbalance rigorously enforced throughout childhood by an abuser and allow a survivor to regain, or attain for the first time, the feeling of being as strong as, or stronger than, the abuser. Many survivors who have filed civil lawsuits against their abusers and lost the suits, often on legal technicalities like the statute of limitations, are still empowered by the process of standing up for themselves.

Survivors can also be empowered through the public awareness that a lawsuit's publicity and openness bring. A lifetime of torture, fear, and shame can be brought to the public's attention, and an impartial judge or jury can determine the truth and decide the remedy.

Family Changes

Filing suit may also bring changes for a victim's family. Children still under the care of the perpetrator can be protected, either through court action against the perpetrator or through individual therapy for the children. The court may order therapy for the perpetrator or may order the perpetrator to pay for therapy for other family members affected or thought to be affected by the abuse. Some courts are more willing to order this remedy than others.

Even if the court does not order a perpetrator to pay for therapy for himself or herself or for other family members, the seriousness of the claims made in the suit and the memories recovered through the legal process may persuade other formerly nonbelieving family members to seek therapy.

Criminal Prosecution of Perpetrator

Some survivors want their abusers to be criminally prosecuted. If the government has not filed a criminal action against your abuser, the publicity of filing a civil lawsuit may cause a criminal case to be investigated. Before filing a civil lawsuit against your abuser, you should discuss the possibility of criminal prosecution with your attorney. Then your attorney can determine the best strategy in your particular case.

If you want to press criminal charges *and* file a civil suit against your abuser, it may be best to wait until the criminal prosecution is completed before filing a civil lawsuit (depending, of course, on whether your statutes of limitations may run in the interim). There are several reasons why it may be best for the criminal case to be tried first. People can be forced to testify more easily in a criminal case than in a civil suit, and there is a right to a speedy trial. Criminal investigation lays the basis for part of the civil case, and a criminal case often uncovers many facts that are necessary for filing a civil suit. Also, if your civil suit is pending at the same time as the criminal prosecution, it may be more difficult to settle your civil case, because the abuser will be trying to clear his or her name in the criminal action and will be unable to settle the civil case and risk the public viewing this settlement as an admission of guilt. Bringing a civil case first may even hinder the criminal prosecution. Your motives may be questioned and your testimony may be less believable because you have a monetary interest in the outcome of the civil case.

Criminal charges can be filed only by the local district attorney (or its equivalent), either at the instigation of the district attorney's office or by the victim pressing charges. District attorneys generally file criminal charges against alleged criminals only if the charges are severe, the evidence is strong (for example, credible witnesses exist to the alleged criminal acts), and the victim agrees to press charges. If you refuse to press charges, the district attorney may decide to pursue the case if the evidence is strong and force you to testify.

The standard of proof in a criminal case (beyond a reasonable doubt) is more difficult to meet than the standard in a civil suit. District attorneys' offices usually have more cases than they have time to handle and, therefore, district attorneys prosecute only the strongest cases. In many childhood sexual abuse cases, there are either no witnesses or the witnesses refuse to talk truthfully (for example, siblings who are protecting the abuser). Most district attorneys would hesitate to pursue your case if the only evidence is your word against the perpetrator's, as it would be very difficult to prove beyond a reasonable doubt that the perpetrator committed the acts.

You should also be aware of certain constitutional protections granted a criminal defendant that are not available in a civil trial. Accused abusers, like other defendants, are granted the following constitutional rights in criminal cases: the right to confront the accuser (you) in court, the presumption of innocence until proven guilty, and the right to cross-examine any witness. Many states require corroboration of a survivor's testimony against any person accused of sex offenses. This is a problem in most cases. Few victims of childhood sexual abuse complain immediately after the abuse about being abused, either because of fear, guilt, or embarrassment.

Depending on your relationship with the perpetrator and the likelihood of future abuse to other victims, you may still want to pursue a criminal conviction. Realize that in most jurisdictions you can bring criminal charges only within certain time limits. If, after discussing the likelihood of conviction with your attorney, you decide that you want to press criminal charges against your abuser, you should decide whether to pursue criminal conviction before or after filing civil suit.

Lose

Although there are many possible gains that might result from suing your abuser, you may also suffer several short- or long-term losses. Some of these detriments are almost sure to occur if your suit does not settle very quickly: you will need to pay money, at least temporarily, to continue the suit; you will lose some of your privacy to the prying eyes of attorneys, your abuser, and ultimately the world at large; and you most likely will see changes in the dynamic of your family of origin.

Emotional and/or Physical Security

Abusers usually operate under the cover of darkness or at least in extreme secrecy. Abusers who are exposed to public view stand to lose everything. If they are financially successful, they can lose good social standing, as well as financial and business or professional success. All abusers stand to lose their former level of power and complete domination and control over their families. These threats will cause some abusers to do whatever they can to keep their transgressions out of the public eye.

Often, the first method used by abusers when their acts are made public is psychological warfare. They may do anything from cajoling to promising reform to threatening suit for defamation. You may even receive threats of violence, either direct or indirect, to you, supportive members of your family, and family pets. Many therapists, however, contend that this threat is not serious, as an alleged perpetrator would be the obvious suspect should a public survivor be assaulted. Despite the remoteness of the possibility of violence by your abuser during the suit, you should still be cautious and stay away from an abuser whom you know can be violent.

Lawsuits are often nasty confrontations. If the lawsuit proceeds beyond its initial stages, you should be prepared to live with the loss of much of your privacy. Attorneys are paid to discover anything that is pertinent to a case. Should your abuser decide to contest the case, you will undoubtedly have

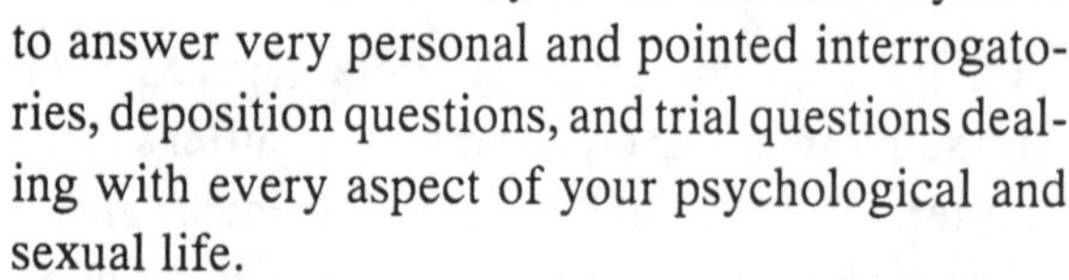

to answer very personal and pointed interrogatories, deposition questions, and trial questions dealing with every aspect of your psychological and sexual life.

Request for production of documents

formal, written document prepared by an attorney which requests specific documents possessed by another party

Also, any party to the lawsuit, including the perpetrator, can gain access through a **request for production of documents** to your journals, diaries, notes, letters, or other recovery work, such as artwork—any written material arguably related to injuries caused or actions taken by the perpetrator. If these works contain information or language that you do not want the public or the perpetrator to see, you should bring them to your attorney's attention before you sue to determine if the statements can be kept private.

Money

You should also be prepared to defend claims made against you by the perpetrator. Your perpetrator may defend by claiming that the statements you made are all false. If one person claims that another person has done something disgusting or immoral, the person about whom the statements are made can sue for defamation.

Please remember, however, that just because anyone can sue for anything at any time, a person can't win unless he or she proves the facts to the **fact-finder** by a **preponderance of the evidence**. Just making a claim does not make it true.

Fact-finder

person or group of people who decide what the facts are in a particular case; depending on the case and court, either a *judge* or a *jury*

Preponderance of the evidence

amount of evidence necessary to persuade a judge or jury it is more likely than not that what one party claims is true; *greater than a 50% likelihood*

Also, truth is a complete defense to a claim of defamation. In other words, if you can prove your claims about the perpetrator's actions, a suit by the perpetrator for defamation is worthless.

Depending on when you file your complaint for sexual abuse, your perpetrator may file suit first, claiming defamation because of your statements to others about the abuse. In practicality, it is not very likely that your perpetrator will file a defamation suit before you start legal proceedings. The perpetrator's attorney should know that filing a defamation action will force you and your attorney to defend against claims of defamation by filing **counterclaims**, which will contain the childhood abuse claims and be, in essence, a suit filed against the perpetrator. Of course, perpetrators are unpredictable and may begin a defamation action against you as a power

Counterclaim

generally, a claim made by a defendant against a plaintiff

move, even though it involves the risk to the perpetrator that you will file your child abuse claims. Similarly, if you sue before your perpetrator, the perpetrator can file claims against you in the form of counterclaims.

Should you fail to convince the fact-finder about your claims, you should be prepared for a judgment against you for the damages your statements have caused to the perpetrator's reputation. These damages can be substantial. You should consult with your attorney about the likely size of such an award should you lose the case. Of course, just as your abuser must have property worth something for you to collect for a judgment, your abuser may not be able to collect against you if you have no, or few, assets.

As previously noted, the financial costs of suing are high. Expenses that must be paid include attorneys' fees, complaint filing costs, deposition costs (court reporter charges, deposition printing costs, and copying costs), experts' fees (for deposition and trial testimony and consultation with your attorney), telephone costs, mailing costs, and general copying costs. Should electronic legal research be necessary or desirable, you will have to pay the hourly rates charged by the electronic service.

Attorneys' fees can range from $50 to $200 per hour or more, and attorneys must spend tens to thousands of hours on typical cases. Attorneys generally bill their services either hourly or under a contingency fee arrangement. Should your arrangement with your attorney be for hourly payment, you may need to spend several thousand dollars before the outcome of the case is known. You may be able to find a low income or sliding fee legal clinic that will cut the costs of attorney fees substantially. The federal government has recently begun a project to help crime victims recover damages through civil suits. You may want to write your representative or senator to urge funding of low-income legal services clinics that represent crime victims in civil suits.

Useful or necessary experts in child sexual abuse cases may include psychologists, psychiatrists, social workers, economists, and physicians. Testimony from social workers, psychologists, or psychiatrists is necessary in almost all cases to prove the survivor's claims of abuse, as usually there are no witnesses to the events. Often, psychological experts bill the time for their testimony at rates above their normal office rates, which may range from $50 to $300 per hour or more. Additionally, if you hire an expert from outside your local area because of the expert's greater professional prestige, you will have to pay for the expert's travel and lodging during depositions and trial. If your abuser's experts must be deposed, you also may have to pay these experts' fees for their deposition testimony, depending on the rules in your jurisdiction.

Trial and all activities leading up to trial will take a substantial amount of your time. You must be prepared and able to take this time from work for court appearances, depositions, and meetings with your attorney, if your attorney cannot meet at another time. Before deciding to proceed with any suit, you should take into consideration the possibility that your business or job performance may suffer or fail because of the time demands and emotional stress of the suit.

Changes in Family and Friends

Lawsuits can also alter relationships with family and friends. You must be prepared for these possible changes.

Families under the stress of lawsuits often break down, even when the suit is by a family member against an outsider. When one family member sues another, the results can be even more dramatic. And when the claim by one family member against another is that of incest, families almost inevitably crack. Family members not named in the suit may choose sides, deciding to believe one member's story over another's. If the perpetrator abused other family members, they may side with the abuser out of their own denial of the horrors of the truth or because they are still under the abuser's control and domination. Other family members may decide to believe neither side and contend that nothing is wrong, but that the victim merely imagined the sexual abuse. Some family members may become estranged from both sides. The survivor may also be blamed for family disruptions caused by the lawsuit. One incest survivor was told by one of her siblings that she was destroying the careers of her siblings because "no one would hire someone whose father was a pervert."

The revelations and stress caused by depositions and trial testimony may cause other family members to remember their own abuse. This may produce extreme hostility and anger toward the victim—anger at being forced to recall events that they don't want to remember.

Families split up by the revelations can recover their relationships, but this recovery may take months or years of self-discovery and/or therapy by other family members before they can believe and cope with the victim's allegations.

Your personal friends, and especially friends of your family, may have difficulty believing the truth of your allegations. If your family had a pleasing facade, as is the case with many incestuous families, you may have even greater difficulty persuading family friends of the truth. You may find that friends who you considered to be lifelong no longer talk to you after word of the suit leaks out. You may also find, however, that you gain new friends or strengthen other old friendships.

Your current family will also be affected, in some cases adversely, by a suit. Your spouse or partner may be unable to handle any more stress than what is present in your everyday lives, especially if you have undergone years of personal therapy and/or couples counseling. The financial pressures of a lawsuit may also add to the strain imposed on your current relationships. Your relationship with your children may suffer, especially if they had a good relationship with the abuser or family members who no longer visit or call. It is extremely helpful, probably crucial, that your partner or another primary friend be supportive of you through the legal process.

Emotional Trauma If You Lose

In addition to the trauma caused by merely filing the suit, you must be prepared for the psychological fallout of losing. Losing any lawsuit can be emotionally devastating. Losing a child sexual abuse case can be even more emotionally crushing. You should be prepared for all consequences of losing the suit, including general disbelief of your claims by members of the public who are not intimately aware of the details of your therapeutic history, disbelief by yourself of the truth of your own allegations, and psychological and financial trauma caused by paying a possible damage award for defamation.

What Won't I Get Out of a Lawsuit?

Quick Resolution of the Dispute

Lawsuits usually take years to resolve. If your perpetrator decides to settle the case before the suit is filed, you will get a resolution to your claims within a few weeks or months. If, however, the abuser decides to defend the case through trial, and possibly through an appeal, you will almost certainly have to deal with the lawsuit and all of its ramifications for years. Most courts in the United States have backlogs of cases that push only the most urgent ones to the judge's attention at any one time. The discovery stages of the case probably won't conclude until months after you sue. The court generally sets a trial date that is several months after the end of the discovery period.

All of these dates depend on how full the court's trial calendar is. In some jurisdictions, several trials are scheduled at the same time, based on the assumption that most cases settle before trial, so only one of those scheduled in each time slot will actually need to be tried. If your case is scheduled during the same time slot as another earlier scheduled case, your trial may be put off several months if the other case must go to trial.

Even if your case gets to the trial stage relatively quickly, you will not get an ultimate resolution for months or years after the trial ends if the abuser decides to appeal the trial court's decision to a higher court. On some legal issues, an abuser may be able to appeal a trial court's decision all the way to the United States Supreme Court. This procedure could take additional years and thousands and thousands of dollars to complete. It is, however, very rare for a case to proceed through several appeals. Also, the abuser may shun the additional exposure.

In general, if your perpetrator doesn't fold almost immediately, you will be looking at years of legal wrangling before any conclusion. Consult with your attorney on the time frames likely in your case.

Improved Relations With the Perpetrator

Although renewing relations with the perpetrator may be the last thing on your mind, you may be looking for some reconciliation with your abuser after an admission of wrongdoing. Therapists and attorneys who have experienced child sexual abuse trials acknowledge that this outcome is extremely unlikely for two reasons: first, perpetrators rarely admit any wrongdoing, even when they settle the case out of court; and second, since abusers do not generally admit any wrongdoing, any hope for reconciliation based on truth is futile.

Chapter 3

How Do I Find an Attorney?

In General, What Should I Look for in an Attorney?

Attorneys are service providers, and you are a consumer of legal knowledge and services. The process of finding an attorney can appear to be very challenging, but in some ways it's similar to finding other service providers, such as therapists, physicians, and hair stylists. Chances are good that you heard about your current therapist from another survivor who, after seeing him or her, said good things. Or perhaps you called a local agency, such as the Y.W.C.A. or Alcoholics Anonymous, and asked for a referral. You can use a similar process to find an attorney.

If you have a friend or acquaintance who has sued, or who is suing, his or her perpetrator, a good place to begin would be with the friend's attorney. Remember that a friend's recommendation is simply a place to start and that you'll need to make your own decision. If one of your friends raved about a stylist after a haircut, but the stylist gave you a crew cut when you asked for a trim, most likely you would not go back.

Don't be afraid to interview attorneys to find one who fits you. Your truth is an indelible, crucial, priceless part of you. Interview attorneys just as you would anyone else with whom you would entrust a fortune—carefully and as objectively as possible. Attorneys are not gods, and you are not a peon. Any attorney who treats you disrespectfully does not deserve to have the honor of representing you.

When you start meeting and interviewing attorneys, you may want to bring a friend, or in some cases even your therapist, to help you through the ordeal. Don't be surprised, however, if an attorney asks that your friend be excluded from any discussions between you and the attorney about your case. This may seem as though the attorney is trying to keep secrets, but it is far more likely to be a protective device for your benefit. Because you and your attorney have a **privilege**, any communications between both of you cannot be learned by your abuser or your abuser's attorney unless you agree to supply this information. If your friend is not also represented by the attorney, however, in most jurisdictions your friend can be questioned by your abuser's attorneys about the conversation between the three of you. An attorney who excludes your friend from consultations is probably trying to protect you by keeping your conversation confidential.

Privilege

a peculiar advantage, exemption, or immunity; an immunity from testifying about conversations between specified people

The attorney you choose should be knowledgeable in the area of the law you need. Maybe even more importantly, the attorney should also have a good rapport with you. Effective attorney representation requires mutual trust and respect. This is especially true in sexual abuse suits, where survivors must be willing and able to candidly disclose and discuss the most intimate areas of their lives. If in the initial interview you feel that your attorney isn't listening to you or makes you feel very uncomfortable, it's probably best to keep looking. The litigation process will be rough enough, considering the probable tactics and strategies of the abuser's attorney, without having to deal with an attorney who makes you feel unsafe or uncomfortable. Remember that there likely will be some initial trepidation at seeing any attorney, because of the magnitude of the step that you're taking and the awkwardness of telling a stranger the details of your abuse. Try to distinguish between this inherent fear and discomfort arising from lack of rapport with the prospective attorney. However, don't discount your "gut" feeling about the safety of potential attorneys and their law office surroundings.

Attorneys are held to high ethical standards in handling law suits. An attorney must listen intently to what you're saying to learn necessary facts, make an accurate assessment of your case, and determine the appropriate legal remedy. If, in the initial interview, you feel that the attorney has only superficially listened to you and has responded glibly, consider interviewing other attorneys to find a better match. You may need to listen to your intuition as much as the attorney's answers to questions to decide if the attorney is right for you.

Ideally, your attorney will have experience representing other survivors and have an excellent success rate in those cases. Because of the novelty of this type of case, though, you may not be able to find an attorney with these qualifications with whom you feel comfortable. Don't give up if you can't find a lawyer who has represented a survivor in this type of case. An attorney may have a basic understanding of childhood sexual abuse and its effects through handling divorce cases, for example, in which child molestation is often at issue. Other good trial attorneys who have not handled any child abuse cases may be willing to "get up to speed" on the relevant case law and psychological and psychiatric knowledge. Attorneys must learn new areas of the law all the time. Law school does not prepare them for every type of case. There are simply too many laws to learn and too many areas of the law, and the law continues to change. Additionally, the differences in factual situations add a slightly different slant to each case. Attorneys are taught to "think like a lawyer," meaning that they are taught the basic legal framework and skills for analyzing situations in a legal context. In many cases, you can get good representation from an attorney who does not have extensive experience in this particular area, but who devotes the necessary time to learning the intricacies of sexual abuse cases.

Other factors, although less important than your general feeling of comfort, may also be important to your selection process. For example, does the prospective attorney have a strong background in litigation and regularly represent plaintiffs? Does the attorney have a particularly good reputation in the community? Sometimes the political strength of a prestigious law firm might be necessary or important to help a survivor gain credibility against a well-known abuser.

Initial Interview Questions for Potential Attorneys

The following questions will give you a general idea of why a particular attorney is involved in sexual abuse cases, how your case looks, how effectively the attorney will guard your interests, and the his or her experience in the area:

1. Why have you gotten into this area of the law?
2. Have you had any other cases like this one? How many? What were the results? What percentage of your cases are like this one? Have you *tried* any cases like this one?
3. Are you familiar with the physical, emotional, and psychological effects of child sexual abuse? How are you familiar with these effects? What are they?
4. Have you ever represented an abuser against a survivor in a case like this one?
5. How much of my story will I have to tell in this initial interview? Can I discuss the details of my abuse at a later time?
6. Will you take the time to read my journals/diaries to get a better understanding of my case?
7. Will you consult with my therapist to understand the facts of my case?
8. Would you be willing to be interviewed by my therapist so I can get a better idea of whether or not I want to hire you?
9. Are you understanding about, and agreeable with, my desire to have my therapist present during some parts of the case, such as at depositions and at trial?

10. What steps will you take to protect me from my abuser and my abuser's attorney?
11. Do you have any problem with being totally frank with me about how my case is progressing?
12. How will you inform me of any changes in the status of my case?
13. To whom will you talk about my case?
14. Will you be working on this case alone or with other attorneys?
15. Do you employ, or are you willing to employ, a victim's advocate to support me through the process, assist with my questions and counseling needs, and generally help validate my feelings about my abuse and this process?
16. How much will this suit cost me?
17. On what kind of arrangement are you willing to agree for payment for your services? How and when must I pay for costs and fees?
18. What are my chances of winning this suit?
19. How far do you think this suit will progress until I recover from my abuser? How much time will that take?
20. (If your state has unfavorable law, such as an expired statute of limitations) Are you willing to take this case to appeal, if necessary, to set a precedent?
21. Will this suit likely require an appeal?
22. What do you expect from me?
23. How will you proceed from here if you take the case?

One survivor was scheduled for a lengthy review of her case with her attorney, possibly with her therapist present, but the attorney wanted to review her personal journals first. The survivor had written extensively during her recovery process. The attorney read every page of her eight journals. After he finished, he felt he didn't need to spend time reviewing all of the abuse with her, saving her the emotional hardship of verbalizing all of the details.

Of course, as the case progressed to trial, she had to go over specifics in preparation for testifying, but her attorney's willingness to read her journals spared her one additional review, and reliving, of the details.

You may learn that a prospective attorney is also a survivor. On one hand, a survivor-attorney will likely have less difficulty understanding you and your problems because of the similarities in your experiences and reactions. A survivor-attorney will probably understand and agree with your actions in, and reactions to, the stages of your lawsuit. On the other hand, survivors-attorneys who have not yet progressed far enough through therapy may actually be vicariously working through their own issues during your lawsuit. As long as the survivor-attorney can remain objective and maintain effective legal representation, this may not be a problem, but you certainly don't want to be cast as a surrogate therapist for your attorney or as a replacement plaintiff for another survivor who didn't get the chance to sue.

Questions for Potential Attorneys Who Are Survivors

If you determine that an attorney you are considering is also a survivor, you may want to ask the following questions:

1. Have you been in therapy to deal with your own abuse? Are you currently in therapy or have a therapeutic support system?
2. Have you sued your own abuser(s)? What was the outcome? Were you happy with the outcome?
3. Do you feel comfortable with representing abuse victims without feeling like their cases were your own?
4. Will another attorney who is not a survivor be

working with you on my behalf?

One attorney/survivor who had undergone several years of therapy for childhood sexual abuse represented a client in a suit against the client's parents for child sexual abuse. The client's parents, who were very wealthy, vigorously defended the case, hiring several expensive experts and several attorneys to represent them. This prolonged the case and made it extremely expensive to litigate and more difficult to win. The parents' attorneys also used every underhanded defense tactic in the book, including abusive, controlling behavior during depositions and at trial.

The attorney had strong reactions to these abusive actions and eventually had to withdraw from the case. This postponed the trial several months. The attorney's therapist determined that "countertransference" had occurred, meaning that at some point in the case the attorney began to view the case as a personal battle.

Just because an attorney is also a survivor does not mean that he or she will be unable to represent you. Many survivor-attorneys advocate for survivors very effectively, understand survivors' needs, and know how to deal with the tactics employed by abusers and their attorneys. However, make sure to the best of your ability that your prospective attorney is psychologically and emotionally able to represent you. If you are unsure about a survivor-attorney's readiness to represent you, ask the attorney if he or she is willing to be interviewed by your therapist.

Post-Initial Interview Questions About Potential Attorneys

After interviewing an attorney, ask yourself the following questions to aid in your screening process:

1. Was I reasonably comfortable in the office surroundings?
2. Did the attorney show some sensitivity to my needs for privacy, perhaps by shutting the office door to prevent other staff members from overhearing or by placing me out of direct window view from staff members or passers-by outside?

3. Did the attorney ease my initial fears of being in a law office, perhaps by offering coffee or soft drinks or talking about less intense topics (*e.g.*, the weather, local news, sporting events), but without diminishing the severity of my abuse, questioning the necessity or length of my recovery process, or demeaning me?
4. Did the attorney appear to be concerned about my well-being and sensitive to any difficulties I had in answering intimate questions?
5. Was the attorney willing to respond to my questions about the attorney's background and reasons for interest in sexual abuse cases?
6. Did I feel comfortable talking to the attorney?
7. Do I feel that the attorney listened to and sufficiently answered my questions?
8. If I started crying or showed other emotions, how did the attorney handle my emotions? Was he or she respectful, perhaps offering tissues, or act annoyed and condescending?
9. Did the attorney appear to be in a hurry, unwilling to talk to me for more than a few minutes?
10. Did the attorney allow interrupting phone calls and staff intrusions?
11. Did I feel like a number or a part on an assembly line rather than a valued human being?
12. Did I come away from the meeting feeling believed and encouraged or foolish and inferior?

The "perfect" attorney doesn't exist. Attorneys make mistakes in the interviewing process that may be inadvertent. Additionally, it may be necessary for the attorney to quickly sign papers that must be filed in court the day of your interview that requires interrupting your session (attorneys must live with the reality of court deadlines). However, interruptions should be the exception rather than the norm.

If you feel shortchanged by the lack of attention in an initial interviewing process and only marginally important to the attorney, chances are good that the feelings will only increase over time. You have the right to be listened to and heard!

Of course, you should still give any attorney who agrees to evaluate your case every courtesy. Attorneys are not therapists and do not have therapeutic skills, so don't expect an attorney to be able to provide a therapy session for you. Emotional reactions of survivors may be difficult for attorneys to handle, especially if he or she is not familiar with normal reactions to such childhood trauma. Give your prospective attorney the chance to respond to your fears, anger, shame, flashbacks, and other reactions. An attorney who can cope with these reactions, or who is willing to learn more about them for understanding and coping in the future, is a much better choice than someone who can't, or refuses to, understand the range of emotions you must experience.

You should also understand that an attorney needs to evaluate you in the initial interview. Attorneys know that one of the most important variables in any case is how their client looks to the other side, the judge, and the jury. If you are in a stage of recovery in which you routinely exhibit anger, hostility, sullenness, and bitterness, or are extremely emotionally erratic, attorneys have no choice but to take this emotional state into consideration when they interview you. Your demeanor and personality are a critical part of your case. Attorneys also know that someone who exhibits these traits is more likely to later direct the anger and frustration against their attorney. Because of this likelihood, most attorneys are justifiably reluctant to represent clients who seem stuck at this stage of recovery. Each of the steps you must take and the emotions you must feel during your recovery are important, but you should understand that your demeanor is an important factor in any attorney's evaluation of you and your case.

Remember, above all else, that you are a consumer and that an attorney's legal knowledge is a service. Shop around if you are dissatisfied with the attorneys you've found. Be mindful, however, that you only have the period of years outlined in the applicable statutes of limitations within which to start your suit (*see* Chapter 2).

What Are Some Sources For Finding Attorneys?

Some organizations keep lists of, or have people who are knowledgeable about, attorneys in your area who have represented childhood sexual abuse victims. The following may be good initial sources for leads on finding the right attorney for you:

1. *The Courage to Heal, A Guide for Women Survivors of Child Sexual Abuse*, by Ellen Bass and Laura Davis.
2. State Bar Association Referral Services.
3. Local Women's Resource Centers.
4. Victim's Assistance Programs through State Attorney's Office.
5. Sexual Assault and Rape Crisis Centers.
6. National Victim Center*.
7. NOW Legal Defense and Education Fund**.

Appendix B also lists attorneys who our research indicates have done, or want to do, this type of case. You may want to interview one or more in your search for the right attorney.

If you are otherwise unable to find an attorney, your last resort should be the local phone book. Attorneys are often listed by specialty. Look under topics such as family practice, personal injury, plaintiffs' litigation, psychological damages, civil rights actions, and medical malpractice. You're looking for someone who is willing to take a case that goes against the mainstream of society and who is not afraid to

---

* 2111 Wilson Boulevard, Suite 300, Arlington, VA 22201
** 99 Hudson Street, New York, NY 10013

rock the boat. For example, most attorneys who routinely represent big business (*e.g.*, defenders of large insurance companies) probably would not consider taking your case.

The considerations and questions listed above are only suggestions. Even if you follow all of these suggestions, we can't guarantee that this process will lead you to a sensitive, effective, ethical attorney. However, these suggestions have helped other survivors find helpful attorneys.

How Do I Pay for an Attorney?

There are several possible ways for you to pay for legal services. By far the most common are *contingency fee arrangements* and hourly payment. If you can afford to pay your attorney's hourly fees as they accrue, he or she will probably ask you to pay for services as they are rendered, through a monthly bill. Some attorneys will not take a case unless they can be assured of monthly payment. Many plaintiffs' attorneys, however, will take your case if you agree to pay him or her a certain percentage of whatever you might recover.

Representation agreements with attorneys are generally in the form of written contracts. Read this contract carefully. If it is in language you don't understand, ask the attorney to explain the meaning of unknown words or phrases. If the attorney is unwilling or unable to explain the meaning of the agreement, you may have some cause to wonder how well the attorney will be able or willing to explain the complexities of your case as they arise. You may even need to seek another attorney to give you an independent evaluation of the proposed fee agreement.

Contingency Fee Arrangements

If you are financially unable to pay for an attorney, some will accept your case in return for a percentage of the recovery (money) you actually receive. This percentage varies depending on the stage your case reaches before you recover the money, and it also varies from place to place and from law firm to law firm. A fairly standard percentage range is 25–30% of the recovery if it settles before trial, 30–40% of the recovery if it goes through a trial, and 40–50% if the case is appealed. In a contingency case the attorney does not collect any attorney fees unless money is recovered. You will be responsible for paying the attorney's out-of-pocket costs, such as court costs, telephone charges, and copying costs.

In some jurisdictions, an attorney can advance court costs, such as the costs of depositions, expert fees, and court filing charges, and then deduct them from any money you might recover in the case or seek payment for these costs directly from you if the case is lost. Other jurisdictions have ethical rules that prevent an attorney from advancing costs. In these areas, clients must pay their own court costs. Ask your attorney for an estimate of the costs and when you'll have to pay them. Some attorneys, while agreeable to paying the bulk of the court costs during the course of the trial, require that their clients pay a certain amount each month toward the accruing costs.

If finances are a major hurdle, you may be able to get some money through fund-raising on your part or with the help of local social services groups such as women's agencies or coalitions. Ask your attorney for suggestions and listen carefully to the attorney's reactions and receptiveness to your suggestion of alternate means of fee payment.

Even if you can find an attorney to your liking who is willing to take your case on contingency, you still must pay for your own living expenses. It is unethical in almost all states for attorneys to pay for their clients' living expenses during a case.

Hourly Payment

If you are financially able to pay for the attorney's time, for court costs, and for other expenses of a lawsuit against your abuser, your attorney may ask to be paid on an hourly basis, through a monthly bill. In such a situation, the attorney will ask you to pay for all costs and fees regardless of the outcome of the case. Attorney fees vary with location and may range from $50–150 per hour in small communities to $100–250 per hour in major urban areas.

Other Payment Plans

Some attorneys are more creative than others when it comes to how they are willing to be paid for their work. If neither hourly payment nor a contingency fee arrangement fits your particular financial circumstances, ask your attorney if another arrangement is possible. You are then limited only by your and your attorney's ingenuity in devising a plan with which both of you can live.

What Should I Tell My Attorney?

Once you have decided who to hire, you might next be wondering, "How much do I have to tell my attorney about my abuse?" How much you are able to tell your attorney has a direct bearing on your chances of success. If you give your attorney only a sketchy picture of who abused you and don't include all the places in which you were abused, all the people who knew of the abuse, all the ways in which you were abused, and all the times when the abuse occurred, you may severely limit the amount you might have recovered or greatly diminish your chances of recovery. Therefore, full disclosure of *all* facts and circumstances that demonstrate who abused you or knew about the abuse; when, where, and how the abuse occurred; and what type of abuse occurred is critical to winning the lawsuit and recovering what is entitled you under the law. It's important to note that full disclosure does not guarantee a just result. Partial disclosure, however, almost certainly guarantees an unjust result.

Each attorney you interview will question you about many of the topics mentioned in the preceding paragraph in your initial interview, and most will try to be as thorough as possible in determining and evaluating the facts of your case as soon as they can. Some attorneys who handle cases in this area, however, are aware of the difficulties many survivors have in recounting the events of their abuse, especially to strangers, and will ask you only essential questions required for an understanding sufficient to get your suit underway. These attorneys will ask for more detailed facts only as they become necessary later on in your case. If you have difficulty telling your story, you should look for an attorney who is aware of the difficulty some survivors have recounting this information (*see* Question 5 in the subsection above titled "Initial Interview Questions for Potential Attorneys").

No matter how, when, where, and by whom you were abused, the more detail you can remember about the abuse, the better. If you do not have clear memories of the exact details of your abuse, you should try to recount as much detail as you remember, such as colors of rooms in which you were abused, specific items in the rooms, clothes you or your perpetrator were wearing, and scents you recall from these times. Don't worry if you can't remember all of the details. Your attorney may hire an expert to explain to the judge and jury that sketchiness of memory is a symptom of repression of trauma, and may even be further evidence of post-traumatic stress disorder.

In addition to these facts, you should recount any past action or character trait of yours that may come back to haunt you later at trial. Tell your attorney about problems unrelated to your abuse, but that someone might view as being somehow related to your claims—problems at school, with the law, with siblings or other family members, or with your abuser—no matter how inconsequential they may seem. Also, if you've had problems with promiscuity or sexuality in any way, or if you are not heterosexual, you should disclose these facts to your attorney, especially if these behaviors, problems, or sexual orientation are common knowledge. Although giving access to this information may seem like a terrible invasion of your privacy, in almost every case you will be much better off disclosing it to your attorney than having your abuser's attorney discover and use the information before your attorney can prepare for it. Some of this information may be totally irrelevant and thus inadmissible at your trial, but you must give your attorney a chance to defend against these concerns, possibly by getting a court order to exclude this information from a jury trial.

In addition to the verbal disclosure you make to your attorney about your story, you should also bring all of your journals, diaries, correspondence, art work, and other written documents relating to your abuse or recovery to your first meeting with your attorney. If the materials are voluminous or not readily available, you should be prepared to have them available at the earliest opportunity for your attorney's review.

The necessity of full disclosure of all details of your abuse, your past problems, and your personal or sexual traits to your attorney underscores the importance of three points:

1. If the applicable statutes of limitation allow, you should be at a point in your recovery where you are comfortable having your childhood abuse publicly disclosed and discussed

2. You should feel comfortable with the person you have chosen to be your attorney

3. You should be at a point in your life where you are comfortable with who and what you are

Opposing attorneys often banter back and forth during discussions about their cases. Some of this is friendly chatter, and some is strategically directed questioning to probe the other side for how the opposing attorney is truly feeling about the case. An attorney's job is to represent a client in a dispute against someone else. Especially in small towns, an attorney will be involved repeatedly in cases with the same attorneys. In one case an attorney may be opposing another attorney. In a later, different case, the same two attorneys may be on the same side. Additionally, your attorney and the opposing attorney may be law school classmates or serve together on professional committees. Attorneys are ethically required to zealously represent their clients' interests, but attorneys needn't necessarily dislike or hate each other. They may even be friends.

You were victimized as a child, and the victimized child in you probably needs to be assured that the attorney is really on the child's side. Friendly chatter between the attorneys may seem to a survivor to indicate that the two attorneys are really on the same side and that everyone is against the survivor. To avoid feeling victimized by your attorney's inadvertent actions, you may need to tell your attorney your concerns and ask that the attorney respect your needs.

On the other hand, despite attorneys' ethical requirement of zealous representation of their clients' rights, if your attorney and the opposing attorney are friends, your case may be easier to settle. In such situations, it's more likely that both attorneys will be more willing to promptly resolve the case.

Attorneys are often very busy professionals, with several simultaneously active cases. Because they must attend to many different cases, they often cannot pay full attention for any lengthy time period to any one case. As a survivor, you may feel the need to be in control of the events of your case and feel left out of the loop when important events occur and decisions are made without your knowledge. If you feel a need to know and approve of events and decisions as they are occurring, tell your attorney. Your active, continued involvement in the case will also help your attorney, as you will have insights into your abuser's mind and about the details of your abuse that no one else can provide. If you haven't heard from your attorney in some time, it's a good idea to call or write and ask for information to emphasize to him or her the importance of your case.

You may want to ask your attorney to be careful in drafting correspondence and other documentation to you and your abuser. Referring to you in a subordinate position/ relationship, like using your first name, while referring to your abuser as Dr. or Sir may seem innocuous to your attorney, but it may have very damaging psychological effects on you. Discuss the use of such seemingly respectful titles with your attorney. In some cases, he or she might be employing them for your benefit (for example, to catch your abuser off guard).

To make sure that your abuser has property to recover if you win the suit, you should ask your attorney as early as possible if it is possible to **attach** your abuser's assets. By using an attachment, your attorney can get the backing of the court system to ensure that your abuser does not abscond with, give away, or sell the property or money that you should recover after getting a judgment. In some jurisdictions, you can attach a defendant's assets before getting a judgment. This is not the norm in most states, but you should ask your attorney about its possibility nonetheless.

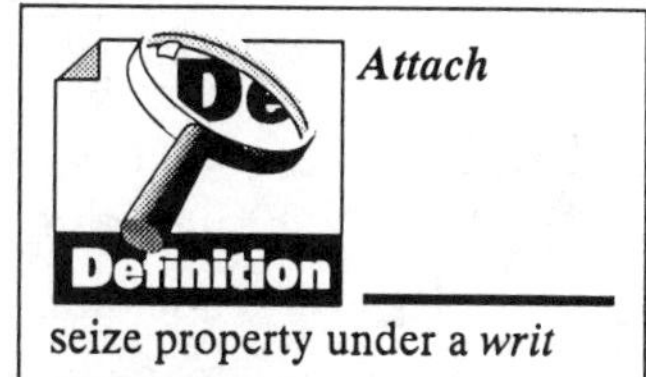

Attach

seize property under a *writ*

How Must Therapists and Lawyers Relate?

Your therapist is an important asset in your case against your abuser. If your therapist is willing to counsel and assist you during the many stages of your lawsuit, you will have a distinct advantage. A therapist's guidance is crucial to helping you overcome the inevitable feelings of anger, shame, guilt, and grief that such a lawsuit will provoke in you, especially if your perpetrator is a close family member.

The relationship between your therapist and your attorney is also critical. For almost all abuse victims, the testimony of a psychologist, social worker, psychiatrist, or therapist about the victim's psychological and emotional states during therapy, and by extension, during childhood, is the cornerstone of both the proof that the victim was abused and has been damaged by the abuse. How well your therapist is able to communicate this information to your attorney is very important. Your attorney will need to be able to structure this information into testimony that is understood to the judge or jury. A good professional relationship and personal rapport between your therapist and your attorney is a solid foundation on which to build a successful case. For this reason, as well as to gain your therapist's insights on how well your attorney will represent both your legal and therapeutic goals, you might want to have your therapist interview your attorney before you hire the attorney. This interview will give your therapist and your prospective attorney a chance to get to know each other and to see how well they work together. It will also give the attorney a chance to question your therapist about you and the facts of your case, to help decide if other psychological or medical experts should be hired to examine you, and to determine if your case can be profitably won.

Chapter 4

What Happens in a Lawsuit?

What Should I Do Before Trial?

One of the major keys to winning any lawsuit is preparation. A better prepared plaintiff and plaintiff's attorney can often prevail over a poorly prepared defendant and defendant's attorney, even if the case is weak. Because of the complexity of the testimony and terminology presented in an incest case, as well as its emotional nature, you and your attorney will probably need more time and put forth more effort than in any other type of case to be prepared mentally, intellectually, and emotionally for the demands of the trial process. Stay on top of the case as much as possible, and get your attorney to tell you the planned strategy in as much detail as possible (with specific regard to the various stages of the case, as described in more detail in the following subsections).

Above all, you should understand that the trial process is like a game. Once you understand this, and know some of the ground rules, through the trial process you'll be able to gain back some of the power you lost to your abuser as a child.

Find a Good Therapist for Self-Healing and Trial

If you can afford it, one of the first things you should do is find a well-qualified therapist. Because childhood sexual abuse cases are often very intense and cause profound emotional responses in survivors, many attorneys understandably will not take your case unless you agree to undergo therapy during the course of your case.

A good therapist will help you prepare emotionally and psychologically for all aspects of trial. He or she will also help you overcome the effects of the abuse, which will better enable you to get through the lawsuit, specifically, and difficult times, generally. You will also need a therapist who is willing to work with you during the litigation process, including testifying in depositions and trials. Such trained professionals are often called **forensic** experts—*e.g.*, forensic psychiatrist. Unfortunately, many therapists are unwilling or untrained to be part of an adversarial trial proceeding, which has a very different emphasis than a therapeutic relationship.

Forensic

pertaining to or used in legal proceedings; *e.g.*, a *forensic* psychiatrist would evaluate someone for litigation purposes

You will need to find a therapist well versed in child sexual abuse issues for both personal healing work and trial needs. One therapist may be sufficient for both purposes, but not necessarily. A therapist's educational achievements are not necessarily indicative of how important he or she will be to your personal healing work, but they are crucial for trial purposes. Academic credentials help sway juries and judges who are trying to decide complex issues regarding psychological damage. Some jurisdictions even require medical (psychiatric) testimony to prove a case. With these thoughts in mind (and with your attorney's help), you should carefully check a therapist's qualifications to determine the therapist's quality of care, level and type of education, and depth of experience in child sexual abuse issues. Ask for any prospective therapist's resumé, which should list his or her schooling and post-graduate training and experience. The therapeutic community is still divided on the prevalence of child sexual abuse and the reality of certain claims made by survivors. Many therapists don't have sufficient training to recognize the effects of child sexual abuse, let alone treat it.

Several other resources can provide referrals to sexual abuse therapists. Call local women's resource centers; the YWCA; rape crisis hot lines; suicide prevention hot lines; hospital and clinic substance or physical abuse programs; battered women's shelters; and local survivors' groups, such as Incest Survivors Anonymous (ISA), Adults Molested as Children (AMAC), or Survivors of Incest Anonymous (SIA). Other self-help groups such as Adult Children of Alcoholics (ACOA or ACA) often have special subgroups or meetings for incest survivors. Some areas have meetings based on the principles in the book *The Courage to Heal*, by Ellen Bass and Laura Davis, a self-help guide for child sexual abuse survivors. Some church denominations also have groups that deal with child sexual abuse. To get the best information about local therapists, attend one or more of these local meetings and ask for referrals.

The Sunday papers in many areas list upcoming meetings for some or all of these groups. You may also be able to find these meetings by looking up the group you'd like to attend in the white pages of the local phone book. If the group you're searching for is not listed in the white pages, Alcoholics Anonymous, which has chapters world-wide, may be able to direct you to other self-help programs so that you can find a competent, compassionate, affordable therapist. Even beyond the useful information they can provide, these groups and the meetings they hold can be extremely helpful in your recovery.

Although using the same therapist for both recovery and trial has many benefits, you may be unable to find a therapist in your area who has sufficient credentials to present to a judge or jury at trial. If you are currently getting good results, at the right price, from a therapist who does not have outstanding credentials, we do not recommend that you quit seeing him or her just because you need a psychological or psychiatric expert witness with better credentials for your case. You should realize, though, that your attorney may highly recommend hiring an additional therapist—an expert—for trial purposes. Recognize, too, that many good therapists will not take you as a patient if they know you are considering suing your perpetrator, because they do not want to be involved in legal battles.

It is important to note that some juries are biased against experts from outside the local area. Through your attorney's local trial experience, he or she should be able to help guide you in hiring necessary trial experts, including psychological or psychiatric expert witnesses, if experts other than your own therapist will be helpful to your case.

Although nontraditional therapy may be very beneficial to your psychological and emotional recovery, these therapies may harm your chances of financial recovery from your abuser. For example, if your therapist wants to hypnotize you to help you retrieve your memories, discuss this therapy with your attorney before you begin it, if possible. Hypnotism is not universally approved by courts or psychological experts as a valid method for the retrieval of accurate memories. Discuss with your attorney, and ask your attorney to discuss with your therapist, any legal ramifications that may come from the use of hypnotism or other non-mainstream therapies.

Therapists differ widely in the amount and type of notes they keep about survivors' therapy sessions. Attorneys similarly differ in their thoughts on how many notes should be recorded, and how detailed these notes should be, to help prepare a winning case. Ask your attorney and therapist to discuss how the note-taking should be handled, to ensure both successful therapy and successful litigation.

Regardless, we would not advise seeing any therapist who would be detrimental to your overall recovery just to help your legal case. Remember that filing a lawsuit is another way of recovering from your abuse and should be viewed as a possible adjunct to your comprehensive recovery plan.

Gather Correspondence, Journals, Art and Memories

Before trial, if you are already in therapy, you should gather all correspondence, journals, therapists' notes, personal notes, and art generated through therapy so your attorney can better evaluate your case's strengths and weaknesses. To do this, send a letter to your therapist asking him or her to release copies of all records of your treatment and therapy. You should also state in this letter that the therapist can talk to your attorney about any aspect of your therapy or treatment. This statement must be included because under the law in most states clients and therapists have a privilege not to divulge any exchanges in the context of the therapeutic relationship. This statement will not revoke your right to demand confidentiality regarding the general public. It will only allow your therapist to talk freely with your attorney about your therapy and treatment, so your attorney can better determine the strength of your case and prepare your case for trial or settlement. You and your attorney have a similar privilege regarding your communications.

Your abuser and his or her mental health care professionals and attorney, incidentally, have the same privilege. In some jurisdictions, at least in criminal cases, the privilege is not applicable to admissions made to mental health care professionals of current, on-going acts of child abuse.

Ask former teachers, classmates, and friends from your childhood if they remember how you acted during the period of your abuse. These people may be able to provide valuable corroborating evidence of the symptoms of your abuse. Don't easily give up searching for corroborative evidence—no other element will give you a better chance of winning your case.

What Really Happens During a Lawsuit?

Although everyone has seen trials on television, the trial process in the real world is a mystery to most. Even those who have been involved as parties or jurors are often confused by the procedures. A general understanding of the trial process, from beginning to end, is helpful as you decide whether or not to sue and progress through the stages of your case.

The procedures and steps detailed in this section pertain only to civil trial. Criminal trial terminology and procedure are entirely different. Because this book focuses on civil suit against a perpetrator, a detailed analysis of criminal trial procedures is beyond this book's scope.

Demand Letter

The first step in any civil lawsuit is the decision to pursue it. Once you have made the decision to sue your abuser, preferably with the aid and consultation of your therapist and an attorney experienced in this area, the next step is often drafting and sending a **demand letter** to your abuser. In the demand letter, your attorney will state that you have been injured by the actions of the abuser, demand payment and/or other action by the abuser, and will file a lawsuit if the abuser does not comply. At this point, your insight to what you want out of the lawsuit becomes critically important. If you do not know what you want, you cannot demand that the abuser provide it.

Demand letter

letter sent by a plaintiff's attorney to a defendant or defendant's attorney that demands that the defendant pay or do something the plaintiff wants

A demand letter is not always the best way to let your abuser know of an impending lawsuit. For instance, it may tip off your abuser about your suit and allow the abuser to begin preparing and planning for the suit. Your abuser might also file a suit claiming defamation before you have time to start your lawsuit. Strategically and emotionally, this may be damaging. You should consult with your attorney to see if you should use a demand letter as your opening move in the lawsuit.

Demand letters take valuable time. If your claims are close to being disallowed because they have not been filed within the limitations periods, you may lose irretrievable time considering possible settlements after sending a demand letter. Your attorney should be carefully monitoring the running of any applicable statutes of limitations and should take these periods into account when deciding whether or not to send a demand letter.

Lastly, demand letters are often futile. Because you have not yet made any allegations public, your perpetrator could consider your threat to file suit as empty and not respond at all or drag any response out as far as possible, in the belief that your threat of filing a complaint will evaporate.

If you are still on good terms with your abuser or your abuser believes you are still on good terms, make sure you've gotten all the helpful evidence you can get from your abuser before you send a demand letter. For example, getting direct corroborative evidence of your abuser's actions is normally impossible. However, in some states it is legal to tape face-to-face conversations without both parties' permission, thus making it possible to get admissions from your abuser about past sexual acts. Demand letters and confrontations arranged by well-meaning therapists often end this possibility before it can be explored, which can be a terrible blunder, as this may be the best opportunity to get irrefutable evidence of the abuse. If it is legal in your jurisdiction to tape such conversations without permission, and you decide with the guidance of both your attorney and your therapist that you want to go through with such a taped conversation, make sure that the confrontation is well-planned and safe for you.

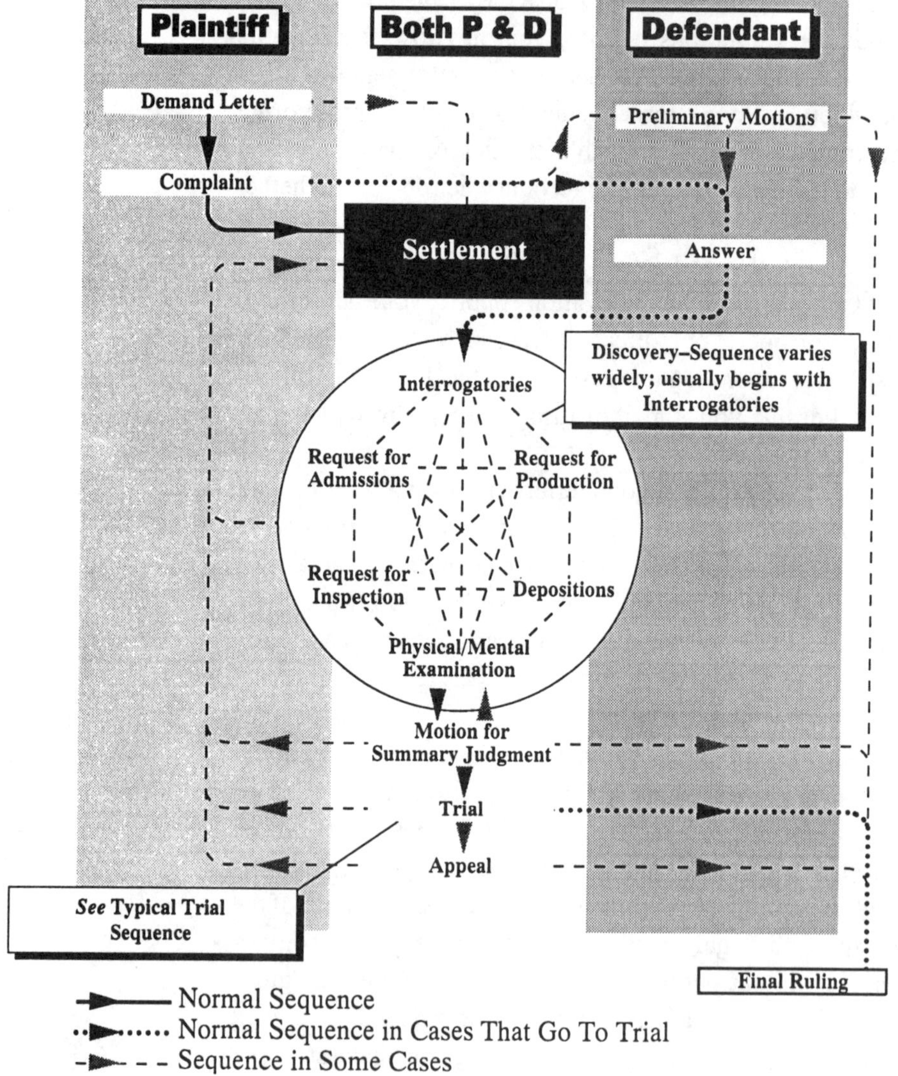

Figure 4-1. Child sexual abuse cases can follow several different sequences of events.

Complaint

A lawsuit itself does not legally begin until a complaint is filed with the court clerk. To prepare to write a complaint, your attorney will ask for all documents you have relating to the claims you are making. He or she will probably want to talk to your therapist and doctor and examine their documents regarding your therapy or treatment to determine what injuries you've suffered because of the abuse. Your attorney will also, undoubtedly, require several hours of your time so you can relate all acts of child sexual abuse as you remember them, as well as any other actions by your perpetrator that may relate to abuses. In at least one jurisdiction, survivors must sign a written statement (an **affidavit**) about their abusers' actions and the effects of the abuse. Your attorney may want to talk to siblings; a non-abusive parent (if available); childhood school personnel; doctors; and family friends and neighbors to determine if they remember any abuse-related behaviors. Your attorney will also want to know everything you know about your abuser's financial situation.

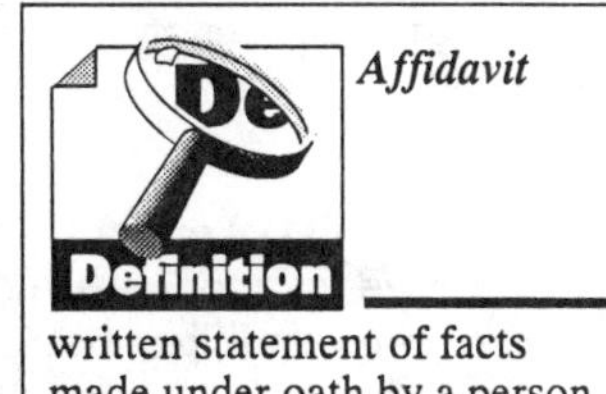

Affidavit
written statement of facts made under oath by a person

You will probably be asked many detailed questions about when and where you were molested. Your answers will help your attorney determine where to file the suit, and within what time period. Generally, defendants can be sued in any jurisdiction in which injuries occurred or in the jurisdiction in which they live. If you and your family lived in several states during your childhood, and you suffered sexual abuse in more than one of these states, you can often sue your abuser in one or all of the states in which you were abused, as well as in the state where he or she now lives. Because the statute of limitations or other law may be more favorable in one state than in another, your attorney may decide to sue in one particular jurisdiction over another on strictly legal grounds.

If your memories of the details of your abuse are

IN THE CIRCUIT COURT FOR THE STATE OF ANYSTATE
FOR THE COUNTY OF EVERYCOUNTY

Caption

```
CORA COURAGEOUS               )
            Plaintiff,        )    Case No. 12345-678
                              )
            v.                )    COMPLAINT
                              )    (Battery; Negligence)
VERNON VILE                   )
            Defendant.        )
______________________________)
```

Claim for Relief

For her First Claim for Relief, plaintiff alleges:

1.

Defendant is plaintiff's biological father. At all times stated defendant was an adult and lived in the same house as plaintiff.

2.

When plaintiff was between the ages of seven years and twelve years old, defendant continuously and repeatedly battered plaintiff by acts of sexual contact.

[Additional paragraphs might describe the acts of abuse.]

...

6.

Paragraph

Plaintiff did not know of any causal connection between said conduct and her injuries until January 1992, nor should she have known of such causal connection.

Prayer for Relief

WHEREFORE, plaintiff prays for judgment against the defendant as follows:

1. On her First Claim, for $100,000 in economic damages, for such noneconomic damages as are shown at trial, and $1,000,000 in punitive damages.

Figure 4–2. The main parts of a complaint are the caption, the claims for relief (with separate paragraphs stating the facts as they relate to the different elements of each claim), and the prayer for relief.

sketchy, you may not have enough information to determine where or when the abuse happened or even all parties involved. Your attorney will need to determine if you have recovered enough details to be able to proceed with a lawsuit.

Elements

parts of a legal cause of action that must be proven by the plaintiff

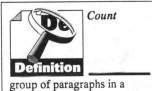

Count

group of paragraphs in a complaint that together state a complete legal claim; also known as a *claim for relief*

A complaint consists of several statements, called allegations, usually set out in numbered paragraphs. These statements present all the necessary information (generally in skeletal form) for a court to find a defendant liable or not liable for the damages claimed. You may be able to recover under any number of different legal theories, such as battery and negligence. To recover, you will need to allege and prove all parts of the claim. Under a battery cause of action, for example, you must prove all of the following:

1. Your perpetrator committed an act
2. The act was intentional (*i.e.*, your perpetrator's purpose was to cause harmful or offensive bodily contact or your perpetrator acted knowing with substantial certainty that harmful or offensive bodily contact would result)
3. The act resulted, either directly or indirectly, in harmful or offensive bodily contact
4. You suffered damages as a result

Prayer for relief

statement in the complaint of what the plaintiff seeks in the case from the defendant, such as money damages

These **elements** for the same or similar causes of action vary slightly from jurisdiction to jurisdiction, and are completely different for different causes of action. Generally, allegations in paragraphs for each legal theory (such as battery) are grouped together in a **count**. Along with the allegations, the complaint contains a demand for whatever a plaintiff wants out of the suit, which is known as a **prayer for relief**. A prayer for relief can ask for many different things. In addition to asking for lost wages, therapy costs, damages for your pain and suffering from the abuse, and other monetary losses you may have sustained,

Process server

person empowered by a court to deliver court papers to a person, generally a defendant

Summons

demand to appear before a court

Served

given a legal document (in a legally binding way)

Answer

legal response to a complaint in which the defendant admits, denies, or denies because of lack of information all allegations made by the plaintiff; may also include affirmative defenses or counterclaims

you may also ask for non-monetary relief, such as a public confession by the abuser of his or her acts, the registration of the abuser as a "Public Sex Offender," or the submission of the survivor to therapy. Although the laws in some jurisdictions do not allow these remedies and the court ultimately may not grant them, it almost certainly won't grant them to you if you don't ask for them in your prayer for relief.

After your attorney drafts the complaint, a **process server** gives it to your abuser, along with a **summons**. After the complaint has been **served**, the abuser has a time period within which to either deny, admit, or deny because of lack of knowledge all allegations in the complaint. The perpetrator's response will usually be in the form of a document called an **answer**. The abuser may also allege affirmative defenses, as well as make one or more counterclaims against you, in his or her answer.

The complaint and answer are both sent to the other party and filed with the court. They then become public records available to anyone. When the complaint is filed, it is often the first time information about an abuser's actions and a victim's injuries gets wide public dissemination, especially if the media decide to report the filing. Courts in some jurisdictions, however, keep the names of the parties confidential when news of the case could be harmful to one of the parties. This court-ordered silence includes child sexual abuse cases in some jurisdictions. Check with your attorney on the rules about anonymity in your jurisdiction. These rules could have a profound effect on your trial strategy, as one of your primary goals may be public awareness of the abuser's actions.

Motions

If your abuser's attorney believes that your complaint does not state a valid claim, he or she can file **motions** (before or after filing the answer) to have some or all of your claims thrown out of court. If any of your claims are not legally valid, the court may decide even before hearing testimony that the law does not allow the claims and disallow them. The person who files a motion is known as a *movant* or *moving party*. The person against whom a motion is made is known as a *non-moving party*.

Motion

a written or oral request of a court to take some action

Motion to dismiss for failure to state a claim

request asking a judge to rule that a claim is legally insufficient based solely on what was claimed

If your complaint does not state sufficient facts to constitute a valid claim, the abuser may file a **motion to dismiss for failure to state a claim**. In this type of motion, the abuser argues that some or all of the claims in your complaint are not valid, even if everything they say is true.

Your abuser may also seek a **gag order** through a motion. In such a motion, an abuser asks a court to keep the names of the parties secret because of the nature of the allegations made. At some point during your case your abuser may also ask the court through a motion to seal the records of the case, making them permanently confidential. (Either or both of these provisions may also be found in a settlement agreement, should you later agree to settle your case.)

Gag order

court demand that attorneys and witnesses in a case not discuss the facts of the case with anyone

Motion for summary judgment

request asking a judge to rule in the party's favor based on evidence

Even if one of your claims is valid as it is written, if the abuser later gets information through the discovery process showing that a claim is totally unsupported by the evidence, he or she can file a **motion for summary judgment**. The abuser's attorney may present statements alleging various facts through the abuser's or someone else's affidavit or may file documentary evidence (*i.e.*, documents indicating that some fact is true). A judge can rule in favor of the party that files a motion for summary judgment only if all facts important to the issue cannot be disputed and support the party's argument. Otherwise, trial is required on the issue.

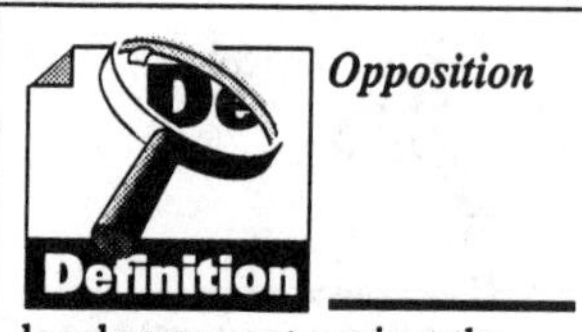

Opposition

legal argument against the arguments supporting a motion

To counter a motion filed by the abuser's attorney, your attorney will probably file an **opposition**. In most cases, the abuser can then file a **reply** to your opposition. These documents must be filed and given to the opposing party within strictly enforced time periods. Although time periods vary from jurisdiction to jurisdiction, in most jurisdictions the opposition must be filed and received by the non-moving party within three weeks of receiving the motion for summary judgment, and the reply must be filed and received by the moving party within a week of receiving the opposition.

Reply

legal argument in response to an opposition to a motion

After the reply is filed, the judge usually hears oral arguments in court from both parties' attorneys in a **hearing**, which can be held at any time from several days to several weeks after the reply is filed. Hearings are generally scheduled whenever the judge can fit them into the court's schedule. If the judge decides that no hearing is necessary, he or she will rule on the motion after the reply is filed. If a hearing is held, the judge will rule on the motion based on the oral arguments and the written motion, opposition, and reply, and can choose to rule on the motion immediately after the hearing or at a later time.

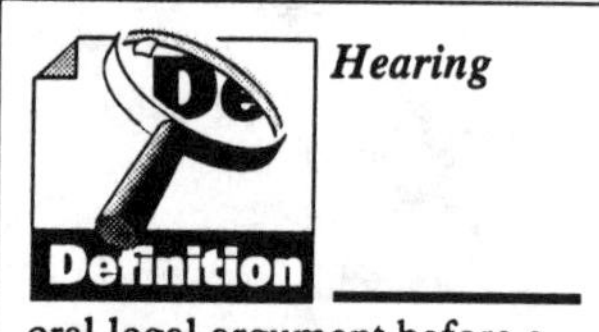

Hearing

oral legal argument before a judge; less formal than a full trial

If the judge rules against you after a motion, you may lose your right to recover for a single claim, several claims, or all claims. Conversely, in some cases your attorney may be able to file and win a motion for summary judgment for some or all of your claims.

If your abuser files pre-trial motions, your attorney fees will increase because your attorney will need to research the law and draft responses to the motions.

Most claims are not decided by motion. Attorneys rarely file complaints that state insufficient facts to constitute complete claims against defendants, so plaintiffs losing their claims on preliminary motions are relatively rare. Losing all claims through a summary judgment motion is also rare, because the facts are almost invariably in dispute. Usually both sides can present evidence, generally through affidavits, that substantiates the statements they made in their complaint and answer.

Remember that it's your abuser's attorney, not your attorney, who comes up with the arguments against you. If your abuser's attorney devises a good, logical argument against one of your claims, don't feel defeated by the logic or power of your abuser. Don't attribute your abuser with skills or powers he or she doesn't have.

Discovery

Once the complaint and answer have been filed and exchanged, each party can attempt to find out what the other party knows through discovery. As noted above, discovery involves a broad range of techniques through which an attorney for one party can gain access to the information known or held by the other party. Included among these methods are interrogatories, depositions, requests for production of documents, and requests for admissions. Discovery is a useful and mostly just method of sharing information. It generally keeps one party from springing information on its opponent at the last moment. Unfortunately, discovery isn't as simple as "give us everything you have." Parties often disagree about what is important to a case, so most jurisdictions require that parties ask specifically for what they want. (Although the discovery rules were written to keep parties from playing cat-and-mouse with the information they have, attorneys still have limited, though expensive, ways to keep information from the other side.)

Drafting interrogatories, requests for production, requests for admission, and replies to these documents is usually a time-consuming process. It demands precision and clarity to ensure that answers comply with the questions without divulging any information that the other party has not requested. You should be ready to spend time with your attorney both to help draft these documents and to answer questions posed to you, and you should be prepared for the cost of such work. If legally objectionable questions or requests arise, you must be prepared for the motions, and the cost of the legal research necessary to fight them, that may be necessary for your attorney to argue their legality in front of the judge.

Other types of discovery are similarly expensive. Deposition preparation can be especially time consuming and costly. Your attorney will need a great deal of time to prepare himself or herself to understand the legal issues and facts of your case clearly enough to depose the witnesses or defend you as you are being deposed.

Don't expect your abuser to readily volunteer information. You should expect your abuser to try to thwart your attorney's every attempt to gain information. To do this, the abuser likely will have his or her attorney use every available excuse to postpone or delay your discovery, including medical reasons, family emergencies, claimed attorney scheduling problems, and financial problems. Your abuser may be able to postpone some discovery, like depositions, for months or even years. To understand how this is possible, you should know that attorneys are often lenient with opposing attorneys in scheduling depositions and conducting other discovery. This is mostly a function of how attorneys relate to one another. Many attorneys (especially in smaller cities and towns) generally grant extensions of time freely, with the implied promise that the opposing attorney will remember this favor and reciprocate in the future. Attorneys know that to get things done they often need the cooperation of other attorneys, and many attorneys go out of their way to do this. Attorneys also often give apparently small concessions to the opposing side to get what they want.

In a child sexual abuse case, however, such friendliness can often come at the expense of a victim-client. Because incest victims are usually totally controlled and dominated as children, such reciprocal behavior can sometimes lead a survivor to feeling victimized again. This is especially true when a survivor is financially strapped and each delay costs more money or when acquiescing to the perpetrator's requests for more time causes a victim to feel like he or she is once again giving in to the perpetrator's demands. To make sure that your attorney's good will doesn't inadvertently victimize you, tell your attorney before you file suit that you want to be informed about and make the decision on *any* concessions or other negotiations, no matter how small.

You should understand that your abuser will likely object to many of your interrogatories and requests. Some of your questions and requests might even be rcturned with the notation that they are irrelevant. Such assertions do not mean that your abuser has proven *you* irrelevant, only that your abuser's attorney claims that the *questions and requests* are legally irrelevant. Don't allow these claims to make you feel you are once again being told that you are irrelevant, as you were as a child. You are not. Your abuser's attorney is merely trying to keep from divulging damaging documents or statements, or to drag the case out in the hope that you will give up.

Information That May Be Difficult to Discover

It is highly likely that your abuser will resist any inquiry about his or her sexual acts with others or about problems with sexuality in general. Despite the obvious sexual nature of childhood sexual abuse, abusers in many jurisdictions will be able to successfully assert in a motion that this information is not relevant to your claimed abuse. Ironically, your abuser may also be able to win a motion about the relevancy of questions about his or her childhood.

If you were abused by one or both of your parents, they may claim that any communications between the two of them about the abuse is protected by a marital privilege. This privilege is similar to the attorney-client privilege, and protects communication between spouses.

If you are suing an organization for abuse by one of their

employees (for example, a day-care worker), you may find that the organization has "cleansed" (removed or destroyed) its files of the employee's records. This may force your attorney to ask questions about the organization's policies on file keeping, to determine if the files were removed in the ordinary course of business, or in response to your lawsuit. Organizations also often plead ignorance of the abusive acts and any propensity on the part of your abuser to commit such acts.

Information That You May Be Able to Shield

If some of your past sexual conduct is embarrassing or may make your story of being abused less believable, you may be able to keep this information from appearing at trial or being discussed during discovery. Some jurisdictions have statutes that protect survivors from having to disclose their sexual conduct with other persons unless they make a claim for special damages, such as for sexual dysfunction. These laws are sometimes known as *shield laws* (see *rape shield laws*). If evidence of your past sexual conduct may be detrimental to your case, ask your attorney whether or not your jurisdiction has one of these laws and if it can help you.

Interrogatories

Interrogatories are the first discovery method used in most cases. They can be either written or oral questions that one party asks another. The written interrogatory is by far the more common. These questions must be answered under oath in writing.

Interrogatories are generally used to get answers to specific questions about pertinent issues. Your attorney will likely draft any necessary interrogatories by using the information you have already given him or her. Your attorney will also likely answer any interrogatories sent to you, with your input, so the answers can be written to comply with the questions as exactly and concisely as possible. Your attorney may object to certain interrogatories posed to you on various legal grounds. He or she will object to these interrogatories in writing in the same document in which you answer any unobjectionable interrogatories.

After one party objects to the wording in an interrogatory (or other discovery methods), the other party may decide to file a motion with the court to force the objecting party to answer the question as posed. The motion will be briefed and argued in much the same manner as the motions mentioned in the previous section.

Interrogatories provide parties with broad background information they may not have had previously. They also help an attorney focus the inquiry into needed areas and prepare for later phases of discovery and for trial.

Requests for Production

When a party wants to see any written evidence that may be in the other party's possession, a request for production of documents is necessary. Requests for production of documents are drafted with the same care and precision as interrogatories to ensure that all documents that a party wants are clearly included in the request's wording.

You will likely be seeking medical, insurance, financial, psychological, and psychiatric records from your perpetrator, and your perpetrator will probably seek the same records from you. Some of these requests may be legally objectionable for several reasons. Your attorney will determine which, if any, requests made by your abuser are objectionable and will decide which objections made by your abuser's attorney are valid. If one party objects and the other still wants to obtain the documents, the nonobjecting party will need to file a motion for the judge to rule the documents discoverable.

Requests for Admission

If one party wants to establish that certain statements are true, he or she can serve a request for admissions on another party. Requests for admissions can address any fact pertinent to the case. Your attorney will answer any requests for admission sent to you, with your help. These requests must either be denied, admitted, or denied because of lack of information. Requests are used to narrow the range of issues a court must address to those about which the parties really disagree. For example, if you remember that you were abused while on vacation in a particular place at a particular time, you allege that your abuser abused you in that place at that time, and you learn through another family member that your abuser has admitted being there then, you can request that your abuser admit this fact.

Physical or Psychological Examination

Parties to civil actions can also seek physical or psychological tests of other parties in certain cases. In most jurisdictions, the person who asks for the tests to be taken must also pay for the tests. Because of the nature of a civil child sexual abuse case, your abuser's attorney will undoubtedly ask that you undergo both physical and psychological examinations. Courts routinely uphold an abuser's right to demand full testing of survivors during this phase, ruling that the survivor has put his or her mental, and often physical, health into dispute by claiming psychological, physical, and emotional damages. Depending on the particular opposing attorney and facts, you may have to have full psychological, psychiatric, and physical examinations. During these examinations, you should be careful about what you say to the testing psychiatrist, psychologist, or physician, because this person will probably testify as an expert for your abuser at trial and will try to use your words against you. Similar to your testimony during depositions and at trial, as outlined in the following section, the best policy is to answer only the questions presented to you, to offer no more information than is requested, and to tell the truth.

Your attorney will probably seek a psychological or psychiatric examination of your abuser. In many jurisdictions, judges have refused to require such testing, despite the nature of the actions and damages claimed. As judges become more aware of the characteristics of perpetrators, this refusal to require psychological testing of abusers may change in many jurisdictions in the future. Should you and your attorney decide to request such testing, however, you should expect a legal battle, with your attorney being forced to file a motion discussing the meaning and requirements of the rules regarding medical and psychological examination.

Depositions

General Considerations

The most costly discovery technique, but often the most enlightening, is the deposition. In a deposition, the attorneys for the parties have an opportunity to question a witness under oath on his or her knowledge about the case before questioning at trial. Attendees at a deposition include a witness (*deponent*), attorneys for all parties, and a court reporter. Witnesses or the opposing party are also sometimes present.

A deposition is conducted in a similar manner to trial questioning, with some exceptions. Unlike a trial, a deposition does not require the presence of a judge or jury. Also, the questioning in a deposition is not subject to as many objections as in a trial, so the questioning is more freewheeling and therefore more thorough and lengthy.

Unlike during other discovery processes, anybody, even a person who is not a party to the lawsuit, can be deposed. Deponents can include any witness to any act or document relevant to the case. The judge can compel a witness to testify, at the instigation of one of the parties, through a **subpoena**. In addition, if people who are not parties to the lawsuit have documents that may be relevant, a party can com-

Subpoena

court order demanding that a person appear before a court or at a deposition

Subpoena duces tecum

court order demanding that a person appear before a court or at a deposition with named documents

Impeachment

demonstration of prior, inconsistent statements; demonstrates witness' lack of credibility

pel this non-party to produce these documents through a **subpoena duces tecum**.

Depositions are important because they allow the parties to directly question witnesses, including other parties, about the facts of a case. They provide an opportunity to see how a witness reacts to certain questions and indicate how the witness will appear to the judge or jury at trial. Probably most importantly, depositions give attorneys a chance to lock witnesses into their answers on important questions. A witness who directly contradicts his or her deposition answer at trial can be **impeached** on cross-examination, thus putting his or her credibility into question.

Depositions, like the trial process itself, can become mind games, especially in child sexual abuse cases. Because most perpetrators use sex to gain power over their victims, expect your perpetrator to use the trial process, and depositions in particular, to try to regain power lost when you filed your suit. You and your attorney should discuss how to prevent your abuser from regaining power during these depositions, and your attorney should understand that it is imperative that you aren't put into a position where you feel like a powerless child again. During depositions, abusers often try the following tactics: arranging chairs so the abuser (and sometimes the nonabusive parent) is seated in a position that dominates either the entire room or the victim (behind the victim, directly in front of the victim, *etc.*) and providing some stimulus/i that triggers the victim back to the dominated role of the past (through various words, phrases, sounds, postures, *etc.*). To prevent such ploys, make sure that you and your attorney arrive before the abuser and his or her attorney to arrange the seating so you feel comfortable and be aware of the triggering actions your abuser will try to use to bring you back to a state of subservience. The help of your therapist may be critical to understanding and overcoming these controlling abuser actions.

Your Deposition

Should your case continue beyond its initial stages, you will undoubtedly be deposed by your abuser's attorney. You will probably be asked direct questions about your sexuality (including sexual orientation), emotional status, marital status and problems, financial status, and childhood, among other things. Writings and drawings in any document provided by you at the request of other parties, including diaries, journals, letters, notes, medical and therapeutic records, and art work, will most likely be questioned from every conceivable angle by your abuser's attorney and by attorneys from any other party against you, including insurance attorneys if the abuser's insurance covers the situation. The questioning may become incredibly heated and pointed. Your attorney will protect you from legally objectionable questions but, for the most part, these questions cannot be avoided, and are merely a prelude to the innuendos that the abuser or those aligned with the abuser will make at trial.

Depositions can be very long—several hours per day and many days in length. Because of the sensitive, emotion-provoking nature of the questions that will be asked, before your deposition is scheduled you should tell your attorney that you will not agree to be deposed for more than a certain number of hours per day, preferably four or less. Tell your attorney before the deposition, with the aid of your therapist, how much you think you can handle per day. You should not be subjected to more questions per day than you can reasonably emotionally handle.

If you are in a stage of recovery in which you are subject to symptoms of post-traumatic stress syndrome, multiple personality disorder, age regression, or memory-induced flashbacks, discuss with your attorney and your therapist the likelihood of another personality appearing or a flashback or other symptoms occurring during a deposition. Discuss with them how you should handle these phenomena during the deposition. If it is at all financially feasible, your therapist should be at the deposition with you, for aid should you begin

to show such symptoms.

If you psychologically can't face your abuser at the deposition, in some jurisdictions your attorney can file a motion with the court to prevent your abuser from being present. If your judge will not grant such a motion, ask your attorney if your deposition can be videotaped. Many jurisdictions now allow videotaped depositions, which can be replayed in court during trial. Although you may not be able to keep your perpetrator out of your deposition, videotaping the deposition will help keep your perpetrator and your perpetrator's attorney from abusing you at your deposition either non-verbally or through blatant verbal attacks, as they can't afford to look abusive to the judge or jury.

Before you are deposed, your attorney will probably try to prepare you for the questions you are likely to hear. He or she will suggest how you should dress, act, and answer the questions. Basic advice includes answering only those questions posed to you. Don't embellish your answers. If a question calls for a "yes" or a "no," answer only "yes" or "no." For example, if you know the time and are asked the question "Do you have the time?," the answer "10 o'clock" is not the best answer. The best answer would be "Yes." You would respond with the correct time only if you're asked "What is the time?" Above all, tell the truth. A lie in deposition, even a seemingly insignificant one, could come back to haunt you at trial.

While testifying, you may want to carry with you, in an out-of-sight pocket, a small doll or other reassuring object that you can touch from time to time, especially if you've used it in therapy and found it helpful.

The Perpetrator's and Others' Depositions

Eventually, your attorney will also get an opportunity to depose your perpetrator, as well as others such as siblings, neighbors, friends, and your non-abusive parent. You may be excluded from attending for reasons similar to those mentioned above. You do not have to attend these depositions, but your attorney may decide that it is in your best interest to be present at some or all of them. Your presence at your abuser's deposition may be advantageous, because it may be your first opportunity to confront him or her face-to-face. Abusers often lose their composure in such direct confrontations, which could both aid your case and strengthen your resolve. On the other hand, depending on your psychological and emotional state, facing your abuser during his or her deposition may revictimize you. Use your own intuition, as well as your therapist's and attorney's guidance, in determining whether you want to be present during your abuser's deposition.

The outcome of these depositions, including your abuser's, depends somewhat on how much information you and your attorney can discover before each deposition. If your memories and your medical and therapeutic records have been corroborated by any other evidence gathered through discovery before your abuser's deposition, for example, you will have gone a long way toward getting a judgment against your abuser. It is much more difficult to argue that objective third-party records like school records are faulty than it is to argue that someone's fragmented memories are erroneous. If, however, your memories and medical and therapeutic records are all the supporting evidence you have, your abuser will likely try to shape the deposition answers to fit scenarios that indicate no abuser wrongdoing and your probable mental illness.

The order of depositions can be important to some cases. Your attorney may want to wait until late in the case to take your abuser's deposition to get a better handle on the case before your abuser is deposed. If you were abused by one of your parents and are able to depose both parents, however, you and your attorney should discuss the order of these depositions. It will often be wiser to depose the less powerful (*i.e.*, the non-abusive) parent (if there is one) first, because this will lock the nonabuser into his or her story and diminish the control the abuser has on the nonabuser's recounting of the facts.

You should discuss with your attorney and therapist how best to draft questions that will trip up your abuser, and how best to take advantage of the fact that your abuser is a lying, domineering, controlling person. An abuser's ego can often be massaged through questioning, provoking him or her to contradict earlier testimony or demonstrating that he or she has the capability to commit the transgressions you know occurred. You may find that you get some satisfaction from drafting either interrogatory or deposition questions to your abuser, as this will allow you, through your attorney, to ask questions you never had the chance to ask as a child and may never get the chance to ask again. Most attorneys are more than grateful for assistance in drafting such questions and will want your insights into your abuser's thinking. Be aware that some of your questions may not be appropriate in the context of a deposition or set of interrogatories and that your attorney may reword some of your questions for evidentiary or other reasons when he or she asks them.

If you choose to attend your abuser's deposition, you may want to make a list of the memories about the abuse you have recalled during therapy and note each of these memories your perpetrator or others admit to having happened. This will give you validation and help you overcome any feeling of denial about the abuse you may still have. You may also want to make a list of the lies your abuser or others tell, so you can discuss them with your attorney and therapist and possibly either refute them or cause the witness to contradict himself or herself through later questioning.

Settlement

Civil cases can be settled at any time. Negotiations between your attorney and your abuser's attorney (and insurance company attorneys, should insurance companies be involved) can occur at any time before filing your complaint up to the end of the appeal process. You will need to be involved with any settlement offers proposed by the parties to ensure that you get as much as possible out of the suit. Before you agree to any settlement, you and your attorney should determine the strength of the evidence for your claims. If your case, however meritorious, has flaws that make further pursuit financially worthless or nearly so, you will need to approach settlement differently than if you have strong, corroborated evidence of your abuser's actions and effects on you.

Settlement of a child sexual abuse case can include several types of demands. You may decide that your most pressing need is a monetary recovery from your abuser to pay for therapy and medical bills and to recoup wages lost because of the abuse. You may want vindication and a public apology from your abuser for the abuse you suffered. You may want to continue to speak to others about your abuse, to help those who have been unable to face or deal with the emotions arising from memories of sexual abuse. You may want the perpetrator to begin therapy to deal with his or her own psychological issues, in the hope that siblings and others will be spared abuse. As in the pre-demand letter phase, before any settlement you must complete a full self-examination to determine what you truly want out of the suit. Your desires may have to be tempered because of the weaknesses in your case, but you should still be fully aware of your innermost needs before accepting any settlement or your most important goals may go unreached.

Achieving all of the goals listed above is unlikely. Very few perpetrators ever admit their perversity. Because of this, it is unlikely that you will get a public admission or be able to get an abuser to enter therapy and honestly address his or her problems.

Settlements are usually agreed upon by the parties to a lawsuit through a contract known as a **settlement agreement**. Because this document is a contract, if one of the parties does not follow the terms of the agreement to the letter the other party can generally sue for breaking the contract.

Settlement agreement

contract by parties settling a lawsuit without a trial that states the parties' agreement about money to be paid and other important matters

Retaining your right to speak on your abuse and recovery may also be difficult, especially if you want to settle the case before trial. Because of the ignominy attached to an admitted or suspected child sexual abuser, most perpetrators who settle before trial insist

Gag provision

a statement in a settlement agreement in which the parties agree to keep certain information confidential; in a child sexual abuse case, this information usually includes the fact that abuse occurred, the name of the abuser, and the amount of the settlement

that the settlement agreement include a **gag provision.** Many abusers have agreed to settlement agreements that contained no provision restricting communication about the details of the abuse, probably because of a greater need to avert a large judgment against them. Other abusers, however, are adamant about including a gag provision in the settlement agreement. Therefore, if speaking to others about your abuse, as well as about your recovery from the abuse, is important to you, you and your attorney may need to devise a creative way to draft the right to speak into the settlement agreement. If full disclosure of all of the details of your abuse is not important to you, your abuser may be willing to agree to a settlement agreement in which you agree to keep his or her identity secret.

Abusers have been known to try to keep control over their victims even after settlement by insisting on provisions in the settlement agreement that put someone else, such as the survivor's attorney, in charge of doling out monthly payments to the survivor. If this type of final control is unacceptable to you, discuss this with your attorney.

Many civil child sexual abuse cases settle before going to trial, most notably because abusers do not want the public attention a trial will bring. Even if all indications point to early settlement, you must be prepared for your case to go to trial. There is no guarantee that your case will settle, and poor preparation for trial because you expect settlement is an almost sure-fire prelude to losing the trial.

Trial

General Considerations

The culmination of most cases that do not settle is a public trial. In certain jurisdictions, child sexual abuse trials are closed to the public to protect the identity of the accused, the victim, or both. In most jurisdictions, however, you will get a full public hearing.

Trials trigger extreme emotions and cause tremendous stress. You should be even more prepared physically and mentally for trial than you must be for the demands of filing suit. Everyone from siblings to long-time friends may make statements and exhibit emotions that will shock and hurt you greatly. Your personal integrity, intelligence, competence, and sanity will all probably be put into question. You must be as prepared as possible for all of these ploys.

Trial courts have fairly rigid guidelines about how trials can be conducted. Testimony and documents are screened carefully by both the court and the attorneys, and only evidence that passes specific tests of trustworthiness is allowed to be heard or seen. Court procedures in each jurisdiction are well defined by court rule and statute and known by all attorneys in that jurisdiction.

Courts must answer both questions of law, legal matters based on how the law is written and construed, and questions of fact, issues about what is and isn't true. After deciding what the law and facts are, a court must apply the law to the facts as they have been presented at trial and make decisions based on this application. For example, in a child sexual abuse case, the judge, who always decides questions of law, determines on which legal theories you have a right to recover, such as battery and intentional infliction of emotional distress. You and your attorney present your case to the court through documents and testimony, with the abuser and his or her attorney presenting contrary evidence. The trier of fact, either a jury or a judge, decides what is fact.

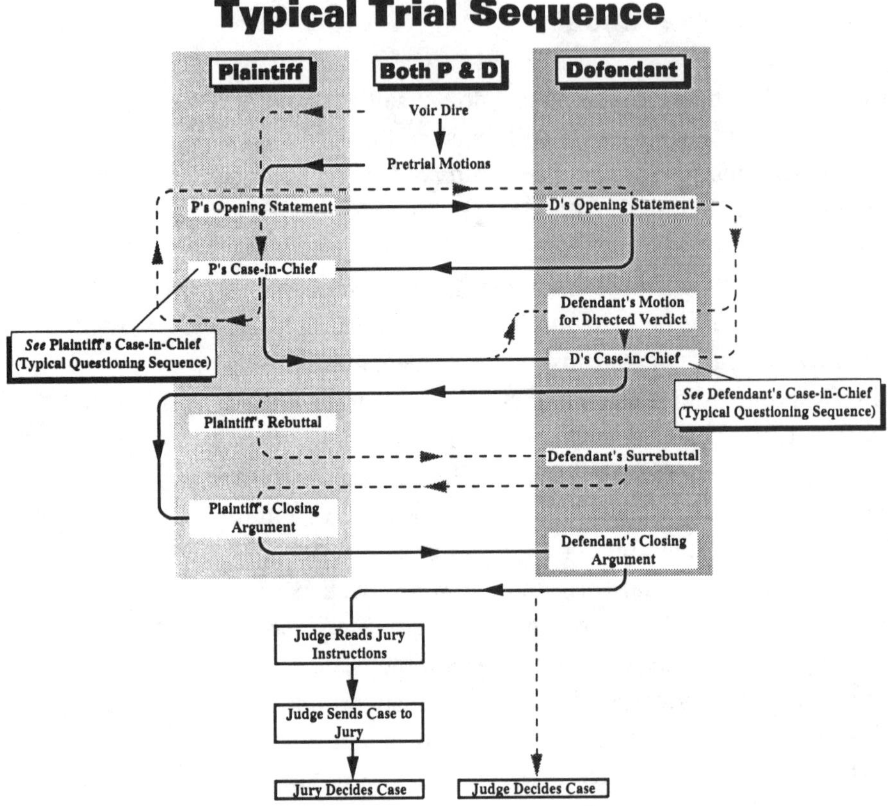

Figure 4-3. Trials generally have a definite order.

If you have a jury trial, the judge tells the jury what the law is, and the jury applies the law to the facts as they see them. If you have a non-jury trial, the judge applies the law to the facts as he or she sees them.

Judge or Jury?

Long before you reach the trial stage, you and your attorney must determine if you want the facts of the case to be decided by a judge or a jury, because either can decide questions of fact in most jurisdictions. You should leave the ultimate decision up to your attorney, because the considerations that go into this decision are somewhat complex and he or she will have a better feel for how particular judges and juries will react to a case like yours. You should, however, tell your attorney your preference before he or she files the complaint.

Some attorneys who have represented sexual abuse survivors feel that people who have difficulty with a claim of childhood sexual abuse will find a way to have themselves excused during jury selection. Other attorneys feel that people who are neither abusers nor survivors often get extremely upset by this type of claim, which can result in a larger jury verdict. On the other hand, because childhood sexual abuse is a widespread problem, your jury panel may include other abusers, who are extremely unlikely to be sympathetic to your claims, and other survivors, who may or may not be able to be objective about your injuries, depending on whether they have been able to remember and acknowledge their own abuse. People don't like to label others as abusers unless they are really convinced, often making it difficult for a survivor to convince a jury that the accusations are true.

If your case includes factors that may prejudice the members of the jury panel against you, you may want to consider having a judge hear your case rather than a jury. Although you may be perfectly accepting of yourself and the fact that you were abused, a jury may not be so accepting. If, for example, you are a lesbian survivor, a jury may be prejudiced against you. Just because a judge is hearing the case, however, does not ensure impartiality. For example, if a judge is a perpetrator you may have little chance of obtaining a fair result.

Jury Selection

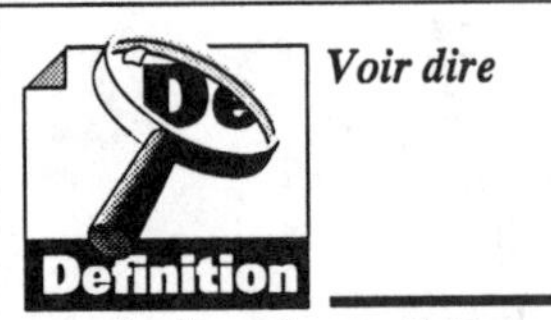

Voir dire

questioning of potential jurors by attorneys

Selecting a jury is one of the first things the parties do when a case reaches the trial stage. Although not widely known, parties to a lawsuit have a limited right to pick who they want to hear the case and decide what the facts are. Jury selection, or **voir dire**, procedures differ widely from jurisdiction to jurisdiction and from court to court. Generally, several potential jurors are seated in the jury box. The parties, through their attorneys, then closely question the jurors on matters that may affect their judgment about issues involved in the case. For example, either your attorney or the perpetrator's attorney probably will ask each juror, in as non-threatening a manner as possible, about possible abuse in their families, including whether or not they are victims themselves. The attorneys will also ask questions that might seem to be unrelated to the issues the jury must answer. The attorneys ask these carefully framed questions for a particular purpose related to your case. After questioning, each potential juror is either accepted by an attorney or **challenged** and excused by the judge.

Challenge

right used by an attorney to excuse a juror from hearing a case; either *for cause*, when a juror shows legal bias toward the other side (each party has an unlimited number), or *peremptory*, when one party doesn't like a juror for some reason that doesn't amount to a legal bias (each party has a limited number)

Because sexual abuse cases depend so much on psychological and psychiatric testimony, you and your attorney may decide that you want as many well-educated people who can understand the psychological factors as possible on your jury.

Again, you must be prepared for the cost of voir dire and other necessary trial activities, like drafting **jury instructions**. Preparing for and completing all of these activities is extremely time consuming.

Jury instructions

explanations of the applicable law given by the judge to the jury; attorneys for both sides to a lawsuit usually give desired jury instructions to the judge, who decides which to use

Opening Statement and Testimony

Opening statement

speech to the court in which attorney tells the facts he or she intends to present during the trial (through witnesses and documents), and how those facts should lead to a decision for his or her client

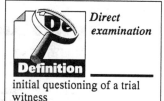

Once jurors have been chosen and the attorneys have argued any preliminary motions over legal issues, the attorneys get a chance to present their **opening statements** to the judge or jury. Trials have several parts. Each party to a lawsuit has the opportunity to present his or her case to the trier of fact (the judge or jury). The plaintiff presents his or her case first, by having people testify and identify and discuss documents (the plaintiff's *case-in-chief*); then, the defendant has a similar opportunity (the defendant's *case-in-chief*). In most jurisdictions, the plaintiff can present additional testimony or documents to rebut what the defendant and his or her witnesses have said. When there are more than two parties, the procedure is more complex, but it follows the same general pattern.

Direct examination

initial questioning of a trial witness

Cross examination

questioning by an attorney opposed to the party who presents a witness for direct examination; follows direct examination

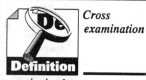

Each witness' testimony is further subdivided into **direct examination, cross examination, redirect examination**, and **recross examination**. When a witness is first called to testify, an attorney directs questions to the witness in the direct examination. The opposing attorney then questions the witness in the cross examination. The first attorney can then question the witness again in a redirect examination. The opposing attorney follows, if desired, with re-cross examination. In most cases, questioning must be limited to issues addressed in the previous questioning. For example, questioning on cross examination must follow up only those questions asked during direct examination.

Redirect examination

questioning by an attorney on issues addressed in cross examination

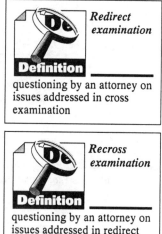

Recross examination

questioning by an attorney on issues addressed in redirect examination

Some of the documents produced during discovery, such as journals, diaries, letters, notes, and art work, are brought into evidence through witnesses' testimony. If you want to introduce a certain page from your personal journal into evidence, your attorney will ask you questions about the journal. Then, your attorney will ask if the other party objects to the journal being entered into evidence. If the other side does not object, you will be able to read selections from the journal. Other documents are entered into evidence in a similar manner. If a party objects to a document being entered into evidence, the court will rule on this objection. Sometimes a court will rule that only parts of a document can be entered into evidence or that a document can be entered into evidence only for a limited purpose.

Typical Questioning Sequence

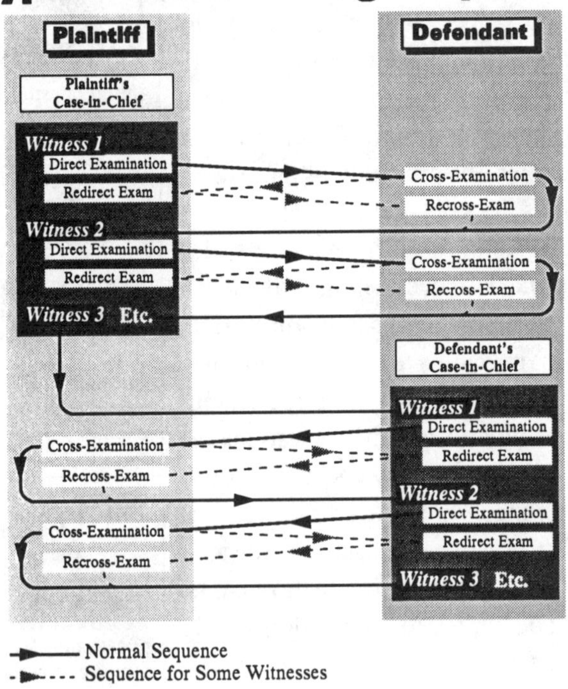

Figure 4-4. Each witness generally can be asked questions four different times, and each party can have several witnesses testify.

In your child sexual abuse case, you will undoubtedly have to testify to prove the fact of your victimization. You will also have other witnesses testify about the extent and causes of your injuries. These witnesses will probably include some or all of the following: physicians, psychiatrists, psychologists, social workers, and economists. If your testimony about being abused as a child can be supported by anyone else, you will also have them testify during the presentation of your case.

In most cases, your abuser will also testify. Although you have the legal duty to provide enough evidence to prove the facts of your abuse, the nature of the wrongs committed and the age at which the abuse occurred may make it difficult for your abuser to directly disprove the abuse. The implication left by the telling of survivor memories not associated with a definite time or place, for example, may be difficult to rebut. An abuser may have difficulty disproving his or her presence during the times and places a survivor remembers, albeit somewhat hazily.

If your perpetrator has status and prestige in the community, through either a distinguished career, financial success, or family ties, you may have a difficult time convincing a jury that he or she could have committed such acts against you. Despite the recent increase in media coverage of child sexual abuse, many jury members and judges still need to be educated about how widespread child sexual abuse is and how it crosses all social and economic barriers. It will be up to you, your experts, and your attorney to successfully educate these people during the trial.

Hearsay

the repeating *in* court of a statement made *out* of court, for the purpose of proving the statement true

Testimony from witnesses to your symptoms of abuse, such as flashbacks, however, may be more difficult to present to the court. If you have made statements about acts committed by your abuser, the witnesses to these statements may be unable to tell the jury what they heard you say because of a doctrine known as the **hearsay** rule. Witnesses can only testify about what they observe. The hearsay rule prevents a witness from saying an event happened if the witness did not observe the event but merely heard about it from someone. For example, if you made a statement to your therapist while you were in a flashback to your youth that "Daddy did it!" and your attorney starts to question your therapist about what you said (to show that your father committed the abuse), your abuser's attorney will object to the question as leading to hearsay testimony. If you have made statements outside the courtroom about your abuser (or others), your attorney will carefully analyze each to determine if it is hearsay and, if so, if it falls under one of the many exceptions to the rule.

If you and your attorney decide that you should not attend the abuser's deposition, trial may be the first time you have seen your abuser in many years. This confrontation could cause severe psychological effects, such as flashbacks or age regression. You should discuss this possibility with both your attorney and therapist, to determine the best way to handle these reactions.

Other strategies may also help you survive the trial. Some attorneys have their survivor clients attend trial only to testify, so the survivor doesn't have to ride a trial's roller-coaster of emotions. You may also want to have your therapist with you during your stay in the courtroom, to help you deal with these emotions and your reactions to them.

Trial questioning is often extremely hostile. It is the opposing attorney's job to make you look as bad as possible in the eyes of the jury. To do this, the abuser's attorney may be confrontational and accusatory and attempt to place the blame for your symptoms of sexual abuse on you rather than on your abuser. The questioning may be sufficiently cruel to revictimize you. It is important that you do not lose your poise on the stand during cross examination. On the other hand, should the questioning become particularly ugly, the jury may decide that the other side is being overbearing. If you should lose composure after one or more of these questions and begin to cry, the jury may realize that you are indeed a victim. In almost every case, being yourself and allowing yourself to react naturally is the best course to take. Although it is entirely understandable that you would be angry about your abuse, letting loose with an angry outburst

or being overly aggressive during trial testimony will probably be counterproductive. Discuss with your attorney what reactions you can afford to allow yourself on the stand.

Because of the nature of most civil child sexual abuse cases, in which the abuse is not witnessed by anyone but the survivor and the abuser, testimony from psychological experts about what happened to the survivor is of great importance. Many child sexual abuse cases become "battles of the experts" in which the testimony of the experts hired by the abuser and the survivor is totally contradictory. In such cases, the qualifications and believability of your experts can win or lose your case for you.

Closing Argument and Decision

After the parties question all the witnesses and introduce documents through them, the attorneys give their closing arguments. In the closing argument, an attorney can state the facts he or she thinks the evidence indicates, as well as argue how the jury or judge should apply the law to the facts. For example, if you have presented evidence demonstrating that your abuser has committed several acts of battery, your attorney will state that this testimony (and possibly documents) demonstrates battery occurred, and the jury should find the defendant liable for damages to you.

If the facts are to be decided by a jury, sometime during the course of the trial the attorneys and judge convene to decide which jury instructions should be read to the jury. These instructions tell the jury what the law is and how it should be applied to the facts. The jury instructions are either agreed upon by the attorneys or objected to by one or more of the attorneys. If the wording of a jury instruction is objected to, the judge may decide that it is fine as written and give it to the jury over the attorney's objection. Should the jury decide the case based on the law stated in the contested jury instruction, the attorney who properly objected has the right to appeal the decision.

The judge reads the jury instructions to the jury after the attorneys give their closing arguments. The judge then sends the case to the jury, who decides the case after studying and deciding the facts. These deliberations can last anywhere from minutes to days, depending on the extent of conflict in the evidence.

If the facts of the case are to be decided by the judge, he or she generally recesses the court and makes the decision. This decision can be made immediately or several weeks after the trial is concluded.

A decision can have many different outcomes. You may win on all or several of your claims or lose them all. If you win some of your claims, either the jury or the judge will name a monetary award for them. This award can range anywhere from one dollar to several million dollars, depending on the law in your jurisdiction and on how the jury or judge views the seriousness of your injuries. If the decision is against you and your abuser has filed claims against you, the fact-finder may also establish your monetary liability to your abuser. After the amount of the award is known, the judge signs a judgment for the winning party.

Chapter 5

What Happens After a Lawsuit?

How Is a Court's Judgment Carried Out?

Assuming you've won some of your claims at trial, after the fact-finder makes its decision and sets the amount of the judgment and the judge signs it you and your attorney can use legal means to recover this amount from your abuser. Typically, recovery can be made by **executing** against property owned by the abuser, including home(s), car(s), boat(s), and other large items that can be sold, and cash or its equivalent (such as stocks, bonds, and certificates of deposit). You can also usually recover a portion of your abuser's wages or salary through **garnishment**.

Execution

carrying a court judgment into effect, usually by seizing and/or selling the debtor's property

Execution

Once a judgment is entered it can be executed. To execute a judgment in your favor, for example, you will collect whatever property is available from your perpetrator. You and your attorney should have previously discussed and discovered

Garnishment

executing against a judgment debtor's wages or salary

what property your abuser owned, so you would know on what property to execute once the judgment was signed by the judge.

The perpetrator may own many different types of property: automobiles, boats, real property (houses, cabins, land, apartment houses, business property, *etc.*), securities (stocks, bonds, mutual funds, certificates of deposit, debentures, *etc.*), collections (coins, baseball cards, stamps, antiques, art, *etc.*), cash, accounts receivable (including future paychecks), and other ownership interests (partnership interests, business goodwill, *etc.*), among other property interests.

Once you have a judgment, you have a right to collect it from the perpetrator. To do this, your attorney must seize the property through legal means and, if it is not cash or its equivalent, sell it at auction. There are limits on what you can recover, however. The law does protects debtors from being stripped of everything they own. A small amount of personal possessions (*e.g.*, clothes) can be kept as well as a set amount for a home. Such property is considered **exempt** from execution. The dollar amounts of the exemptions vary by jurisdiction, but are usually relatively low (*e.g.*, \$500 for clothing, \$25,000 for a home).

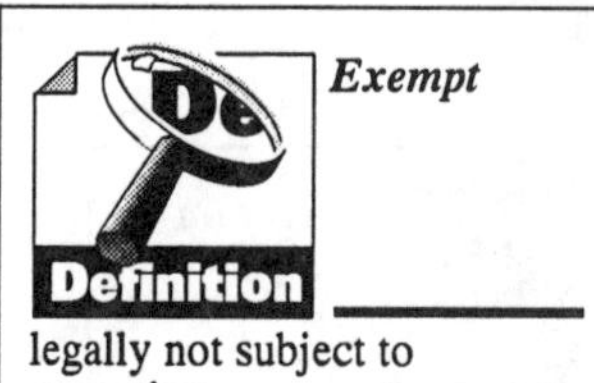

Exempt

legally not subject to execution

You should also be aware that a bank or other lender may have an ownership interest in property apparently wholly owned by the perpetrator. The bank or other lending institution probably has an interest in the perpetrator's home and car, for example, as lenders generally require security for loans to buy these types of properties, and the best security is often the property itself. Under these agreements, a bank generally has a better claim to any proceeds from this property than you do, so you will get only the amount that remains after the bank has been paid in full. Be aware that this remainder is often small or non-existent.

As noted in Chapter 6, you may also be able to recover against one or more insurance policies the perpetrator had when the sexual abuse occurred.

Bankruptcy

Your abuser may be able to escape paying the damages the court awarded you in several ways. He or she can hide any property owned, fraudulently and secretly transfer the property to someone other than you either by sale or gift, or file for bankruptcy. If your abuser hides or transfers the property, recovery from your abuser depends on the success you, your attorney, and possibly a private investigator have in finding and seizing this property. Each state has its own laws on how property can be seized and sold after a judgment against someone, so a listing of the steps necessary to turn seized property into money is not possible here. Ask your attorney what steps can be taken to gain possession of the property and what you must do once the property is seized.

If your perpetrator decides to file for protection under the bankruptcy laws, a complex set of legal rules will govern how much, if any, money you will receive.

What Happens If the Case Is Appealed?

If the trial judge rules that you lose certain claims on legal grounds (the law does not allow the claims) or makes a legal ruling that otherwise adversely affects one of your claims, you must decide, with the legal assistance of your attorney and the therapeutic assistance of your therapist, whether it is in your best interest to appeal the decision. If the judge or jury finds for you and your perpetrator appeals your case, you will be faced with the similar decision of whether or not to **respond** to the appeal. Your participation in an appeal depends on several factors, including your emotional and psychological health, your perpetrator's willingness and ability to extend the case, and your financial situation.

Respond

make arguments, either legal or factual, to the contrary

The parties to an appeal are the *appellant*, the

person who appeals the trial court's decision, and the *respondent* or *appellee*, the person who responds to the legal arguments presented by the appellant. In most appeals, the appellant files an *appellant's brief*, a document setting out the legal arguments against the trial court's decision. The respondent then files a *respondent's brief*, which is a rebuttal of the arguments presented by the appellant. The appellant usually files a shorter *reply brief* to rebut the arguments the respondent made in the response brief. The appellate court decides which arguments have the most strength and rules for one party or another on the questions presented. The appellate court can rule that the trial court's decision was totally correct, partially correct, or totally wrong on all contested issues.

If the appellate court rules that the trial court was entirely correct in its rulings, the trial court decision stands. If the appellate court rules that the trial court was partially or totally wrong on issues contested by the appellant, the appellate court may rule that the trial, or parts of it, should be conducted again or may simply order that the trial court grant a different judgment on some or all issues.

It is important to note that appeals rarely change the trial court's determination of the facts. Appeals are usually concerned with the trial court's determination of what law should have been applied to the facts. For example, after hearing all testimony, if the trial court determines that you were abused on a particular occasion on which your memories are clear, but not on another occasion you recall very hazily, the appellate court will almost certainly not overturn this determination.

If, on the other hand, the trial court rules a particular statute of limitations should be applied, and the appeals court disagrees, the appeals court will overturn the trial court's ruling and allow the trial to proceed on any causes of action that should have been heard under that statute of limitations.

Appeals are very costly, mostly because they require many hours of legal research. Appellate briefs are often 50 pages long, and sometimes contain hundreds of citations to cases supporting the party's position on the legal issues in dispute. Each of the cases cited, as well as hundreds more that do not quite fit the issues, must be read and digested to come up with the legal arguments presented. Such cases are found in *legal reporters*, volumes of appellate court decisions, or in computer databases of legal decisions. Finding this information takes either extensive attorney time, if your attorney uses legal reporters, or money, if your attorney uses computerized legal databases. Either way, the process is expensive.

Additionally, if you are paying your attorney on a contingency fee basis, you will likely pay a larger percentage of any recovery to your attorney if the case is appealed. You may also need to hire a new attorney, as some trial attorneys do not handle appellate work.

Some states and the federal courts have more than one level of appeals court. In some cases, you may have to appeal or respond to an appeal in more than one appellate court. For example, if one party appeals a trial court's decision to an intermediate appellate court (called a Court of Appeals in many state jurisdictions and in the federal system), the case may end in this court or one of the parties may decide to appeal the intermediate court's decision to the jurisdiction's highest court (usually known as the Supreme Court).

The decision to appeal or respond to your abuser's appeal should be made with particular reliance on your attorney's recommendations. Your attorney will have the best understanding of the strength of your legal arguments.

Chapter 6

Of What Other Issues Should I Be Aware?

This section covers situations and legal principles that don't easily fit into any other section of the book. It explains where you can sue, how insurance may be available to cover your damages, and how the law, procedures, and reactions to your suit will likely differ if your abuse was perpetrated by someone other than a parent, stepparent or adoptive parent, by multiple perpetrators, or in a satanic or ritualistic cult.

Where Can I File My Suit?

Jurisdiction

As noted before, you will need to discuss all aspects of your abuse with your attorney before suing your abuser. Without this information your attorney will not know in which jurisdiction to file your suit.

Although you can sue anyone at any time for anything, you can't successfully sue anyone *anywhere* for anything. Courts have strict rules on what parties can be sued in their jurisdictions. Your attorney will be able to determine the best jurisdiction and type of court for your suit only if you have given him or her complete information about what happened to you.

In state trial courts, the most common rule is that defendants can be sued in any jurisdiction in which they live or in which the injurious acts were committed. Suing anywhere else will result in the court refusing to hear the case because of lack of **personal jurisdiction** over the abuser. Thus, your attorney must know both where the acts occurred and where the abuser now lives.

When recounting your story, be sure to tell your attorney every place that abuse occurred. This information is important because your abuser can likely be sued in any state in which you were molested. When describing where you were abused, don't forget to include vacation locations and states in which you lived or went to school.

Personal jurisdiction

court's power to hear a controversy involving a person

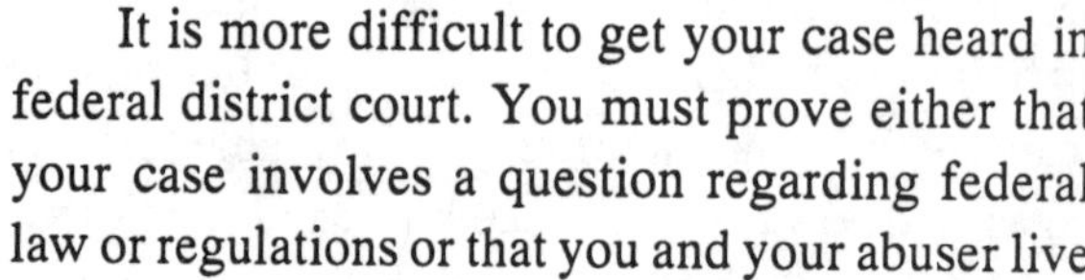

It is more difficult to get your case heard in federal district court. You must prove either that your case involves a question regarding federal law or regulations or that you and your abuser live in different states. It is unlikely that your case involves issues related to federal law or regulations, but you may live in a different state than your perpetrator. In addition, the amount of money in controversy must be greater than $50,000. The nature of the injuries involved in child sexual abuse cases makes this figure almost a certainty in most cases.

The decision of where to file the lawsuit is an important initial determination that should be left to the discretion of your attorney. The ability to choose where to sue is important because different jurisdictions have different laws, including different statutes of limitations. Without complete information on your abuse, however, your attorney may not have the opportunity to file suit in a jurisdiction that has laws favorable to you, even though filing in that jurisdiction is possible. With complete information, especially if you were abused in several states, you may have the opportunity to "forum shop" for the state with the most favorable laws to you and sue in that state.

Venue

You and your attorney must also determine in what court in your chosen jurisdiction to file your suit. This is a question of **proper venue**. For example, Minnesota is a single jurisdiction, but there are many trial courts in Minnesota in different locations. If you have chosen to sue in a Minnesota state court, you must choose the correct Minnesota court in which to sue.

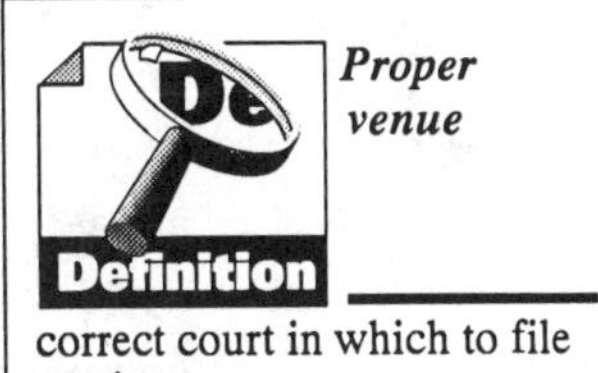

Proper venue

correct court in which to file a suit

Picking the proper venue is important for similar reasons to those for picking the proper jurisdiction—if your case is filed in an improper venue, you may lose time and money. Generally, if the facts of the case are not intimately tied to a particular venue, filing suit in that county will probably lead to a challenge of incorrect venue from your abuser's attorney.

In some cases, several locations are correct venues for the trial. In such cases, the more your attorney knows about your case, the better able he or she will be to pick a venue that has advantages for you such as a good judge.

Full disclosure of all events related to your abuse figures prominently into what venue your attorney chooses. Because the requirements for proper venue vary widely from jurisdiction to jurisdiction, there is no standard rule on this issue.

It is often advantageous to have the case heard where you were raised or in which your abusive parent currently lives, because your abuser will not want his or her reputation tainted or ruined in his or her home town or current home area and may be more willing to cooperate or settle.

Does Any Insurance Cover My Abuser's Acts?

Besides suing your perpetrator directly, you and your attorney will probably consider suing one or more of your perpetrator's insurance companies. If either you or the abuser has included the insurance company as a party to the case, you may be able to make a claim against the insurance company and eventually be awarded a judgment against it. Depending on where and when you were abused and on your abuser's job or profession, you may be able to make claims under several different types of insurance policies.

Contract

agreement to do or not do something, in return for an agreement to do or not do something else; can be written or oral

Beneficiary

person whom another person intends to receive payment should some named event happen

Insurance policies are **contracts**. In most insurance policies, in return for the payment of money by a policy holder, insurance companies agree to pay for damages suffered by people named in the insurance policy (**beneficiaries**) when certain things happen. Your attorney will have to determine if you are an intended beneficiary of each insurance policy. If not, it is unlikely that you will be able to collect from the corresponding insurance company. Depending on their wording, these policies can cover both intentional and negligent acts by the abuser that lead to damage to someone else. Your attorney will probably ask your abuser to hand over all of the insurance policies that were in effect during the time you were being abused. By doing this, all insurance companies that insured against the actions you claim happened can be brought into the case.

Types of policies that should be reviewed for possible coverage include home owners', rental, umbrella liability, automobile, and malpractice (for example, if the perpetrator is a medical care specialist who was also your doctor). In addition to proving that you are an intended beneficiary of the policy, you must prove that the perpetrator's actions fall within the actions covered by the insurance policy.

Up until the early 1980s, most insurance policies did not exclude coverage for child sexual abuse. If you were abused prior to the 1980s, you may have a better chance of collecting damages on a claim against one of your abuser's insurance policies than if the abuse occurred later. Courts have almost universally ruled, however, that the language in home owners' insurance policies exclude the coverage of intentional torts and that most acts of child sexual abuse are, by definition, intentional. Ironically, many deserving survivors have been denied the coverage of their abusers' home owners' policies because courts have ruled that their abusers were acting intentionally when they sexually abused them.

Despite the general lack of coverage for intentional acts under liability policies, some home owners' policies may provide coverage in cases of incest if both the abuser and a nonabusive parent were covered and the nonabusive parent was negligent in protecting the survivor.

Because of the growing number of cases of survivors suing their abusers, insurance companies are now writing their policies to specifically exclude intentional acts of child sexual abuse. Some newer policies have even been written to exclude the negligence of a nonabusive parent. As a result, even though new decisions and statutory limitations periods have given survivors more rights to recover from their abusers, insurance companies have been systematically removing any chance of recovering insurance money for abuse.

Modern malpractice insurance policies usually cover only negligent acts committed by the covered person. Some, however, are either sufficiently vague about what they cover or plainly cover both negligent and intentional acts.

Your attorney should review the applicable policies and pursue those that appear to cover the actions you remember.

If insurance coverage is claimed by either you or your perpetrator (who may claim coverage to help pay for attorney fees and court costs) in many jurisdictions the insurance company can be brought into the case as a party. The court may eventually enter a judgment in your favor against an insurance company. Insurance companies generally have far more resources than individuals and can lose their licenses to operate in jurisdictions if they do not pay judgments, so you should have less difficulty recovering from insurance companies after a judgment against them than you would from your perpetrator. Because of their greater resources, however, insurance companies can also generally provide stronger opposition to every move you make in the trial process than an individual abuser can. Insurance companies may also appeal the case to the jurisdiction's appeals court, thus prolonging the case and increasing your costs.

If you were abused by someone in a position of authority outside your family and friends, you may be able to sue the institution or organization for which your abuser worked when you were abused (see the section below entitled 'What If I Was Abused by Someone Other Than a Family Member?').

What If There Was More Than One Perpetrator?

Sexually abusive families sometimes contain more than one abuser. If you recall being abused by more than one person, whether they were family members or not, you should disclose this to your attorney. If you were in contact with people who are publicly known sexual abusers but whom you do not recall as abusive to you, disclose this fact to your attorney.

If you were sexually abused by more than one person, your attorney may decide to sue more than one abuser. Because some child sexual abuse survivors have somewhat hazy memories of their abuse (for example, after recalling repressed memories), the existence of multiple abusers may also present your attorney with a significant proof difficulty—by whom were you abused? One or more of the abusers you name as defendants will probably claim that you were actually abused by one or more of the *other* alleged abusers. Similarly, if you recall being abused by only one person but you were exposed to publicly known abusers, your abuser will undoubtedly claim that the publicly known abuser is your actual abuser.

The decision about whether or not to sue more than one perpetrator ultimately rests with you, but you should listen carefully to your attorney's reasoning on why or why not such a move should be made, as he or she will understand all the strategic legal aspects.

What If I Was Abused by a Sibling?

Child sexual abuse is defined in all jurisdictions as sexual abuse of persons under a certain age, generally between 16 and 21 years. However, all states do not define how old the abuser must be to fall within the definition of "child abuser." In some jurisdictions siblings can also be sued for child sexual abuse, depending on whether the jurisdiction's definition of child sexual abuse includes minors in the definition of "child abuser."

Attorneys who have handled cases of sibling abuse report that such cases are often more difficult to win, as judges and juries are not as outraged with sibling abuse as with adult-child abuse, especially when the abuser was "only a minor" when the abuse happened. Also, placing blame on one child when both were in a dysfunctional family situation is difficult for many judges and juries.

Judges and juries have even more difficulty understanding how a sibling of a similar age, size, and apparent power can abuse another sibling. A person's sexual victimization doesn't depend on the victim being a child, or the abuser being an adult. Victimization doesn't even hinge on the victim being chronologically younger, or physically smaller, then the abuser. In some families, the power structure enables a younger or smaller member to be sexually abusive to a larger, older sibling. This type of case is difficult to win, as judges and juries have great difficulty seeing beyond the sizes or ages of the abuser and the victim to grasp the underlying family power structure.

Because of societal norms, survivors who are male and were abused by a female or who were older or larger than their abusers generally have more difficulty finding attorneys willing to take their cases and less chance of winning the cases at trial.

Depending on the ages of the survivor and the abuser when the abuse occurred, an abusive sibling may also try to defend by claiming that his or her actions were merely healthy sexual exploration.

If your parents allowed one of your siblings to abuse you, you may have a claim against your parents for negligent child supervision, even if your parents did not know of the abuse. In such cases, because their essential component is parental negligence rather than an abuser's intentional act, recovery against the family's home owner's or other insurance is much more likely than it is in a case directly against an intentional abuser.

What If I Was Abused by Someone Other Than a Family Member?

If you were abused by someone other than an immediate family member, additional factors must be considered. In some respects your case will be easier to prove, and you may get more support from those around you. In other respects, your case may be more complex and difficult to prove.

Cases against authority figures other than family members usually differ from familial sexual abuse cases most notably in how much support a survivor gets from his or her family and close family friends. If you are suing a non-family member, you will likely get more support from your family and friends. Making claims against an outsider is much less likely to upset the family balance, and family members and others close to you will not be forced to choose sides.

You may also have more avenues of recovery if you were abused by a non-family member. If an authority figure abused you while connected in some way with his or her employment, you will probably also sue the institution, company, or organization for which the person was working when you were abused. A survivor who was abused by a clergy member, for example, would probably also sue the church for which the clergy member worked. One of the first things you and your attorney will probably try to determine is whether or not any organizations can be sued in addition to the actual abuser.

If the organization is insured, the insurance company for the organization will most likely also be brought into the suit either by you and your attorney or by the organization itself. This may lead to a more costly suit, as insurance companies often have vast financial and legal resources which allow them to fight extended, expensive battles to defend claims. If the organization is well known or highly respected, the media will undoubtedly pick up the suit's existence and highly publicize it, thus adding more pressure. This publicity may bring out invaluable corroborative evidence in the form of other survivors speaking out about abuse by the same person or someone else in the organization. On the other hand, if other survivors of your abuser's acts want to join in the suit against the abuser and the organization, the case will probably become more lengthy, complex, and costly.

Vicarious liability

indirect legal responsibility for the acts of another; also known as *respondeat superior*

Negligent hire

hiring someone a reasonably prudent person would have foreseen would harm someone (usually because of the employee's background)

Proving a sexual abuse case against an organization and its employee differs markedly from proving a sexual abuse case against an individual alone. You will be trying to prove not only that the abuse occurred and that the abuser should be liable for it, but also that the institution should be liable for the abuser's actions.

Negligent supervision

failure to provide sufficient supervision of an employee

Employers and supervisors can be held liable for the torts of their employees or other people they hired or supervised through three main theories: **vicarious liability**, **negligent hire**, and **negligent supervision**. Under the doctrine of vicarious liability, an organization that hires a person is liable for the person's actions if the person is acting within the scope and course of his or her employment. What actions fall within the phrase *acting within the scope and course of employment* depend on the facts and circumstances of each case and the law in each particular jurisdiction. Generally, however, it means that the person's job involves actions that were similar to what caused the plaintiff's injuries. Most states consider intentional or criminal acts to fall outside the scope of employment unless the intentional or criminal act is related in some way to the abuser's job. Many organizations successfully defend themselves in sexual abuse cases by arguing that sexual abuse is so totally unrelated to what the abuser was hired to do that the organization should not be held liable for the person's actions.

The Church of the Implausible Denial trained and employs Minister Maurice Lester. Minister Lester has for years taken elementary school-aged church members into the church bookstore after Sunday School for "spiritual training." This training consisted of sexual molestation of various kinds.

As a child, church member Jonathan was molested in one of these "training" sessions. He repressed the memories and did not remember the abuse until he was 25 years old. When he was 27, he filed suit in civil court against Lester for sexual abuse and against The Church of the Implausible Denial for vicarious liability as Lester's employer.

Jonathan and his attorney argue that Lester was acting within the scope of his employment. The court may rule that a minister's normal job function does not contain anything related to sexual abuse, so the church cannot be held liable.

If an organization knows or should know that a person it hires has a history of sexual abuse it can be held liable under the doctrine of negligent hire. Proving negligent hire requires that you and your attorney find information about the abuser's tendencies that was or should have been apparent to the organization before it hired the abuser. This may require extra investigative work.

(Assume the same facts as those in the example above.)

Before allowing Lester in its ministry program, high church officials become aware that Lester has been convicted of child sexual abuse about ten years before he applied to become a minister and has served two years in prison on the charge. Despite this knowledge, the church leaders, in their infinite wisdom and compassion, decide to put Lester in charge of one of their church's Sunday School programs.

Jonathan sues Lester individually and the church for negligent hire. The jury may rule that the church was negligent in its hiring practices and give a verdict to Jonathan.

An organization can also be sued for negligent supervision of its employee. You will have this cause of action if the organization did not sufficiently supervise the employee's activities.

What If I Was Abused in a Ritual or Satanic Cult?

Sexual abuse in cults presents more legal, social, and psychological obstacles to recovery than any other type of sexual abuse. Recovering from a sexual abuser who perpetrated his or her acts on you during cult activities will be more difficult than a typical case of child sexual abuse for several reasons:

1. You are more likely to have been subjected to cult training or brainwashing that demanded that you not tell about the cult, whether you remember the training consciously or not, which will make it more difficult for you to tell the truth in a legal setting;
2. You may have more difficulty convincing a potential attorney of the truth of your story;
3. You may have more difficulty finding an attorney who is willing to take such a case because of the

possibility of cult retaliation against the attorney;

4. You and your attorney have an increased chance of receiving threats of violence against your persons, your possessions, your families, and your family pets;
5. You will have a more difficult battle in the courtroom between your experts (psychologist/psychiatrist/therapist or physician) and your abuser's experts, as the therapeutic and medical communities are not as uniform in their agreement about the prevalence of satanic or ritual abuse as they are about non-cult related sexual abuse; and
6. You will have a more difficult time convincing judges and juries of the truth of your story, as society has not been able to admit the prevalence of satanic and ritualistic abuse.

If you are eventually believed by your attorney, the judge, and the jury, you can expect the judge and the jury members to be very sympathetic to the pain and suffering you have endured, and award damages that will be much higher than in a typical sexual abuse case. Because of its severity and cruelty, satanic and ritual abuse horrifies, repulses, and angers people like nothing else.

Chapter 7

What Else Can Be Done?

What Can I Do?

Sometimes suing your abuser is not possible. Your state may have outmoded statutes of limitations that make the chances of prevailing in a suit against your abuser very unlikely. You may not be able to handle the emotional trauma that a suit against your abuser could cause. Your evidence may be weak enough that a verdict in your favor is doubtful. If you do not sue your abuser, there are other things you can do to help both yourself and other survivors.

Speaking

Many survivors have found that speaking to others about their abuse has a healing effect on them. Of course, depending on the facts of your particular case, you may not want to speak to certain people or groups. Always make sure that you feel safe about the people to whom you are speaking about your abuse. Don't let speaking about your abuse come back to reinjure you.

Your attorney may also tell you to refrain from speaking about your abuse during your case against your abuser, as such speaking may have detrimental effects on your case.

Don't immediately think your attorney is trying to silence you, but ask questions about the reasons why such restraint is necessary in your case.

For some survivors, speaking to others frees emotions bottled up for years or decades. Just being able to tell the truth can be a very cathartic experience. In addition, speaking about your abuse educates the public about the reality of child sexual abuse in this country, whether you're speaking to one person or to thousands. Like a pebble thrown in a pond, this will cause reverberations far beyond any person or group to whom you speak. Your speaking will give other survivors a better chance than you had to get some justice from their abusers.

Writing

If you see a story about child sexual abuse on television, in the newspaper, or in a magazine, write to the newspaper's or the magazine's editor, the show's producer, or the network's president and tell them the importance and accuracy or inaccuracy of the piece. Use a pseudonym if you feel uncomfortable or unsafe using your real name. Every time you encourage the truth about the reality of child sexual abuse to emerge, you make every survivor's case a little easier to prove to a judge, jury, or appellate court.

If you cannot file suit against your abuser because of your state's current statute of limitations, write to your state legislator about the problem and stress the current statute's unfairness. Even if your state legislature is not yet considering amending or adding a more just statute of limitations for child sexual abuse actions, your letter may prompt your legislator to get some legislation started. Make copies of the delayed discovery-type statutes of limitations in Appendix C and send these along with your letter. To see how survivors have been able to get their statutes of limitation changed, see Chapter 8 and the stories by "Patti" and "Mark."

Testifying

If your state has a draconian statute of limitations for child sexual abuse cases and your attorney tells you that the trial judge will not extend the statute of limitations in your case, about the only direct legal self-help avenue left to you is to testify to your state's legislature about the realities of child sexual abuse. If you feel strong enough to present yourself and your situation to the highest body of lawmakers in your state, you can often testify to a committee set up to hear testimony on whether the legislature should pass a new statute of limitations. Your opportunity to testify, of course, depends on your state being enlightened enough to consider adopting such legislation.

You might also want to testify on behalf of proposed legislation that protects children from child abuse to help limit or prevent the kinds of injuries from which you're recovering.

What Else Should Be Done?

There is currently a backlash against plaintiffs and the recoveries they've gotten in trial courts in this country. Legislatures have limited recoveries to specific dollar amounts and denied other types of damages altogether. Victorious plaintiff-survivors should not be denied full recoveries by this trend. Appellate courts and legislatures should exclude recoveries in child sexual abuse cases from any such limitations, as child sexual abuse is vile behavior that should not be countenanced or encouraged in any way.

Children should be loved, encouraged, protected, and nurtured, and any act of sexual aggression by adults against children should lead to swift and sure punishment. Legislatures should enact laws that add automatic punitive damages of a certain percentage, 200-300%, of the actual damages awarded in actions against child sexual abusers, unless the abusers admit their actions and complete court-supervised therapy to rehabilitate and heal them. If an abuser completes such treatment the trial court can later reduce or eliminate any punitive damages assessed. This will encourage abusers to confess their wrongdoing, both to avoid the large punitive damages and to try to heal the injured family. Generally, however, other damages should still be borne by the abuser. In most cases abusers are adults who are responsible for caring for children. Along with this duty, an abuser should have the resulting responsibility of compensating the survivor for past, current, and future losses and problems that the abuser caused, no matter how truthfully apologetic the abuser becomes or how responsive the abuser is to therapy.

Legislatures should enact statutes of limitations that mirror the reality of child sexual abuse. An ideal standard in cases of child sexual abuse would be no limitations period at all. Child sexual abuse is a vile, despicable, horrific, absolutely inhumane act. Many states have exempted certain particularly unconscionable acts such as murder from any statutory period in cases of criminal prosecution. Child sexual abuse is unquestionably as repugnant and, in some ways, is more repulsive than even murder. Therefore, child sexual abusers should not have the benefit of a statute of limitations on which to fall as a technical crutch for escaping justice. The arguments in favor of retaining a statute of limitations are particularly inapplicable to this type of case, especially where a survivor represses the memory of the abuse. Neither making sure that evidence is fresh nor ensuring that witnesses' recollections are accurate have much bearing on cases in which the damaging act occurred out of the sight of anyone but the survivor and the abuser and little or no physical evidence of the act remains other than the physical and psychological ailments that persist in the survivor. Also, few, if any, acts or series of acts could possibly remain more firmly locked and preserved in memory than acts of child sexual abuse, both for the survivor, who often remembers them suddenly and vividly years after the fact, or for the abuser, who *must* remember them, at least subconsciously, from the time they occur. Arguments that innocent people will be harmed by disgruntled children who make up stories of their abuse are not persuasive. Studies of the truth of allegations of abuse indicate that a very low percentage of claims of abuse are false. Also, the complexity and range of emotions and psychological effects seen in survivors would be hard to live with on a full-time basis (which would be necessary to fool other witnesses of a perjuring plaintiff's behavior) and difficult to reproduce accurately enough to fool mental health practitioners. Any such acting job could be debunked effectively at trial. As one court noted, while arguing that no statute of limitations should apply:

> [C]hild sexual abuse survivors are hostage to their own thought processes, implanted by their abusers, and from which they may never be totally released. Indeed, the mental and emotional dysfunction suffered by such victims may virtually prevent them from seeking relief against their tormentors until the period of limitations has long since expired. To place the passage of time in a position of priority and importance over the plight of childhood sexual abuse victims would seem to be the ultimate exaltation of form over substance, convenience over principle.*

Because the legal system is slow to change and statutes of limitations are so ingrained in the system, however, a more realistic proposal for a statute of limitations must be made, or most legislatures will be unable to agree to any lengthening of the time period. A compromise statute should include provisions that allow a survivor to bring an action within a certain number of years after the last act of abuse is discovered (such as Washington's), as well as a provision allowing a survivor who is incapacitated by the childhood sexual abuse and therefore cannot file suit to subtract the time he or she was incapacitated from the time within which the suit must be filed (such as Vermont's). The statute should not require filing suit within any time period based on when

---

* *Petersen v. Bruen*, 792 P.2d 18, 24 (Nev. 1990).

the survivor *should have* discovered that the abuse caused the injury and should not be limited to only intentional torts. Below is a proposed statute of limitations for child sexual abuse cases.

A civil action brought by any person for recovery of damages for injury suffered as a result of childhood sexual abuse shall be commenced within X years of the act alleged to have caused the injury or condition, or X years of the time the victim discovered that the injury or condition was caused by that act, whichever period expires later. The victim need not establish which act in a series of continuing sexual abuse or exploitation incidents caused the injury complained of, but may compute the date of discovery from the date of discovery of the last act by the same perpetrator which is part of a pattern of sexual abuse or exploitation.

When a person entitled to bring an action for damages as a result of childhood sexual abuse is unable to commence the action as a direct result of the damages caused by the sexual abuse, the period which the person is incapacitated shall not be taken as a part of the time limited for commencement of the action.

Under such a statute, a survivor would be able to sue when he or she was emotionally able to sue, free from the mental control of the abuser, and after remembering more details of the abuses. This type of statute would also take into consideration the phenomenon under which many abuse survivors, though cognizant that they have been abused from the time of the abuse itself, find themselves psychologically unable to attribute any later physical, emotional, or psychological infirmities to the abuse.

You are now an adult seeking justice for what happened to you as a child. You have every right to seek comfort, protection, and recompense through the courts. We must not, however, lose sight of the real focal points, and the real victims, of this blight. Children are damaged by child sexual abuse. Children are those left defenseless at the hands of depraved adults. Until surprisingly recently, children were treated as less than human. Courts and legislatures, and society in general, held children to be chattels, things, owned by their fathers. As mere things, children had very few, if any, rights. Society has been slow to shake off these antiquated ideas. Unless and until children are accorded full rights as human beings and citizens throughout this country, full justice for children will be an illusion. Adding statutes of limitations that enable survivors to sue their abusers is merely an effort at damage control, a band-aid on a psychological and emotional beheading. Stronger laws must be passed to protect children *before* they are injured, to deter depravity before it becomes activity.

Chapter 8

Case Histories

Hundreds of people have filed suit against their childhood sexual abusers. The outcomes of these cases have varied widely, depending on the particular facts of each case, the laws in the jurisdictions in which the cases were filed, the emotional and psychological resiliency of each survivor, and the resourcefulness and craftiness of each perpetrator, as well as a host of other lesser factors.

This section recounts several case histories of victims who have filed suit, or are still pursuing suit, against their abusers, their abusers' insurance companies, and others. The stories are mostly in the survivors' own words. The alleged abusers in each of these cases has denied the charges of abuse.

These stories are provided to demonstrate not only how the legal process works, but also how real people have responded to the legal process. Each of these case histories has different facts and is from a different jurisdiction, so its processes and outcome differ from, and are not necessarily indicative of, what might happen in your case. The names, dates, and places in some of these stories have been changed at the request of the survivors to protect the survivors and to keep safe the survivors' legal rights against their abusers.

Caitlin

Long and expensive... but necessary

I am the oldest of seven children. My father was an active alcoholic until I was nine, when he went into a rehab program. He routinely attended AA until his death in 1979 and, as far as I know, never drank again. He was a white collar professional and my mother was a housewife.

From my earliest memories until I was approximately 12 years old my father would orally and, as I got older, vaginally and anally rape me on a regular basis. My mother knew this and would send me into their bedroom, knowing he was going to rape me. My father worked midnight to 8:00 am. The rapes often took place when he would be waking up in the late afternoon. He also sexually abused me in the family car when he would take me with him on errands. It was clear to me that my mother was fully aware of the fact that he was sexually abusing me, so there was no point in trying to get any help from her. I'm not aware of any teacher, pediatrician, extended family member or anyone else approaching me or my family about what was going on. I do not remember directly telling anyone about the fact that my father was sexually abusing me.

In the late 1940s, my family moved to a new house in New England. Sometime later the next door neighbor, Frank Smith*, began raping and torturing me. He would do the following things to me: orally rape me; put me on a workbench in the basement of his house, put my arm in a vise so that I couldn't get away and torture me by applying pliers to my nipples and chest area and by inserting things in my vagina; if I whimpered he would torture me more, saying he was doing it because I had whimpered; if I did not whimper he would torture me more, saying that obviously it didn't hurt me or I would be crying; sometimes he would hold a

---

* All names in this story are pseudonyms.

blanket over my face until I passed out; he made me watch him burn a baby doll in the furnace, saying that this was what he would do to my baby sister if I told; he would hide in closets and jump out to scare me; and he would hide under beds and grab my legs as I walked by; he would pin me down on wooden stairs and tickle me for 20-30 minutes while I begged him to stop. The reason I would be at his house was that he had a daughter Karen who was 2 years older than my friend and me. My friend and I vied for Karen's attention. Karen would only play with one of us at a time; if I did not go over to her house to play then my friend would go over there to play and I would be alone. Throughout all of those years, the late 1940s to the early 1950s, my friend was the only source of support I had and my contact with her was essential to my emotional survival. Frank Smith would tell me that it was my fault that he was torturing me; he would tell me that he knew I liked what he was doing to me.

The rape and torture continued for the five years that I lived there. It stopped only because we moved. After we moved, the Smiths would stop by our house without calling ahead. During those visits Frank Smith would say things to me to terrify me.

During all of the years of the torture my parents never did anything to protect me or ask what the marks on me were from. There was no way they couldn't have seen the marks from the pliers, vise, and other instruments of torture. I don't know whether each of my parents believed that the other parent was responsible for the marks.

My father's rapes of me continued until I was about twelve years old. When I was eleven years old my father impregnated me. The pregnancy was discovered when I was five months pregnant and an abortion was performed.

At 18, after one year of college, I married my first husband, Paul, in an attempt to get out of the family home. The marriage was not good from the start. I later realized that I had chosen to marry this brutish man because I thought he would protect me from the "Frank Smiths" of the world. It took me 19 years to be able to end this marriage because I was afraid to be on my own if someone like Frank Smith came into my life. There was one incident of wife assault; this was not reported to the police. Paul did not abuse our three children.

When I was approximately 30 years old I went into therapy for the first time. I was in therapy for approximately one year. An inkblot test my therapist administered suggested I was preoccupied with violence and was enormously fearful. I do not think we talked about abuse. The precipitant for entering therapy was my general unhappiness.

In 1979 I entered therapy for the second time, this time with a former professor of mine. The precipitant for entering therapy was my fear of going out into the world and losing my role of student. I was in therapy with this therapist approximately seven and a half years. A minor incident was the only abuse I became aware of during my treatment with this therapist. We talked about how I felt unloved and unprotected by my parents. This therapist was the first gentle, accepting man I had known.

In 1987 I met the man who was to become my second husband. He was warm, kind, gentle and very caring. In 1988 we signed a contract for a house we would buy together. For the first time in my life I felt that there would be a loving, consistent partner in my life. That week I had my first memory of being sexually abused and tortured by Frank Smith. With my partner's support and listening ear I began to recover more and more memories. I remembered being forced to fellate Frank Smith often. I realized that the sharp horizontal pains I frequently experienced in the back of my legs were body memories of being pinned down on stairs by Frank Smith; I also realized that the sharp, take-your-breath-away pains I frequently had in my chest were body memories of Frank Smith torturing me with pliers. In 1989 I began to remember the abuse by my father. With the help of a therapist with expertise in sexual abuse I remembered more and more about what was done to me by Frank Smith and my father. With that therapist's help and the assistance of a therapy group for survivors of childhood sexual abuse, I have been able to sort out the different effects of the different abuses I experienced.

In 1988 I confronted Frank Smith by telephone. As I expected, he denied sexually abusing and torturing me. I telephoned my mother and my siblings, told them of the sexual abuse and torture by Frank Smith, and alerted them to not give out my address or telephone number to anyone. I was fearful of retaliation from Frank Smith for revealing the "secret" of his abuse of me.

In 1989, in a joint session with my mother and my individual therapist, I confronted my mother about her lack of protection of me from Frank Smith's abuse and torture. As I expected, my mother denied knowing that I was abused by Frank Smith; she denied ever seeing any marks of torture on my body. I decided that for my own sake I would not have any more contact with my mother until she acknowledged the truth that she had known I was being harmed and had done nothing to protect me. Knowing the likelihood that my mother would rally my siblings around her and against me, I wrote to my siblings and told them that I knew mother had known about the torture and that I would have no contact with mother in the future. I invited all of them to come down for a group session with me and my group therapist. In a joint session in 1989, with my brother and my group therapist, I told my brother that our father had sexually abused me, forcing me to engage in fellatio and cunnilingus, from my earliest memories until I was about twelve years old. He expressed shock and pleaded my mother's case, saying that even if she had known about the incest by our father and the rapes and torture by Frank Smith, "she is an old lady now and might die or kill herself" if I didn't put this in the past and resume a relationship with her.

I initially considered suing Frank Smith in 1988. I contacted the bar association and the women's collective in that New England state to get the names of attorneys and began contacting attorneys to find out about the process. In 1989 I began to remember the abuse by my father. I put the idea of suing on hold both because remembering the incest was consuming my energy, and also because I feared that in a court case Smith's attorney would say that all my symptoms were the result of the incest and not Smith's abuse of me.

In 1990 my group therapist suggested that there were ways to distinguish effects of incest from the abuse by Smith, so I again began to contact sources in the New England area to identify attorneys who might be interested in taking my case. My reasons for suing included the fact that I know perpetrators continue to abuse until they are forced to stop; I felt that I was in a better position to sue than many other survivors (because I'm well educated, well spoken, have credentials in a field generally seen as trustworthy, have a significant support system, and I was at least 50% through the healing process).

I had telephone contact with about 40 different people in the New England area trying to locate attorneys familiar with, and interested in, cases such as mine. As a survivor I possess a common trait of not trusting many people, so I do a lot of checking and data retrieval before I interact with someone I don't know well. I mailed summaries to four attorneys who sounded like they might be appropriate after interviewing them on the phone. I talked to them after they received my summaries and I narrowed it down to two attorneys. In 1990 I went to New England to meet with the two attorneys who seemed most appropriate. I took a friend along because I was so apprehensive about putting myself in a position to risk not being believed; I felt I would need her support if the interviews went badly.

The two attorneys were very different. The first appeared to be a wheeler-dealer; the eight cases he said he'd been involved in all settled out of court and for minimal amounts of money. He did not appear interested in trying to set legal precedent. When I asked him how he and I would negotiate it if he felt I should settle for less than I felt was reasonable, he said, in effect, that I could get myself another attorney. He wanted a 50% contingency contract.

The second attorney was very different from the first. She was conservative, she wanted to try to set precedent, and she was willing to be in this for the long haul. I met with her and her colleague. Their firm was willing for her to take the case and agreed to do it on a contingency basis with me paying disbursements. This attorney recommended that I meet with a psychiatrist of her choosing before we met. I decided to work with the second attorney.

I went home and did a lot of thinking. The issue was how much energy, time and money I was willing to put into this case. The attorney said that the case would probably take four to six years (2-3 for the first court, 2-3 for the appeals court) and that disbursements would probably run $10,000 to $40,000. As a single parent with sole financial responsibility for my children, I had to think long and hard before committing myself financially to this.

Over the winter I wrote letters to the editors of survivor newsletters asking for suggestions on how to raise the money. I contacted NOW and other women's groups. I approached a local columnist and tried to get her to write about my situation as a way of identifying possible resources. She said that what was done to me was "too heavy" for people to read about.

Finally, as the statute of limitation time was running out, I decided that I had to go ahead with the suit in order to be able to say to myself that I had done all I could. Abusers must be held accountable for their actions.

The attorney I had chosen had taken a government position. I was told by her firm that another attorney would be assigned to handle my case. In 1991 I went to New England to meet the new attorney, and we had a long meeting to decide if we wanted to work together.

Regarding my suing Frank Smith: my oldest child wished I could "forget it all and put it behind me"; my younger children felt I should do whatever I wanted as far as suing. I decided to include my mother in the suit. Most of my friends have been very supportive, and some less so. A couple of survivor friends seemed afraid that then they would be expected (by me or themselves?) to also pursue suits against their perpetrators.

Long before I made any decisions about suing anybody, my brothers had chosen to have no contact with me because of my decision to have no contact with our mother unless she acknowledged knowing that I was being abused and went into her own therapy. My sisters and I have minimal contact, by their choice. One of them said, "When I think of you, I think of the abuse and I don't want to think of the abuse so I try not to think of you." None of them knew about my plans to file a suit against anyone until my mother was served with papers. There has been no contact since then.

My group therapists were in complete agreement with my decision to file suit. My individual therapist is very supportive of my decision to sue and to include my mother in the suit.

Defendant Smith filed a motion asking to defend himself under a pseudonym, to impound the documents filed with the court, and for a protective order. The court denied all these requests. My mother, who I am suing for neglect and failure to protect me from Smith in ignoring the torture marks on my body, asked that the case be dismissed based on the expiration of the statute of limitations. The case has not yet gone to trial, and no depositions have yet been taken.

I would advise others to really think through the decision of whether to sue and to consult with others. This is neither a decision to undertake lightly, nor is it one that, once made, can be easily backed out of. I'm glad I made the decision to file the suit. It was the right decision for me.

Mark

Attorney, heal thyself

I was molested by a close family friend who occupied the position of being an uncle by virtue of his growing up in my mother's childhood home. This "uncle" seduced and molested me beginning when I was 12 years old. The sexual relationship continued throughout my teenage years and on into my adulthood. I was able to break off the sexual relationship when I entered law school at age 25, but the man dominated my life throughout law school because I lived at his home and we were involved in some business dealings together.

A couple of years after I graduated from law school, and early into my marriage, my perpetrator presented me with some veiled threats about how he knew so much about me that he could easily blackmail me. He made these threats in a jesting way at a family gathering. He and I both knew the extent of the power he had over me. I decided to free myself from his emotional and spiritual blackmail.

My best support throughout the process, apart from my wife, was from my lawyer and from a professor/mentor from law school. Because of extreme denial, it took me some months after the threats to recognize that I was indeed damaged by the childhood sexual abuse.

Overall, I have had only positive support from my therapists. I owe a great personal debt to a now deceased pioneer in the field of therapeutic treatment of male victims of sexual abuse, Jayson Bischoff. The bulk of my therapy was through his treatment program in Minneapolis, Minnesota. As trial approached, however, I anticipated a battle of the experts, so I decided to supplement this therapy with a better-credentialed therapist—a psychiatrist.

My family of origin was understanding, at first, but within a year or so was tired of hearing about my therapeutic progress, and about the painfully slow development of my legal case. I was soon met with suggestions that it was about time that I get on with my life. I found this to be terribly shaming. To a degree, my wife got tired of hearing me process the same old stuff over and over again. For that matter, despite a tremendous growth through therapy over five or so years, I still consult my therapist from time to time as the need arises.

I was quite public with the facts of my abuse, appearing on numerous local television talk shows here in Minneapolis. When the lawsuit was finally over, I also appeared on the Sally Jesse Raphael Show, a nationally syndicated talk show. The public confessional of the television interview or talk show was fairly helpful to me. I would caution others from appearing on television. Some talk show hosts are more interested in pandering to the public than they are concerned about the talk show guests, themselves.

Most recently, I have begun communicating with members of a local chapter of Survivors of Incest Anonymous. This has been a part of my support system.

Finally, I have dedicated a part of my law practice to helping survivors of sexual abuse.

My attorney was a classmate of mine in law school. He was recommended by a mutual friend, a law school professor. My attorney did an excellent job for me. Most importantly, he took the case when the statutory and case law background in the area of statutes of limitations in Minnesota was squarely against the facts of my case.

My lawsuit was commenced in January, 1984—*Mark Earl Douglass vs. Stephen P. Gillies*. No demand letter was sent because for a variety of reasons I wanted the lawsuit to start immediately. My attorney's interaction with my therapists was minimal, except at depositions and at trial.

In 1984, the statute of limitations in Minnesota for intentional torts was two years. My attorney plead the case in a variety of theories to get around the harsh statute of limitations. My attorney and I hoped that my case would become a test case in which the Minnesota courts would judicially modify and expand the strict and oppressive two year statute of limitations to a delayed discovery statute.

Almost immediately a motion to dismiss based upon the

statute of limitations was filed. My perpetrator's motion was denied on the grounds that there were some facts that were within the statute of limitations—namely, the veiled threats. In a bit of ***dictum*** the court said that the discovery of sexual abuse was rather like the discovery of asbestosis and silicosis—it is delayed. The district court's decision on this pre-trial motion was not appealed. No other motions were filed prior to trial.

Dictum

a statement by a judge in an appellate court decision that shows how the judge thinks a particular issue should be decided, but which has no current or future legal effect on anyone (*precedential* value)

My perpetrator first tried the motion route. He failed. Later, he discharged his first attorney, and attempted to scare me by hiring one of the most well-known criminal trial law firms in our area. That did not dissuade me. By the time trial began, he tried to hire a well-known sexual crimes defense lawyer who had an office two doors down the hall from my own office. He consulted this attorney throughout trial but this attorney did not ever represent my perpetrator in the trial. Finally, my perpetrator decided to handle the case ***pro se***.

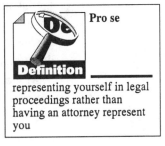

Pro se

representing yourself in legal proceedings rather than having an attorney represent you

One tactic my perpetrator used was to propose settling the case, which I agreed to consider only if he would disclose his assets. My perpetrator then delayed and finally refused to disclose his assets.

Delay was a major part of my case. It was commenced in January, 1984, and we finally got to trial in May, 1988. Some of the delay was caused by my perpetrator—through his changing of attorneys. Some of the delay I welcomed, because I wanted to focus on my therapy. Another reason for delay was that I was paying my attorney hourly, and could not afford to keep current with his bills.

No settlement was ever reached in my case, and it went to trial in May, 1988 before a jury of six. Because my usual reaction to psychological stress is to intellectualize, the first part of my trial testimony was dry and professorial. I tried to discourse on sexual abuse victims in general. During a lunch break, my attorney demanded that I let him do his job, and that I directly respond to his questions—minus my professorial lectures. My testimony was more effective thereafter.

My perpetrator, by acting as his own attorney and by bald-faced lying, cooked his own goose at trial.

The hardest testimony for me to hear was from my therapist, simply because he spoke directly and pointedly about the vulnerability that I had to my perpetrator when I was a child, about the degree that I came to be emotionally dependent upon my perpetrator, and about the damages that I had suffered at the hands of my perpetrator.

I won a substantial moral and spiritual victory at trial. The jury awarded me the actual damages assessed by one of our experts, plus punitive damages in the amount of one million dollars. The case received a good deal of print and broadcast media attention. However, this was a pyrrhic victory in that I was never able to collect on the judgment because my perpetrator had lost a good deal of his means to bad business decisions and poor health—and he had hidden the rest.

My case was not appealed. This deprived me of an opportunity to seek a judicial revision and expansion of the Minnesota statute of limitations then in effect. Fortunately, this, in part, led me to pursue a more comprehensive legislative revision and expansion of the statute of limitations in Minnesota.

Although my attorneys' fees and costs were in the neighborhood of $12,500, I would do it again. As a lawyer, it was important for me to have the legal system, my own personal priesthood, vindicate me.

From a personal standpoint, I disrobed my perpetrator in a public trial, showing him to be the sick person that he is. I also helped several of his victims empower themselves by giving them the opportunity to testify as rebuttal witnesses in my trial. (My perpetrator, on direct examination, was asked if he had ever had sex with children. He replied, "No. Never." We called as rebuttal witnesses other child victims of his that were now adults—a police officer, a student, a salesman, and a housewife.)

Several weeks after "winning" at trial, I became depressed and despondent. Most of my life and career for the preceding 4–5 years had been focused upon this trial, yet I had been unable to get the statute of limitations changed through the courts.

A few weeks after my trial I appeared on the Sally Jesse Raphael Show along with other victims of childhood sexual abuse. There, I learned that Patti Barton had lobbied for a change in the law in Washington, in light of the decision against a child sexual abuse survivor in *Tyson vs. Tyson*. Based on her example, and giving due credit to her, I got the legislative ball rolling at the Minnesota Legislature in its 1989 session. I involved our attorney general and a prominent local sexual abuse lawyer in the legislative process. I testified at two committee hearings. I also joined in contributing the idea that the proposed Minnesota statute ought to apply retroactively, rather than prospectively. The result was Minnesota Statute § 541.073. (*See* Appendix C for the full text of Minnesota Statute § 541.073, Minnesota's delayed discovery statute of limitations for sexual abuse cases.)

Susan

Gaining control

I was sexually abused during a period when I was between eleven and thirteen years old. I decided to sue when I learned that such a suit was possible. Since I had begun to experience repercussions from the abuse and could sue, I did. I wanted to let the abuser know that I would not be quiet and that I would fight for my rights and regain control. I was in law school at the time, and had chosen to do my major paper on the topic of suits by adult survivors, so I was quite knowledgeable about the process.

Most of my family members and friends were supportive. I had problems with friends who did not understand the emotional distress I was suffering due to the abuse. My therapist was very helpful. I was able to see a psychiatrist who charged a reduced fee due to my income level.

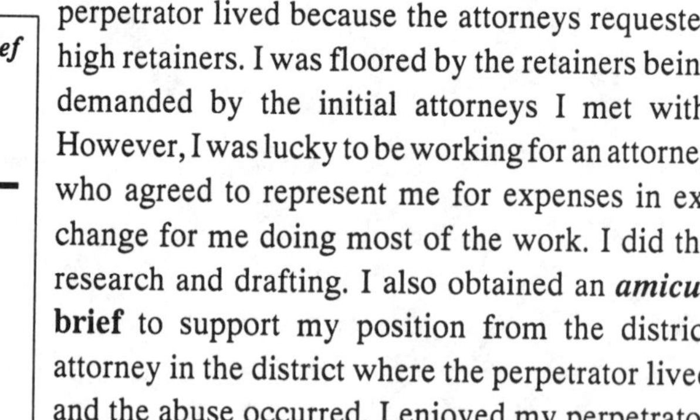

Amicus *brief*

a document filled with legal arguments, and referring to legal authorities (cases, statutes, or persuasive articles) (a *brief*), dealing with a particular issue, filed by someone who is not a party to the lawsuit, but is interested in the case's outcome (*amicus*–a friend [of the court])

I had a hard time finding an attorney in the town where the perpetrator lived because the attorneys requested high retainers. I was floored by the retainers being demanded by the initial attorneys I met with. However, I was lucky to be working for an attorney who agreed to represent me for expenses in exchange for me doing most of the work. I did the research and drafting. I also obtained an ***amicus* brief** to support my position from the district attorney in the district where the perpetrator lived and the abuse occurred. I enjoyed my perpetrator learning that the district attorney knew of him.

My attorney took my case all the way to the Court of Appeals for the Sixth Circuit. We sued in Tennessee, where I was living, and claimed diversity of citizenship for federal court jurisdiction. My attorney protected me by acting as a buffer between me and the perpetrator.

My attorney had good contact with my psychologist, considering how short the case was. The psychologist who did my psychological testing called her to recommend that I see a psychiatrist to obtain medication because of my level of depression and anxiety. This communication and their concern led to my acknowledging that I needed help.

We sent a letter that included an offer to settle the case for $10,000. As I expected, he refused the offer, but I felt good knowing that I made him spend this much defending my lawsuit.

The abuser filed a motion to strike the portions of my complaint that detailed the sexual abuse. This didn't cause me any problems, as I liked that these allegations concerned him. He then filed a motion to dismiss my case, claiming that the court did not have jurisdiction over him. We lost this motion. I did not, and do not, agree with this decision, so I appealed it. Even though I lost the appeal, which disappointed me, I made my point. I decided not to try to file again in Alabama, and am okay with my decision.

Taking this case to court helped my mental health. Waiting for responses and making or knowing about telephone calls increased my anxiety, but overall the suit helped combat the emotional effects of the sexual abuse. The suit damaged relationships, but I'm not sure how healthy they were to begin with.

Filing the suit was worth it, and I *would* do it again. I turned the tables and let my abuser know what I thought and felt about the abuse. I was no longer helpless, and I had control. Potential survivor-plaintiffs should remember that they are in control, and that their abusers are on the "hot seat." I recommend taking legal action. If you can obtain a financial recovery, so much the better. But therapeutically, filing and pursuing suit can be very beneficial.

Cynthia

The dark side

Cynthia filed suit in federal district court in New York City when she was 33 years old. In her complaint, she alleged that her father began having sexual relations with her from infancy into her teenage years, and that he repeatedly and regularly fondled her on her private areas of her body, and repeatedly warned her that severe harm would come to her and to her family if she disclosed the incidents. She also claimed that she became pregnant in 1968 as a result of her father raping her, and that her father took her to Puerto Rico for a traumatic second trimester abortion. She sought $900,000 in damages from her father in the suit.

New York's statute of limitations at the time limited suits to within three years of the plaintiff reaching adulthood (at age eighteen), so Cynthia had to argue that because she had involuntarily repressed all memory of the abuse and was therefore unable to file suit within the prescribed time, her suit should not be dismissed. She said that she did not remember the abuse until her recollection was rudely refreshed when she received a letter from her father, in which he said that his granddaughter reminded him of Cynthia when she was at that age.

The suit, and the disclosures it required, greatly upset Cynthia. On an Easter Sunday three years after making the incest public, Cynthia, distraught because of the emotional pain this disclosure had brought her, committed suicide.

Her attorney said afterward that bringing suit too soon had been too much for her.

Lynn

Frustrated and uninformed

I was between two and four years old when the abuse started. I was raped by my father both orally and vaginally. My siblings and I were also beaten and psychologically abused. We were all terrified of him and his erratic behavior. I think the abuse continued until I was about 14 years old. I don't have all my memories back, so I can't guarantee that it ended at that age.

I initiated the suit because it was the last opportunity I had to say "no" to my abuser. I was unable to say "no" as a little girl. Because my father is now a vegetable (mentally disabled, probably because of alcoholism), it is not an ideal time for me to file a law suit. However, it is the only time I have. I was not offered a better time, because I did not remember the abuse until after he was in this state, when I was more than 45 years old.

To prepare for filing suit, I went back to the houses in which I grew up, and asked the strangers living inside to please let me go through the house to regain memories, and I explained why. I contacted everyone from my childhood I thought could help me. I have taped programs and read articles pertaining to others going through the same process. It helped to validate my actions. It is easy to doubt that you are worth the effort. What I heard in my support groups, though, made me angry at all abusers of young children and helped give me the energy to speak out against abusers and the child abuse that still goes on.

In short, I have educated myself, strengthened myself emotionally, and remained in therapy throughout, so I could stay grounded.

The therapeutic community that supports me has been encouraging, and it has left it open for me in case I change my mind about filing suit. Recently I found a support group of people who were all abused as children.

Other than therapists, I have very little in the way of a

support system. I filed suit two years ago and until recently had no support other than my husband and children. My family has stood behind me even though they too have had to pay for my decision. Friends have been almost neutral about the suit. I don't think many of them understand why I am putting this much energy into it.

Filing the law suit has seriously damaged my relationship with my younger brother. We had a very close relationship prior to the suit but he is unable to deal with the discord and probably the memories he may regain as a result of the law suit. My sister told me she would have nothing to do with me if I filed suit and would not testify on my behalf. Two years and several memories later, she is in the process of changing her mind.

I interviewed several attorneys and, through referrals and interviews, I found two in one law firm who were both enthusiastic about the suit as well as experienced in this area of the law. In the initial interview, I felt that my attorneys were very sympathetic and understanding. Originally, they agreed to handle the suit whether it remained in the Seattle area or was transferred to the smaller town. I thought I would receive good representation.

My attorneys sent a demand letter to my abuser and his attorney, who treated it like a joke that I would not follow through on.

I went to Seattle to file suit because that was where my abuser and I lived while I was growing up. He has since moved to another county in Washington.

Since I filed suit, I have received numerous threats from my father's wife (my step mother).

My abuser filed a motion to change the venue of the case to the smaller town and, although we opposed it, two years into the case it has been transferred to the smaller town, and my attorneys have left me high and dry. They now say that they do not want to travel that far and that I must find another attorney in that area. Now I am disappointed in them and feel it would be unwise for me to try to push to have them live up to their original agreement. I think they would not be my best advocates if they no longer want to handle the case.

I dread going to the smaller town to look for an attorney all over again. I don't yet even have any recommendations from anyone on attorneys in this area. Although I've run into difficulties, I'm not ready to terminate the suit.

Some attorneys have told me that because my father is in a vegetative state, I could have problems with the **dead person's statute**. I hope to hell that this isn't going to be a problem. I feel that he is at no greater disadvantage than I was when the incidents occurred. So far the attorneys don't have an answer to this question.

Dead person's statute

rule of evidence that prevents testimony by the surviving party about a controversy if the other party to the controversy is deceased

I have been paying the out of pocket costs to the attorneys who have represented me so far, under a contingency fee arrangement. Now that they are leaving me to fend for myself in trying to find another attorney in the small town, I will have to strike a new agreement with the next attorneys.

My attorneys could have been more available to me. I understand that it is difficult when the attorney is in another state, but I have had no help except bare legal maneuvers from my attorneys.

I would like to see an attorney I felt supported me more. I would also like to know what is happening in the case at all times. As the wife of an attorney, I expected that I would be better informed either by my attorneys as a matter of course, or because my attorneys would be anxious to appear to be good attorneys knowing that my husband was watching them.

The lawsuit has cost me in relationships with my immediate family and other relatives. I have been surprised, however, to find a few that strongly support me. The suit has caused me headaches, other physical ailments, anxiety, and a number of emotional problems. Even with these results, I respect myself for pursuing the case, and am not ready to give up. I want my day to say "No! It was wrong!"

Patti

Making the law work for you

I was abused by my father* in Alaska from the time I was a baby up through age ten. The abuse ranged from fondling to penetration. I decided I wanted monetary compensation for my counseling right away after discovering I had been sexually abused. I found that in the state of Washington, where I lived, there was nothing I could legally do to gain this. My husband and I worked at changing our state law to allow me as well as other survivors with blocked memories of abuse, and survivors who did not know the damage their abuse caused, to file civil suit against their perpetrators. I decided to use the new law, which was the first in the nation, shortly before it went into effect in June of 1988.

I had zero support from my family of origin for suing, but my total support system throughout the four years since I discovered the abuse has been very good and remains good. I have total support from my husband and my young children, and good support from my in-laws, from a church I formerly attended, from my husband's fellow employees, and from the community and media.

I had an easy time finding an attorney, because Washington was one of the few states at the time that had several of these lawsuits, and because I had worked at changing the law with several attorneys. I located these attorneys by calling sexual assault centers and the Northwest Women's Law Center in Seattle. The National Organization of Women (NOW) is also involved in this issue.

[Authors' Note: The NOW Legal Defense and Education Fund maintains an attorney referral list and other resources. It can be reached at 99 Hudson Street, New York, NY 10013.]

I had good interviews with both of my attorneys (I have two because my case is being tried in Alaska and I live in the

---

* Patti's case is currently pending. Her father has denied all charges.

Seattle area). They are very good about telling me everything that will happen, what information the defense will ask for and have rights to get, and also what they don't have rights to get though they ask for it. They are very good at returning my calls and explaining things to me. I feel included in the decision-making process.

My attorneys thoroughly discussed the statutes of limitations. I don't think I would have filed had there not been a specific law allowing these suits because of the emotional strain that could have be caused by my family gloating over getting the case dismissed based a bad statute of limitations and misrepresenting it as their win.

I requested that a demand letter be sent to my father. My attorney wrote it and we discussed the amount of the demand. We also discussed what my parents' reaction might be to the demands, one of which was that they might flee the state of Washington in order to avoid being served. This is what they did indeed do, so my statute of limitations was put on hold until such time as they returned to the state. My attorney explained all of this to me. My parents did not return to the state, so they were served in Alaska after my husband and I worked at changing Alaska's law.

My father threatened me at least once during the deposition, tried to make all present feel sorry for him, tried to make me think he loved me (stating it several times), rambled on incoherently, and accused me of things. My mother told all of our family members and friends that I was mentally ill. She carries my letter of confrontation in her purse to show to people, has told many lies about me that had nothing to do with the case (including some she had to make up to cover my father's guilt), made my attorney ask the questions repeatedly by avoiding directly answering the questions, and tried to sit in on my father's deposition. The stories my parents made up in depositions about me helped confirm their character and the fact that my father should be held accountable.

My attorneys made sure my mother could not enter the room while I was testifying, made my father shut up while I was testifying, told me I could leave if their attorney got

disrespectful or my father upset me, told me I could have breaks whenever I wanted, made me feel in control of the deposition process, told me to ask their attorney to slow down, and told me to tell him his questions were too vague or broad and to be more specific.

Little things also helped, like being at depositions first so I didn't have to walk through the middle of them and anyone they might bring with them for support, and asking for a volunteer from our sexual assault center to accompany me to depositions.

During my deposition, my parents' attorney also criticized me. It was like he was an abuser, twisting my words and meanings up, mitigating anything my parents did, suggesting other reasons than what I gave for things, trying to put words in my mouth. This was hard to deal with, since it was so similar to the way my parents have treated me. It made me feel stupid and non-affirmed, with no reality of my own, just like my parents did. Breaks during the deposition helped me interpret what was going on.

I don't think I could have handled being present at my therapist's deposition. It would have been very difficult for me to hear his testimony, even though he was testifying for me. It was difficult enough to hear my husband's testimony.

By the end of four days of depositions, I wanted in the worst way to settle and not drag these poor people through the courts! I talked to my attorneys about it and they complied with my wishes and talked to their attorney, who said they would never settle. I shed tears over it even. I told my husband about it. He knew I was being swayed but he had made up his mind that he would not interfere. If he had I would have been terribly upset with him. I was afraid he wouldn't understand that I just couldn't bear to drag these pathetic looking people through the courts no matter what they had done to me. So he went along with me, just as my attorneys went along with what I wanted. I do not know if my attorneys realized at the time how swayed and under the influence I was by my parents. It was like I was seeing things totally their way. I had slipped back into their mold, their image of me, their desire not to be held accountable. I even discussed with my attorneys agreeing on a settlement and giving it to some mutually agreed upon charity.

By the end of the weekend, after I was back home, I got my head on straight again. I called my Alaskan attorney and told him that I no longer wanted to settle, and that I had been swayed by them. I did not want him to pursue settlement further with their attorney. It was a real lesson for me that I was still very much their victim after four years of almost no contact with them. I think the best thing an attorney can do is to say, "Wait, you may change your mind after you have been away from your parents for awhile."

It took me about a week after my parents' and my own depositions to recover from the awful feelings it brought about the underlying unresolved abuse issues.

I am under a great deal of stress, part of which is caused by the suit. I have had skipped heartbeats, which are caused by stress or fatigue, regularly now for at least the past month, which have been checked by a doctor and are benign.

My parents have tried to make everyone believe they are indigent. My attorneys informed theirs that they have property completely paid for that they did not disclose to him.

I haven't heard from my extended family, except what my parents said in depositions, which of course is negative. Family friends are the same way, but my parents have been in contact with them rather than me, giving their version of the story. It causes me a lot of pain to think of those relationships, some of which are years old. Some of them are definitely "former" friends and will always be enemies.

Survivors who want to sue should have a good support system of people who support in various ways. Someone to talk to who has gone through the process is helpful. Get the best, most knowledgeable attorney you can find, and get the best expert witness, someone who is well respected and well credentialed who understands victims. It's hard, but try to think long-term. Will you be happy with yourself ten years from now if you don't use your only opportunity to sue? Would it be better not to sue because you may be losing an inheritance, or worse, psychological health? Though these suits are often done on a contingent fee basis, be prepared for great cost, including the cost of depositions, expert witnesses, travel, and hotels for yourself and your attorney when suing out of state. Be prepared to do long hours of document hunting, information gathering, and preparing questions for your abuser's and others' depositions for your attorney.

So far it has been worth it and I would do it again. I think there is a healing from it that you can't get from a therapy room that does not confront an abuser head-on for what he's done with some kind of power that can make it stick. For me, it is important to at least try to get justice. It is also important for the community and for other survivors to see some sort of resolution to this issue.

[Author's Note: Kelvin and Patti Barton are working as advocates to change statutes of limitations for child sexual abuse actions and have become knowledgeable about the progress of such efforts in all fifty states. For information, send a self-addressed stamped envelope to them at P.O. Box 7651, Everett, WA 98201.]

Rachel

Sometimes the system breaks down

The abuse started when I was an infant. My mother would insert objects into every body orifice. She also used needles to inflict pain. From childhood until I left home at 18, I performed cunnilingus on my mother. The abuse with my father lasted approximately from age 3 or 4 until age 10 or 11. Fellatio and sodomy were his favorite activities. Sometime between the ages of 4 and 6, he brought his drinking buddies home to join him.

I have inner parts that I refer to as Suzanne, Patricia, Peggy, Penny, Shelly, Sheila, Gina, Laura, and Sharon. These parts endured various aspects of the abuse. I hesitate to call them alters because I do not lose time in the present. *[Authors' Note: The following paragraphs are, in essence, one story told by two of Rachel's parts. Unfortunately, it is but one of many horrific stories remembered by Rachel's parts.]*

My father owned a bar in a Midwestern city. His father owned the building. On street level were the bar and a cafe. Above the bar were two apartments. Above the cafe was only the "roof," the play area for the children who lived in the apartment. When one of my brothers was born, a fence was put up around the perimeter of the roof. There was a wooden staircase leading from the roof to the parking area below. Across the gravel parking area was the blacksmith shop. It was not well built and one could see the flames between the boards that made up the siding.

The northwest corner of the stockyards was directly across the street. Dad would take my younger brother and me on the walkways above the pens. On Sunday evenings, trucks filled with cattle would be backed up for miles waiting for the market to open Monday morning. Business must have been good as the farmers came to quench their thirst at the tavern.

The door leading to the apartments opened onto the main thoroughfare through town. The steps were old and creaky. At the top of the stairs was the bathroom for the smaller apartment. Down the hall to the left was the rest of the smaller apartment. Straight ahead was the entrance to the larger apartment. It opened into the kitchen, a square room with a table. The dining room was only partially divided from the kitchen. Only the decor made the difference. There was a larger dining table, a buffet, and an oil heater. The dining room opened to the living room. The right-hand door led to one bedroom. The door straight ahead led to the master bedroom. A closet separated the master bedroom from the children's bedroom. The only other way out of the children's bedroom was a window that led to the roof. To the right of the dining area was the bathroom, a linen closet, and the laundry room with a door also leading to the roof.

Peggy was playing in the living room. She heard footsteps on the stairs. Dad was coming home. She ran to greet him. He wasn't alone. He was having fun with his friends. Dad always talked in a loud voice. And laughed above everyone else. They looked at her. She was frightened. They made jokes she didn't understand.

"She has to be tighter than the wife."

"Take your clothes off." She froze.

"Didn't you hear me?" Tears came.

"If you cry, I'll take my belt off."

The tears stopped. She attempted to unbutton her dress. She was too slow. He took it off for her. They put her on a table. She was lying on her back. Dad held her shoulders down. They ached against the hard table. The men touched her all over. Moved their hands over her chest and abdomen and stroked her nipples. Then they licked her, the shameful parts of her body. Then they held her legs by her ankles, holding them up to their shoulders. Then they hurt her. There was pressure against her backside.

"How's this for tight?"

"I told you it would be good," he bragged.

She didn't hear any more. She was gone.

He left with the men. Back down the noisy stairs.

She went to the bedroom and covered herself. It was the middle of the day.

Then she heard him come back. He was angry. He came into her room. Took off his belt and beat her as she lay in bed.

"Don't you ever treat my friends like that again. You understand? They have just come back from the war. You better show them a good time when they come again."

They did come again. She heard them. She tried to hide in her bedroom. He found her. Reminded her that she had better do a good job. Once in the dining room, she began to undress seductively, leaving her clothes in a heap on the floor. Then she walked over to one of the men and started to stroke his crotch. That caused a whoop from the men. They put her on the table face down and took turns penetrating her rectum. One of them went so deep that she passed out.

When she woke up, she was standing on top of her discarded clothes. Mother came home. Took her into the bathroom, put her into the tub and washed her. She stood. It hurt to sit down. Then Mother took her into the bedroom, lay down on the bed, removed her panties, spread her legs and had Penny lick her. Penny knew how to do this well. She took pride in her abilities to please.

I was in and out of therapy from 1966 to 1986. In May, 1986 I began therapy with my eighth therapist. I went to him in desperation. Nothing else had worked. I was severely depressed and unable to hold a job. I made a promise to myself that I would commit suicide if he couldn't help. In July, 1986, the first memories came to consciousness. My therapist mentioned that he was assisting other survivors in lawsuits against their perpetrators. I told him I could never do that to my parents.

In late August, 1986, the *Tyson* appeal was handed down. This ruling effectively denied the use of the delayed discovery doctrine in cases of repressed memories.

In January and March, 1987, I wrote a couple of letters to my father. I did not mention the incest. I wrote about the emotional and physical abuse. This was my father's response: "I'm sorry that you are living in the past. I'm 66 years old and what happened in the past can't be changed. All I'm trying to do is live each day as it comes and enjoy life on this troubled planet. I hope and pray that you do the same. Dwelling on the past, especially if all you can recall are the bad times only makes you miserable. Irregardless [his word] of what you think happened or what actualy [*sic*] happened, try to live life today. Maybe we can resolve some of these misunderstandings by talking to each other. I don't think that writing letters will solve anything. If your [*sic*] looking for answers, I think it would be a lot better if you, Mom and I got together and discussed it. You name the time and place and we'll be there."

I couldn't have asked for more. I requested them to come and meet with me and my therapist. They refused. They said dad was too sick to be so far from his doctors. A year later I learned from my sister that they had flown to San Francisco with an aunt and uncle. I checked my geography. I couldn't understand why they thought Seattle was too far and San Francisco was not. But then, what do I know?

In June and July, 1987, another of my brothers went through a suicidal depression. On July 2, 1987 I called my parents asking them for backup financial support, if my brother should need it. I hoped that if he could rely on my parents that he would be able to take two or three months off work to deal with his problems. They flatly refused. When I finally, in desperation, told them he was suicidal, my mother's cold response was, "Let him do what he has to do."

One day in July, my brother, after a five-day binge, went into his garage, turned on the ignition, and lay down in his truck bed, head toward the exhaust, clutching a pillow. A friend found him. He survived without physical or mental problems. To this day, my sister and I are the only ones who know about his suicide attempt. This brother and my sister are the only ones who have been supportive of me.

After the phone call, I knew that it was of no use to talk to my parents. They refused to help in a crisis. They were not about to accept any responsibility for what their adult children were going through.

The following year, a bill was introduced in my resident

state legislature to allow the recover of repressed memories to be the start of the statute of limitations. After the bill was signed into law in April 1988, I wrote to an attorney whose name I had received from a survivor's group. We met in person sometime in May.

I don't know how long I was in his office. He grilled me for a long time. When he was satisfied, he apologized for putting me through that. He said that he did not take cases of this kind unless he believed his client. He also said that he would need to talk to my therapist and that he would like the result of a psychological test. And he wanted to talk with any siblings who might be able to substantiate my story.

We also discussed the importance of money. If my parents didn't have assets, it would not be beneficial to take them to court. My parents did have assets. They owned their own home and had a number of certificates of deposit.

This attorney then told me that I would have to sue in my birth state, since the abuse happened there and my parents still lived there. The attorney's staff researched the law there. He called to tell me that I would have a tough time there, since my birth state had no law comparable to the one recently passed in my state of residence. He advised me that I would probably not be allowed to go to trial, and that there was a greater than 50-50 chance that my case would be dismissed on statute of limitations grounds. I decided I still wanted to go on. I felt it was important to take a public stand.

Then he informed me that my birth state had a two-year statute of limitations. I found myself in the position of having to find an attorney 1500 miles away in six weeks.

I turned to a woman who was the mother of an acquaintance. She was a retired educational psychologist who had been on the governor's council for education for six years in my birth state. She didn't agree with what I was doing, but she did give me some good advice. Following her suggestions, I called the legal and psychology departments of two universities in my birth state. I was given the names of attorneys who practiced family law.

After a number of calls, I spoke with a woman who said she was interested. She explained that she would have to clear the case with the partners before going any further. She promised to call by the end of the following week.

She did not call. I called her. She was not in. I continued to call. She would not talk to me. Finally, I asked her secretary to please ask her if she was going to take my case or not. The attorney still would not talk to me. I was on the line waiting. But she told her secretary to tell me that she would not take my case.

I had three weeks left.

I went through periods of frantic phone calling and periods of giving up. Some attorneys were supportive but simply didn't have time on such short notice to help me. Others told me I was wasting my time. They let me know that they felt that any attorney who would take such an unwinable case was foolish at best.

I had two weeks left.

I decided to give it one more try. This time I reached an attorney in the capital city. He said that he had had only one abuse case, and that one involved a teenager who had clear recall of the abuse. However, he said that he was intellectually interested in my situation. Because I had the support of my first attorney, this attorney agreed to prepare a petition and summons. My first attorney graciously sent his notes and a copy of the *Tyson* case to him.

My parents were served one day before the two-year statute of limitations expired. My attorney felt that my parents would settle before the end of the month they had been given to respond. They did not settle. Their attorney, instead, sent a list of interrogatories and a request for copies of checks substantiating the amount I said I had paid for therapy from 1984 to 1988.

It was at this point that I learned a lesson on why the legal system moves slowly. The interrogatories and check copying requests were reasonable. I had a problem, however, because for a year or so I had allowed the bank to retain my checks for "safekeeping." Bank personnel were not pleased when I asked for a copy of around 100 checks. I actually had to show the bank vice president a copy of my attorney's request before they would proceed. This alone took about six weeks and cost me $100.

After receiving my answers to the interrogatories, my parent's attorney requested depositions from my therapist and from me. Again, there were delays. My new attorney felt that my costs would be minimized if the depositions were to be held in my first attorney's office. So we had to reconcile the schedules of busy attorneys. The depositions were finally set for January, 1989.

In the meantime, my sister had invited me to her home in the Midwest for Christmas. I flew in, and we both drove to meet my new attorney in person. I knew that he had a deep, sonorous voice over the phone. In person, he looked like the bearded Perry Mason. He was a large, imposing man.

He spoke with my sister and me for an hour or two. He said he was interested in any information that my sister, who is younger than I am, had that would corroborate my story. He was pleased with her answers. He said that she would make a good witness if we went to trial. My sister was concerned, however, that she would have a difficult time talking about Dad if he were in the courtroom watching her.

He was concerned with me. He couldn't understand why I spoke so softly. He didn't understand why I wasn't stridently angry. After the suit, I learned that incest survivors often speak in slow, measured, soft tones.

I was sorry we went to meet him. After that I did not feel that he supported me with the same conviction he had before the meeting. He did not feel I would be a credible witness.

The depositions were held as scheduled. My therapist was deposed first, in the morning. My turn came in the afternoon. I was so nervous I was unable to eat breakfast and had only a bowl of soup for lunch. I do not do well when my blood sugar is low. Toward the end, I knew that my answers were not as clear and straight-forward as they could have been. If I had to do it over, I would insist on going first—even if I had to pay my therapist more for his extra hours out of the office.

At the time, though, I was relieved that he went first. My parents' attorney had sent his son, a junior partner. My first attorney felt that this was his first deposition. Obviously this case had a low priority for the firm. The advantage to me was that he was gentle when questioning me. He did not try to put me on the spot or to contradict or confuse me. He could have been much tougher.

Both my therapist and I believed that this junior partner believed me. I later learned, however, that no matter what an attorney believes, he has a fiduciary responsibility to protect his client.

I feel that my attorney and my therapist should have asked a Ph.D. to interview me and be deposed on my behalf. My therapist is well-known for his work and lectures in the areas of incest and child abuse, but he does not have any educational credentials, not even a B.A. He comes across well in person and verbally, but his transcribed answers did not read as well. These answers were all the judge had to go by. A Ph.D. on my side may not have made any difference in the final outcome, but I believe that the judge would have given a Ph.D. more credence than a well-meaning therapist without credentials. My attorney should have known this, and my therapist should have known this. In addition, even though my therapist had told me when I first started therapy with him that he was assisting several clients in legal actions, this was the first deposition that he had been required to take part in for a client in such a case. He wasn't as experienced in legal matters as he had led me to believe.

The judge heard briefs from both attorneys sometime in March or early April. It turns out that my attorney did not go in person to the hearing. He said that it was sufficient to have his brief available to the judge on a timely basis. His failure to be there gave my parents and siblings a moral victory. "He didn't even bother to show up."

I asked my attorney for a copy of the briefs. He promised to send them to me. He did not do so.

My suit was dismissed on statute of limitations grounds.

Two weeks later, at the beginning of a session, my therapist handed me a letter from my attorney telling me about the dismissal.

It turns out that my attorney had written to my therapist a week before. My therapist did not let me see the letter because he felt that my attorney should tell me directly instead of using him as an intermediary. My therapist did allow my attorney to address the second letter to me in care the therapist.

In the meantime, my therapist had shown the first letter from my attorney to every colleague and client so that they could express their rage about the inadequacies of the legal system when it came to survivors of incest.

I felt betrayed by both of them. It was my lawsuit. I had initiated it. I had found attorneys in both states. I had paid over $2000 to go through with it. Yet I was the last to know the results.

I think my therapist expected me to cry. Actually, I was angry. I think I was more angry with them and their discounting of my feelings and my relationship with them than I was about the dismissal. From the beginning, my first attorney had prepared me for this eventuality. Yes, the money would have helped. But that was not the primary reason for filing the suit. It was important to me to take a public stand on behalf of myself and other incest survivors.

Since my suit now gave the courts a precedent against the use of delayed discovery with repressed memories, I decided that it was important to change the law in my birth state. My attorney said he would help, but he did not.

I had notified my siblings by letter about both the filing and the dismissal. I invited their questions, but I received only two phone calls. One told me, "If Dad has a heart attack and dies, his death will be on your shoulders. I will never forgive you for depriving my children of a grandfather." The other, who has no children, called to ask what kind of inheritance would be left for the grandchildren if my parents paid for my therapy. Since then, I have been ostracized by four of my brothers.

My sister has been in contact with our parents and other family members. I get feedback from her occasionally. She said my mother takes any opportunity she has to call me crazy and to call me a liar. It turns out that she was labelling me "crazy" long before I filed the suit. Some of the grandchildren had taken to calling me "crazy aunt Rachel." Mom never misses a chance to comment on what a good mother she is. Finally, in regard to money, Mom said, "I would rather spend every dime we have on legal fees than give Rachel anything." Mother continues her hatred of me. She no longer decorates a tree at Christmas "because of the lawsuit."

The benefits of going through the suit to me were: 1) I stood up to my parents; 2) I found that at least some people outside the therapeutic community believed me—and these people were in positions of authority in the legal/justice system; and 3) I took a small step in the process of shedding some light on the darkness and secrecy surrounding incest.

Crystal

Survivors and *abusers: Scared, but not sorry*

My abuser was my stepfather. The sexual abuse spanned many years. My earliest memories of abuse being at age 12 and end when the abuse finally stopped at age 23 in 1985.

His pursuit of me was relentless. It didn't matter whether it was day or night, holiday or not. There was no place I could go that he couldn't intrude upon. There were no safe places within the home and very few outside in the world.

My mom worked outside the home for many years, and as the oldest of three children, many of her responsibilities were passed down to me, including care of the younger kids (my mom's and stepfather's two children).

The sexual abuse began with fondling and inappropriate touching and got progressively worse. Before long it included oral sex, the use of a vibrator on me, using my hand to bring him to orgasm, intercourse, and being forced to allow the family dog to have oral sex with me. The last is the worst of all in my mind. Only recently have I begun to work through the pain.

When I was seventeen, I reported the abuse to the Department of Human Services. A child protective worker took my report and investigated. My mother was called in to get me and my stepfather was confronted. He, of course, denied everything.

Due to harassment from various members of the family, such as being called a liar and other names and being physically threatened with a gun, I stopped talking and cancelled a doctor's appointment the protective worker had arranged for me. The investigation was dropped and the abuse continued for over six more years.

In September, 1989, I confronted him again. This time I included my stepfather's two children, who were then old enough to understand. I needed to know if he'd molested them and I felt they deserved to know the truth. To this day, they both say they haven't been molested.

That confrontation changed my life. My mother says she believes me, but she never talks about it and knows none of the details. The first time I confronted I got no support from her. My stepsister believed me immediately and still does, although she has lately been less supportive than when she first found out. My stepbrother is the youngest, but he is also an adult now. He and I were really close. I was his substitute mom, and he confided in me a lot. Now, we rarely talk. I understand his need to have a father in his life and I never asked him to stop loving his father. I only hoped he could also love me.

It took many years of therapy before I even realized that I had a right to sue. It just never occurred to me that it could be dealt with in a legal way and it wasn't until several months after my second confrontation that the issue was mentioned by my therapist.

I decided to look into a civil suit because of the total lack of remorse on my stepfather's part. Also, although I haven't lived in the same house with him since 1983, every time something went wrong in the family he brought me into it and told people I was to blame for his marital problems and that I was crazy and making up lies.

Another consideration, although by no means my purpose in doing this, has been financial. Why should I have to pay physically, emotionally, spiritually, and financially for something he did to me? I have spent thousands and thousands of dollars in trying to heal from the abuse and reclaim my life.

Believe it or not, I found my attorney through a newspaper ad. The ad was well written and had a warm tone to it. I wrote a letter to the firm briefly explaining that I was a survivor of incest and was wondering what legal options were available to me, if any. Within a week I got a reply that was extremely validating of my pain and an offer to call and set up an appointment, which I did.

I had my first appointment in April, 1990. It was a tremendous step for me. The simple act of speaking about what was done to me produced this feeling of impending doom. I felt like "something bad was going to happen" because I "told on my stepfather." However, it was also very empowering to take action and state clearly that what he did was not acceptable.

In August, 1990 I got a call from my attorney's office informing me that they'd researched my case and the statutes in my state, and that I had a case. The next day I went in to sign some papers, and the case was filed in court that same week.

In October, 1990 the sheriff's department served papers on my stepfather informing him that I was suing him for sexual abuse. I feared he would become violent and come after me in a rage, but this did not happen. Suddenly, he made it known through the rest of the family that he was willing to talk. "Can't we get together and work this out?" I would have considered this if I felt he was truly sorry, but I feel that the only thing he is sorry about is that I opened my mouth. He is scared, but he is not sorry.

The whole process seems very slow and frustrating at times. In June, 1991, I completed the written interrogatories from my stepfather's attorney—twenty-eight very detailed questions that were very difficult to get through. One question that stands out was "Describe in complete detail each act of abuse of which you complain, including in your answer for each: the date it occurred, the time, what the defendant did and said, what you did and said, and the names of any witnesses present." It took me pages to answer that question. I found it very intimidating regarding the dates and times. I have some strong memories, but they act as if I charted it on a calendar or something.

Shortly after the interrogatories were completed, I went into the hospital for the first time in my life. I was severely depressed, having nightmares and flashbacks, and finding it impossible to work. It seemed like a drastic thing to do at the time, but it saved my life.

I've been in therapy for five years now. My therapist and my attorney have not yet met, but are in contact by phone when the need arises. I'm sure as the case progresses the three of us will be spending a lot of time together.

I've gotten valuable support from a friend of mine and

from the staff at the local Sexual Assault Crisis Center, as well as from a few other close friends. They are consistent, caring, and most of all they believe in me. That's a nice feeling after years of feeling that no one believed or cared enough to do anything about it.

Would I do it again? The case is still in its early stages, but I would have to say yes. I cannot imagine anything the opposing attorneys could say that could come close to the pain I lived with on a daily basis. They may scare me, but they can't scar me like he did.

Chelse

Standing up, speaking up, fighting back . . . and winning

My story is a long, intense one, from which I grew and got stronger and took my power back. I had a very positive experience, for which I am grateful. I know how fortunate I was. I drew to me loving people—strong, supportive, effective people who have been there for me and helped me to believe in life and stay alive. I only hope to stay alive to give some of this back.

I know I was abused from at least age nine until I was seventeen. My dad said that the sexual abuse actually started when I was a baby, and that he had sexual feelings toward me when I was less then six months old. However, overt touching, genital touching, didn't occur until I was nine years old, although there was a lot of other inappropriate touching exposure both before age nine and after. It stopped when I was seventeen, because I reported it to a high school counselor. At the time, I didn't realize it was wrong. I just wanted it to stop. I had gotten some information from school and news suggesting it was not okay. Also, I didn't want it happening to my younger sister, as I was a senior in high school and soon to go off to college.

After I reported the abuse, the child protection agency got involved, along with the legal systems, and our family got involved in ineffective therapy. It was a crazy time, but eventually we got hooked up with a better therapy center. My dad was forced to move, which was hard because my Mom and I had no relationship. She blamed me and life became even more difficult.

In addition to the sexual abuse, I was also physically abused, and of course emotionally abused on many levels.

A criminal lawsuit was brought by the county, but I was not involved in it because I was a minor. My dad delayed it, plea bargained, and slid through the system. The county attorney was mostly concerned that my dad keep his job and continue to pay taxes. Because my dad had a top secret clearance job working with computers and defense systems, a felony on his record could have jeopardized his job, which concerned the county attorney greatly. Since my dad was being a good guy and going to and paying for therapy, what was my problem? In the end, dad got a ten-year probation to be a good guy and pay for therapy for the family for a year.

At that time I made a deal/contract with my dad. We agreed that I could get as much therapy as I could in the next year and he would pay for it, or he could pay for what I needed over time. He agreed to pay for the therapy I needed, when I needed it.

I continued on with the therapy as needed and tried to go to school. In the course of my therapy I needed to be hospitalized in a psychiatric unit. I had no insurance to cover the bill, so I handed the bill over to my father. He decided he didn't want to pay for the bill, and said it wasn't his fault. I got angry because he was breaking his contract, and tired of his games. I hired an attorney and threatened a lawsuit. Eventually I filed the suit and went through the whole thing.

I don't think my father thought I was serious, or that I was that strong. Sometimes I feel guilty for being strong and for my father being dumb and underestimating me.

I wanted a strong, feminist attorney, but I couldn't find one who was interested in taking the case. They wanted money and weren't hopeful about the outcome. Finally, I hooked up with another survivor who was pursuing his own case. He referred me to his attorney. This attorney took my case on contingency. I was his little charity case. He didn't get much money when it was said and done, but he got publicity and my undying loyalty and love.

The next couple of years of my life were very hard. I had a serious suicide attempt and ended up living in group homes and on psychiatric medications for sleep, flashbacks, and depression.

I found a good therapist who had been through her own abuse issues. She became a role model for me. She was very loving and supportive. I also had a psychiatrist who watched me go through the process and tried to make my life as easy as possible considering the circumstances. The hospital I went to is a top-notch institution that was years ahead in its approach to survivors. All of these people and institutions helped me feel safe, and allowed me to begin to take back my power.

My attorney handled me well. He knew I needed to be very much in charge of the whole process. He copied everything for me and kept me updated. He worked closely with my support system and knew when we were out of his league and needing to connect with my therapist or doctor. My attorney continued the lawsuit even when my mouth told him to stop. He understood my semi-irrational fear of my father coming to get me. He made no judgments of me as I struggled through hospitalizations and group homes. He believed in me, stood up for me, fought for me/with me, brought me cigarettes when I was locked up in hospital units, and believed he could right a wrong.

My attorney also handled my dad very well. He treated him like the asshole he was—very firmly, professionally. It was like having someone beat up my dad for me and fight for my life, my rights, my voice, my power.

Every time paperwork came from him my stress level increased. Every time something happened with the case, my whole life was put in upheaval. The process psychologically and emotionally ripped me up. My attorney tried to avert as much pain as he could, but he wasn't going to settle unfairly. He tried mediation with my Dad. He tried to prepare me, he educated me, and he let me gather information and add feedback.

The court process started in the fall of 1984, but the trial wasn't complete, and judgment wasn't handed down, until April, 1986. It was a very agonizing time. I had to be reminded what I could accomplish, which was to tell my truth to a court system. After that it was out of my hands. The only real thing the court system can do is hear testimony, gather facts, and hand out justice as it sees fit. The only justice possible in my case was money. The court system can't give anyone the family they never had. It can't make someone say they are sorry or did wrong. It can't promise

things will get better. The main reason I did the court case was because I knew I had to live with myself. The biggest questions someone considering suing has to answer are "Can I live with myself if I do this?" and "Can I live with myself if I don't?" I knew I couldn't live with myself down the road if I didn't fight and speak when I had the chance.

We were concerned about the statute of limitations, and brought the case in the nick of time. However, a statute of limitations argument would have been valid and possibly blocked us had it been argued. I personally believe that there should be no statute of limitations on these types of cases due to delayed discovery and the unpredictable process of therapy, but I doubt this is a realistic expectation of the law.

My therapist and psychiatrist were in contact with my attorney throughout the process, educating him about their areas of expertise. Everyone worked very closely together toward my recovery, whatever that involved.

My deposition was taken in a locked psychiatric unit. My dad wasn't present, only his attorney, my attorney, the court reporter, and a nurse.

I was hospitalized in the month prior to trial, in a locked psychiatric unit. I was very crazy, and I didn't want to live through the procedure. I was scared out of my mind. Needless to say, the month went by. I was moved to an open unit and lived out of the hospital during the trial. My lawyer would pick me up and drop me off at the hospital. I was really in awful shape and on lots of medications. My blood pressure was that of a person in shock. I'll never forget those four days of trial—things that were said, scenes, names, faces. It's been five and a half years and I remember it like it was yesterday.

At some point in the process, my dad hired an attorney, but it was too late—he'd put the cart before the horse. He hadn't taken me seriously, and he paid deeply for his stupidity. My dad had the decision of whether to have a judge or jury trial, and he exhausted all the judges from our area. The judge who finally heard the case had to be brought in from another district.

My dad and then my mom were called up to the stand.

During their testimony, my attorney made sure I had a lot of support and even had someone (my therapist) just to hold my hand the whole day.

I testified after my parents, for 2½ hours one day and three hours the next day. The judge was very empathetic. He wanted to know how much a day of abuse costs and multiply it by years. The judge told me I didn't have to say anything, just look at him if I needed a break. I let my attorney go with my testimony. I wrote several of his questions to me to clarify my dad's denial and minimizing. I didn't care any more, and had a chance to tell my truth.

The day my witnesses were called to testify it was great to have all my therapists, doctors, hospital personnel, and friends all there at one big table—I felt very supported and strong.

I wrote most of the questions for my dad's cross-examination, because I couldn't sit there and listen to him lie. It was very painful to hear him and watch him. It was also difficult to listen to my mom say she "had never loved me," and that I "was born crazy."

It was hurtful to hear professional "hired guns" who were paid to say what they said, which was very sick. These doctors and psychologists said that I "was born crazy, and always would be crazy, and eight years of abuse had nothing to do with it." They also said I had gotten "bad" therapy, which was the real problem. The defense also said a lesbian therapist made me file suit, and the real cause of my problems was PMS. Actually, my therapy was very effective, and the efforts of all the helping professionals were well coordinated.

The judge wouldn't hear any of this. He was able to see through it, thank God. My attorney once again let me be very much in charge. After going into chambers with the judge, he would come out, we would have a cigarette, and he would tell me what had been said so I knew everything.

When it was over, we knew we had won, even though the judge took it under advisement. I watched my mom and dad leave court, and I cried and went back to the hospital. My lawyer asked for two million dollars, crazy guy that he is. We received a judgment of $243,000. My dad didn't have that kind of money, but I am seeing little pieces of it, and all my court costs, my attorney, my doctors, and my therapist were paid for.

It's been 5½ years since trial. I am still in therapy on a weekly basis, and am still on medication to help deal with flashbacks. I have no contact with my happily married parents, which is best for me. I am a nursing student and hope to graduate someday to help other survivors. I try to help my attorney by being a support person to other survivors as they go through court procedures, and am working on being a qualified advocate in this capacity. I don't pretend to be a therapist, just someone who has been there and has done it. My attorney can't handle all the emotional stuff and do his job too. He is smart enough to know that.

I don't hate my father or mother, or wish bad things to happen to them. I understand why this happened on some levels. I work on forgiving myself regularly. I'll neither forget this history, nor should I—it has made me strong and shaped me. I get angry at my parents from time to time, but no longer wish to change them and realize I can't. I have learned a lot from all of this, grown through it, and feel that court procedures were the only way to let go of some stuff around it. I still work on letting go and going on. I am grateful for the love and support I've received from professionals, friends, and others along the way. Going through the legal process was the hardest thing I've done in my life, except living through the abuse, and it was the most painful, yet I would do the whole thing again tomorrow.

There is no real way to prepare for how you'll feel at trial. Be honest, tell your truth, be strong, keep your power, get lots of support, do what you need to do to feel in charge and not victimized by the court system, and allow yourself to feel angry—let the anger empower you.

Connie

Breaking the cycle of abuse

[Authors' Note: Most of Connie's story is reprinted with permission from Civil Litigation: One Incest Survivor's Experience, *by Connie Nesbary, in* Sojourner: The Women's Forum, *Vol. 17, No. 1 (September 1991) (42 Seaverns Ave., Jamaica Plain, MA 02130: $17/year for 12 issues).]*

When I offered to write my story, I imagined that it would be easy to discuss my experiences of recovering childhood memories and suing both of my parents for incest and ritual abuse. Reality set in when I sat down to write and found myself mired in a quicksand of feelings. I heard, again, the emotional abuse I experienced as a child: "If you write or say anything, it will be used against you," "You're asking for it," "Who do you think you are?" My parents had also threatened, and proven their capability, to kill me if I ever told. Thus the threat of death loomed over my computer. I had to complete this task, however, because speaking out about the horrendous abuse I endured is a necessary part of my healing. I was fortunate to be able file a civil suit as another step in reclaiming my identity and as an attempt to stop the cycle of abuse for the next generations.

In February 1989, at the age of 34, repressed memories of my horrific childhood suddenly began to surface. My husband and I had initiated an adoption process a few months prior and my autobiographical statement compelled the adoption worker to ask if I was an incest survivor. I had laughed and told her that the word incest meant nothing to me. I remember the following weeks as one would think of a volcano preparing to erupt. The flashbacks that followed, in relentless frequency, were no laughing matter.

The trauma-induced, partial amnesia of my childhood has, and will continue, to effect every aspect of my life. One of the most important ways in which the abuse has affected me, and which made it imperative for me to pursue legal remedies, was the notion of my "responsibility." As the oldest child in a family of four girls with two incompetent parents, I became the parent. My mother and father were eager to let me believe that I was responsible for their abusive actions. I heard constantly how their actions were my fault because I was "born on the wrong day, had the wrong name, should have been a boy," ad nauseam. The civil suit was a way for me to state, and receive acknowledgement, that I never asked for it. I didn't deserve it. I was not, and am not, responsible for my parents' (abusers') behavior.

Making the decision to seek legal remedy in any situation is complex, but suing family members for incest has to be one of the toughest. Because the statute of limitations only gave me one year from the time I began to remember the abuse in which to file, I had little time for consideration. No one could tell me how long the intense flashbacks would last. I wasn't sure I could handle the stress of a lawsuit at the same time I was re-experiencing the horrors of my childhood. I questioned whether I was physically and mentally capable of withstanding several years working with the legal system and dealing with the social stigma of coming out as an incest survivor who was suing her parents—all with virtually no support from any biological relative. I considered whether I had adequate support from my immediate family, friends, the mental health experts, and my lawyers. In the end, my children tipped the decision towards filing.

My children were seven and eight at the time the flashbacks began and had to be told something. I told them that I was spending a lot of time crying because I was remembering that my parents had been "very mean" to me. They wanted to know what I was going to do to protect them from my parents. I saw the fear in their eyes and I knew that if I didn't have the courage to stand up for myself, for the innocent child that I had been and that was still a part of me, my children would never believe that I could protect them and they would be right. I decided to use every means possible to break the cycle of abuse for my children. The respect, love, and support that they have given me since has made the struggle worth it a thousand times over.

Another reason I made the choice to sue and to continue speaking out is the fact that most perpetrators of sexual abuse don't stop with one victim. My father and mother had multiple victims beyond the family and used that fact to reinforce our hopelessness. Sexual abuse continues as long as the status quo of secrecy is maintained. Survivors have the power to influence societal norms and legislation through relating their experiences. When we begin to recognize that each survivor most likely represents several victims for each perpetrator, the importance of acknowledging these experiences is magnified.

My first thought was to file a criminal complaint against my parents. To my dismay, the criminal statute of limitations in my case had expired when I turned 21. This statute seemed totally unjustified, since child sexual abuse promotes long-term amnesia. How could anyone criminally prosecute a perpetrator of child sexual abuse, if they were unlikely to remember the events until much later in adulthood? I decided to file a civil suit, the only option open to me.

I was spending over $150 a week on psychotherapy alone, and I naively began to hope that the court would demand that my parents take responsibility for their actions. I decided to sue even though, in most recent cases alleging incest, the plaintiffs had been unable to collect the substantial sums of money they had been awarded because the defendants had left the country or failed to disclose assets. But then, what amount of money could ever fully repay someone for this extensive damage?

In July 1989, just five months after my memories surfaced, I filed a civil suit in a federal district court in the Midwest, naming both of my parents as perpetrators of incest and ritual abuse. After almost two years of protective orders, depositions, and a summary judgment (request for dismissal by the defendants), both parents settled in April 1991. The legal system can be used effectively, however there are barriers which hinder victims from exercising this right.

One of the main barriers is financial. I was fortunate that my attorneys felt strongly enough about my case to take it on contingency and to cover their legal expenses until a decision was rendered. Even so, my costs of travel to the Midwest for court-related appearances and meetings with my attorneys, phone bills, copying, and fees for an expert witness went in the thousands of dollars quickly. At the same time, the emotional strain made it nearly impossible to do any kind of work.

Social norms, some of which are created as a reaction to fear, rule institutional systems. The long-established norm insisting that family business be dealt with "in the family" creates a social barrier for survivors. As a society, we are reluctant to air a family's "dirty laundry." Spouse-battering and incest have, until very recently, been considered taboo in the courtroom. The media has only begun to address family violence.

This insistence on keeping family secrets is based on the fear and pain of having to recognize that the rape, torture and murder of children in this country is not uncommon. Even more frightening is the fact that the perpetrators live right next door to you and me, and sometimes live within our own houses. At the beginning of my lawsuit, friends and acquaintances who clung to this norm became suddenly recognizable. I didn't anticipate the peer pressure to keep quiet and the loss of a few friendships. Both were emotionally difficult.

Social barriers extend to the court system and media as well. Because there are those who would rather avoid the painful truth of incest than deal directly with domestic violence and child sexual abuse, the court system and the media are given license to focus pressure on the victim ("blame the messenger" syndrome). This avoidance strategy is accomplished by requiring the plaintiff to produce absolute evidence in as many forms as possible (much like Cinderella's stepmother demanding more and more work of Cinderella as a ruse to keep her out of sight). One lawyer refused to take my case because I didn't have photographs of my parents in the act of abusing me when I was a child. Fortunately, most attorneys and judges are more realistic.

Another example of this occurred during the time of "discovery." Supposedly discovery is a time when plaintiffs and defendants may examine each party's evidence before trial. My parents' attorneys argued that since I was making "crazy" allegations and I had the burden of proving them, my parents' psychiatric stability was "not in question" and "irrelevant." I was required to relinquish an entire life's worth of medical reports and undergo a psychiatric evaluation in order to prove my case, but was not allowed to examine my parents' medical records or to require them to undergo psychiatric evaluations (which I contend would have strongly supported my allegations). When someone has been accused of a felony such as incest, how can their psychiatric history and stability not be relevant?

My parents used several tactics to deny my allegations. Hearing and reading their excuses, their "blaming the child" statements, and their blatant lies, was painful—and validating. Their attempts to gain power during the depositions by wearing black and using other "triggers" were also validating—and actions that I had to be well prepared for.

Some segments of the population believe that force (violence, intimidation, and threats) is the answer to everything and, to a certain extent, the court system reflects this societal norm as well. Lawyers in depositions and in courtrooms are allowed free rein to verbally and emotionally abuse those being questioned. Only personal ethics guide the degree to which this abuse is controlled. I held onto my confidence and self-esteem during a time when this intimidation was at its peak, by viewing the anger from the opposing attorney as a measure of his fear of the subject. Going through seven and a half hours of questioning (accusations) seemed to be a breeze, since I viewed it as educating a five-year-old having a temper tantrum. However, he was an adult and his behavior was unnecessary and unwarranted. I would like to see courts and lawyers begin to take strong action toward barring this behavior to send a clear message to unethical lawyers that the damage done to a survivor's psyche by the initial abuse does not need to be compounded.

Under court order, my parents may not be named here, and I am not allowed to use my maiden name. Some would argue that court orders like these protect everyone involved by ensuring the personal privacy of all parties when, in fact, it only perpetuates the secrecy of incest and sexual abuse. Sexual abuse perpetrators use the same philosophy of "I'm doing this for your own good" to justify sexual abuse. It is a fallacy that everyone, or anyone, is protected by perpetuating the secrecy of incest. In reality, society has created another barrier to protect itself from the knowledge of childhood sexual abuse and, as a consequence, is allowing perpetrators to continue to abuse.

The most disturbing part of the civil suit process is that it is set up as a win/lose proposition, much like a game of chess. But with childhood sexual abuse, everyone loses. Even though I "won" the civil suit, I continue to struggle with the extensive physical, emotional, and spiritual damage done by my parents. My parents remain lost in their cycle of abuse. Society loses the creativity and productivity of all parties and continues to pay daily for the suffering and damage resulting from continued sexual abuse. These costs are incurred in foregone wages, social services, medical costs, mental health fees, costs of incarceration, loss of life, and more. The legal decision made in a civil suit is, in this way, irrelevant.

Would I file again? Absolutely. To use the system, when I had the ability, gave me a chance to have a voice in making changes within that context and to reclaim some of my own power. The legal system is not yet as sensitive as it could be and those who sue are taking risks; however, with each new case, the courts and legislatures are becoming more aware of these issues. More survivors are filing every year and that gives all survivors a greater voice. Through a judicial decision, my civil suit made the process more accessible for others. By sharing my experiences here, I hope that the next survivor to file a civil suit will find the process less intimidating and revictimizing.

Judi

The right remedy for each wrong

[Authors' Note: As a Canadian citizen, Judi is subject to laws and procedures that are somewhat different, and have different names, from comparable U.S. laws. Her story, however, gives a hint of the universality of the problem of child sexual abuse, and shows that courts in other countries are also trying to determine survivors' rights.]

I have chosen to use my real name with my story as I no longer feel ashamed of what happened to me as a child or the desire to keep quiet about what I've needed to do in order to heal. Rather, I feel pride and honor in putting my name to this story for others to see.

I was sexually abused for most of my childhood by a number of different people, including my brother and a neighbor for whom I baby-sat. In both cases the abuse lasted for about five years and included intercourse, fellatio, and other types of sexual touching and talking as well as the humiliation and degradation that goes with having one's body, being, and soul so violated. These were both people who I adored, loved, looked up to and respected. I wanted and needed their love and attention. I did not want their sexual advances.

As a result of the strong positive emotions I had towards these people, I found it difficult to face the betrayal and anger I had buried so deeply. I trusted my psychiatrist, who insisted the anger was there and that my depression, eating disorder and self-mutilating behaviors were the result of not dealing with it. I knew I needed to do something. I just didn't know what.

I found out that legal action was possible even though it had been over ten years since the abuse had stopped. I did not know whether this would help me feel any better, but I was desperate and willing to try anything.

The motivation for me to consider legal action came

mainly from my daughter, who was one at the time. The knowledge that my daughter was at risk of being abused as long as I was powerless against my past gave me the determination and strength to do everything I could to take control of my life.

The first step was to make a police report. I was terrified and uncertain, but I had nothing to lose. I wanted my family to hear about the report from me first, so I phoned them the night before. They weren't thrilled. I went ahead with it anyway, and ended up meeting with a police officer for about five hours over three days. It felt like a lifetime. Although the officer was very gentle and understanding, I told my story without emotion, as if I were talking about someone else.

I received validation from this process alone, as here was someone not from the therapeutic community who believed me. This gave me the courage to go on. I then met with the Crown Counsel [Canadian district attorney], who was also very understanding and supportive. She felt she could only go ahead with the prosecution of the neighbor who abused me. Although she said she wished she could go ahead with the others, there was not a solid enough case.

In Canada there is no statute of limitations on crimes as horrible as sexual assault. It is the official position of the Crown Counsels to proceed, where possible, with the prosecution of these cases even when outdated. These cases, however, must be tried under the laws as they were written at the time of the offense. With my brother, it was felt that although he was five years older than me he was still a juvenile at the time of the abuse, and would only receive a "slap on the hand" for his crimes. My brother was also living in the United States at the time, and would not be extradited to face the charges due to the cost of such proceedings and the unlikelihood of a conviction or sentence.

My neighbor was an adult at the time of the offenses, and he had become very much a father figure to me. The way the laws were written, it was illegal to have intercourse with someone under sixteen as I had been. I also knew of another girl who had baby-sat for the same people after I had. I phoned her and asked if she had had similar experiences. She had and agreed to testify, as did the neighbor's ex-wife. All of this made for a pretty good case, considering the amount of time that had passed. This was very empowering for me. I no longer felt I was the only one. I was not alone.

The investigation continued with the officer I had reported to and eventually led to him leaving town and going to this man's place of work to take him into custody for questioning. I couldn't believe that what I had said was getting this kind of response.

It was decided that the case should go to a preliminary hearing and a date was set. I was scared to death, but I had a lot of support, mainly from the therapeutic community. That was the most important thing for me. I don't think I could have gone on without those people backing up my decision.

At the preliminary hearing I got to tell my story again. I testified last and all the judge said when I was finished was that there was definitely enough to go ahead with a trial. Wow! I couldn't believe it. All these people listened to me and heard what I said. Where were they when I was little?

It was at about this point in the process that I started feeling victimized by the system. A trial date was set. I don't remember how long a wait it was, but it felt like the courts were booked up for the rest of the century. Before we made it to trial the Crown Counsel who had done all the work on the case left town for another community. I felt abandoned yet again in my life. I felt very uncomfortable with the idea of someone new doing the questioning. I wanted to quit, but felt that too many people were involved and I couldn't let them down. Perhaps these are wrong reasons, but I'm glad I continued.

The trial date approached and I prepared. It was to be a jury trial, and I felt as ready as I could be. The week before the trial was to start I still hadn't heard from the Crown Counsel, so I called, only to find out the case had been postponed because the accused had fired his lawyer. I was upset that he could use such tactics to stall. I was more upset that no one bothered to notify me. I was crushed. I had been ready and now I felt like I had to put my life on hold again.

Another date was set. Again I prepared. It was no longer

a jury trial. Now it was going to be heard by only a supreme court judge. I felt I had no choices in this system and I didn't. I had no control over what took place. As the date approached, I found out that my childhood had been reduced to "plea bargaining." I was devastated. My minimal self-worth plummeted. The week before the trial was due to start I discovered that the Crown Counsel was going to be out of town during the trial and an *ad hoc* counsel would be handling it. The attorney chosen was totally unacceptable to me. He was someone I didn't respect, trust, or have any confidence in. I couldn't take it any more. I decided to throw a tantrum and refuse to show up unless they got someone else to present the case. I guess I yelled loud enough. I finally got my way. The entire chaotic experience left me shaken and uncertain. I kept waiting for another bomb to drop.

It came the morning the trial was to start. I found out they had reached an agreement and the charges had been lessened in exchange for a guilty plea. I was mad! I wanted to testify, but I didn't get a choice. I decided to stay and watch the sentencing. I soon became very glad that I was not testifying. The judge was upset that this case was even being presented before him after such a passing of time. He claimed that the accused had a right to speedy justice so he could get on with his life. I just chuckled to myself in disgust and thought "He could have walked into court fifteen years ago and plead guilty." I wish he had. Then I could have gone on with my life as well. I was sure glad I had taken a lot of support people with me. It was very difficult to not feel guilty about what I was doing to this *poor* man. All the judge was to say to him was that he should know better than to "diddle" young girls. I couldn't believe it. I immediately wondered who this judge was abusing. I gained tremendous strength from the collective outrage of my group of supporters. It was very beneficial for me. I was able to really get in touch with my anger. For the first time, I truly despised this man who had added to the horrors of my childhood.

In the end victory was mine. The judge claimed that cases similar to this one were receiving sentences and therefore sentenced my ex-neighbor to six months at a corrections facility. I was elated as this man who had had so much power over me was led from the courtroom defeated. I felt that justice had finally been served.

At the time that the Crown Counsel made the decision not to proceed against my brother I felt a bit of a letdown. Having been a victim for so long, I took defeat easily. I was surprised when my psychiatrist sensed that I wasn't satisfied with the situation, and suggested that I look into other alternatives for dealing with my brother. I knew suing was possible, but it wasn't done very often and few people had any information on how to go about it.

I spent some time thinking about my brother, about what he had done to me and how it was still affecting my life. I knew I needed to sue. It was a difficult decision to make. It wasn't about revenge or getting rich quick, although I was sure there would be some people who would think so. I wanted my brother to have to take responsibility for his actions. I wanted him to know what it felt like to be powerless against a sibling. I knew that money was something he cherished. I knew that this was his weakness and as such would be the perfect avenue to help him understand how much he had hurt me.

The first step here was to find a lawyer. I telephoned all of the local ones that I thought were competent, and explained what I wanted to do and that I needed to do it on a contingency basis. In my fairly small home town there was only one lawyer who was willing to take it on and definitely not on contingency. I didn't have the money to work with, so I approached an attorney in another community who I had heard had experience in prosecuting sexual assault and child abuse cases. I was hoping he'd be willing since he had spent some time as a Crown Counsel specializing in this area. As it turned out, I met with him and he was interested in taking my case on contingency as he wanted to try a couple of these suits to see how they would go.

I felt great. I felt like I was doing something instead of letting the world trample me down. Pretty soon, though, the realization hit. I had thought the criminal proceedings were slow. They suddenly felt lightning fast in comparison to the civil action. It seemed like months would go by and I would receive another piece of mail that would inform me of some paper being filed or some response from my brother's lawyer. Although initially I felt like I was doing something, that was quickly reduced to waiting. It was unbearable at times and I really felt like a good portion of my life had been put on hold until this was settled.

My brother and his lawyer were able to slow things down even more because he lived out of the country and they had numerous excuses. I was consistently reminded that it must be harder on him not knowing what the outcome would be. I felt, however, that he still had all the control and I found it frustrating that there was so little I could do.

Eventually we opted not to do the examinations to discovery of him as I would have had to pay all of his expenses. The time finally came for his lawyer to examine me and my evidence (after being twice re-scheduled). I had to travel to another town that was more convenient to everyone else, but I just wanted things to move on.

There were a number of uncertain areas in my case. The statute of limitations was 7 years. However, my lawyer felt he could get around that one. The difficult part seemed to be whether or not what my brother had done had caused any harm to me. My brother had confessed to the abuse when I had confronted him in my psychiatrist's office, so proving he had done it was no an issue—we had witnesses. Since I had been sexually abused by others, it would be difficult to figure out what portion of my troubles were due to my brother. My attorney was unsure as to how the courts would decide.

The examination to discovery came at a difficult time for me. I was suffering another serious bout of depression and had pushed all but one of my support people away. I felt very much alone, and going to a different town was really frightening. I spent a sleepless night in a strange hotel bed and then drove for two hours in horrible weather conditions to reach the examination, which lasted about 5 hours. Afterwards, I was exhausted and relieved. I had told my history again, and it seemed to be getting easier to talk about.

At the end of the examination, the two lawyers met

privately. I was then able to talk to my attorney, who informed me that my brother was offering me $3,000 to shut up and go away. I said no way. My lawyer asked me how much I wanted . It was a difficult question to answer and he gave me a couple of days to come up with a number. It was an issue of self worth. If I accepted the $3,000, that was like saying that the hell I had lived through was nothing. If I said I wanted $100,000, which was maybe more in line with what I wanted to believe I was worth, I knew he wouldn't pay it and we would go to trial. At this point I was tired of the waiting and I wasn't sure I wanted to do this in court, since I knew only too well how some judges may feel. When I finally phoned my attorney, I gave him a figure of $25,000. It was purely an arbitrary number. I just felt it was a nice round figure and was an amount that would help get me back into school, which was something very important to me.

More important than the money, I told my lawyer I wanted a letter of apology from my brother and a baseball glove of my father's that he had given me and my brother had taken some years ago. I never received the letter, and the figure my attorney asked for was $15,000, but when the glove arrived in the mail I knew it was settled. That was a sweet victory, as the glove meant more to me than any amount of money. It held a lot of sentimental value for me and was one of the few things from my childhood that I had cherished. My father and I had been trying to get my brother to return it for years, and it was very satisfying to hold it once again.

It was a while before I realized what had happened and let it sink in. First, I slept for a couple of weeks, suddenly feeling how exhausted and stressed out I was. My depression started to lift. One day I had this wonderful mental image of my brother and me. He started out big and strong, towering over me. I was very small and fragile, shaking with fear. Miraculously, in my mind he started to shrink while I was growing, and suddenly I realized he no longer had any power over me. I was free. That, more than anything else, made it all worthwhile. He had been forced to give in.

Some months later I found myself thinking about my

brother and wishing things had been different. I miss the parts of our relationship that weren't hurtful. I felt that maybe a time would come when once again I would have a big brother. I realized suddenly that forgiveness, something I had always thought impossible, was sneaking up on me as I sat unaware. I don't know if it will happen, but I feel it may be possible at some time in the future.

Unfortunately, my brother has since chosen to divorce the family and wrote a letter to both of my parents informing them of this. His reason was their lack of support for him during the legal action. I felt some guilt and responsibility initially when I heard about this, but I quickly realized that it was his choice. Although I was sorry that what he was doing was hurting my parents, I was glad that I wasn't trying to protect them any longer or him by suffering in silence. I also felt I received little support from my parents, but I chose to accept them for who they are—the parents of both sides—and I got support elsewhere. I am very thankful to all those who understood what I needed to do and believed in my ability to heal.

Debbie

Hope for the future

I was in the fourth grade in a Midwestern state when my adoptive father began touching me ever so gently. I was just beginning to start puberty, and it was a very awkward stage for me, let alone the start of years of incest. He would touch my breasts to show me that I was beginning to "become a woman" and, as the years went by, my body became his to do with as he pleased.

He performed both overt and covert sexual abuse on me. My adoptive father would come on to me only when my adoptive mother was absent from the house. He would touch me all over my body and vagina while he laid there with an erection. He would force me to touch him. He used my body as a means to sexually arouse himself and would leave me in my bed, to the silence of the night, to deal with my fear of him coming back.

He was like a Jekyll and Hyde. He projected the day persona of the most ideal successful father and businessman a little girl of any age would want. At night, though, he become a sexual maniac who neglected my little girl specialness for his own sexual needs.

He loved me, affirmed me as a human being, adored me—and he sexually abused me. This was the most difficult statement for me to formulate in my heart and my mind, but once I did, I was able to embrace the ugliness of my abuse—he misused his love for me. He didn't stop coming to my room until I was a junior in college.

It has taken me years and many geographical moves to feel safe enough and strong enough to reclaim myself. Only in the last three years has the legal system begun to listen to survivors. By processing my feelings of a need to speak out and act on my own behalf legally with my therapist, a long time wish has begun to form. It is only thanks to my therapist, my boyfriend, selected friends, and my attorney that I am even in a position to think about suing. To sue the perpetrator is to break many rules that are imparted in incest: I am worth it, and I can speak out. Once I started pondering the question "Am I going to seek legal action?," all of my incest issues came up. I have never processed so deeply as I presently am. It is like it happened yesterday.

My therapist was instrumental in helping me connect with my legal support. It helps tremendously to know that there are survivors even in the legal profession. There is hope for the future.

I have the right people supporting me both legally and emotionally. I have received no support from my other family members, but with my history this is healthy. If I had looked to my family for support, I probably never would have made the decision to sue. My partner has been very supportive of my decision. I have lost a few friends along the way because of my decision to sue, but I don't feel sad about it. I am relieved to know who is for me and who is not. Knowing helps give me much needed safety, so I don't revictimize myself in the process.

I know that my process has just begun. It gives me hope knowing I am not alone in making the most important decision of my life. Gaining college degrees, deciding to marry, giving birth to a wonderful son, succeeding in my career—none of these things compare to addressing and making the decision to sue my perpetrator. Whether or not he is successful in dodging the truth of my reality of incest, I have gained something no one will ever be able to take away from me—*my own self respect and love.* I am somewhat envious of those who have completed this difficult task. They are free in some fashion. It's okay that I don't know the outcome. Hearing about the survivors who have gone before and attained hard-won changes has given me courage to go ahead with my lawsuit. I will forever be grateful to those who have gone before me. I hope all those who are just beginning know they have friends and support from all over. Just making the decision to sue has changed my life for the good.

As an incest survivor, one of the most precious parts of my core being was stripped from me—the choice to defend myself whenever I felt scared or threatened. My decision to sue gave me feelings of self worth, self acceptance, love, and self forgiveness. Whether or not I win my case, I feel I have won a major battle on my own behalf by being able to speak my truths. This has healed many areas in my soul that words can never describe.

It is not yet realistic to look to the legal system to defend us. As incest survivors, we are having to change the rules, laws and definitions state by state so the next generation may be protected, which is important to me. My decision to sue came easier because of the need to protect future generations. I am fully aware that I may need to appeal the question of the statute of limitations all the way to the state Supreme Court. I am willing to do this to change the state's law on delayed discovery. I am preparing myself for a possibly lengthy process.

Chapter 9

Questions & Answers

Italicized terms in the answers are defined in Appendix A, as well as in the margins in the main body of the text. The answers are based on general legal principles followed in most state jurisdictions in the United States. Consult a competent attorney in your area for possible local variations.

Question: *If I file a civil child sexual abuse suit against my perpetrator, is there a chance the perpetrator will go to jail?*

Answer: Yes. If the state, federal, or city prosecutor believes that the evidence you can present against your perpetrator is strong enough for conviction or if the *claims* are egregious enough that the prosecutor wants to make an example of your perpetrator, *criminal* charges may be filed, which could lead to conviction and jail time. You can also press *criminal* charges against the perpetrator. Conviction depends on a number of factors, including the strength of the evidence (often quite weak in cases such as these) and the running of the criminal *statute of limitations*. Many states have criminal *statutes of limitations* that expire well before survivors remember or can emotionally handle filing charges against their perpetrators.

Prosecutors often have so many cases to handle that they will not bring criminal charges unless the victim is willing to press charges and testify against the perpetrator.

Question: *Can I lose money by filing suit against my abuser?*

Answer: Yes. If the judge or jury does not believe your evidence, you may lose your claims. If this happens, you could owe your attorney for his or her work (if your attorney is being paid hourly rather than on a *contingency fee* basis) and also have to pay for court costs, without any recovery from your abuser. The judge or jury could also find you *liable* to the abuser for *damages* for *defamation*, if your abuser has *counterclaimed* against you for *defamation*. However, even if the abuser *counterclaims* against you and wins, if you have few or no assets, he or she may be unable to recover anything from you.

Question: *What is the difference between a civil and a criminal suit?*

Answer: In a *civil* suit, one *party* sues a second *party*, generally for money *damages*. because of some action of the second *party* that hurt the first *party*. For example, if person A hits person B with a baseball bat in a heated argument, A can be held to be *liable* to B in *civil* court for monetary *damages* to cover medical costs, lost work time, and other losses that occur as a result of A's action.

A *criminal* suit, on the other hand, occurs when someone does something that society, in general, finds offensive. For example (using the same facts as those above), a government attorney (district attorney, attorney general, or U.S. attorney, depending on the case) can bring *criminal* charges against A for hitting B, which could result in A serving jail time.

Many criminal actions lead to civil *liability*. If no particular person is harmed by a person's *criminal* actions, however, such as in cases of arson to public property, only a *criminal* suit can be filed against the wrongdoer.

Question: *Has any trend appeared in civil child sexual abuse suits?*

Answer: From our research, most cases are being settled in the survivor's favor before trial. Attorneys we've talked to are carefully screening cases, so mostly the best cases with the strongest evidence are being litigated. This may account for the generally positive results to date.

Question: *If my perpetrator has a lot of money, will he or she put up a stronger legal fight?*

Answer: A wealthier perpetrator will be able to hire more expensive, proficient attorneys, and more impressive *expert* witnesses. These attorneys and expert witnesses may be able to make it more difficult for you to prove your case against your abuser.

On the other hand, because abusers who have more money, power, and prestige probably have more to lose, they may decide to settle quickly and avoid protracted public litigation.

Question: *If I tell an attorney my story, will the attorney tell the police or my perpetrator what I said?*

Answer: No. You are protected by a *privilege* from having your attorney tell anyone what you tell him or her. If your attorney were to violate this *privilege*, he or she would be subject to disciplinary and, possibly, court action. The law in some *jurisdictions*, however, may require an attorney to tell authorities about knowledge of ongoing abuse of children.

Question: *If I tell an attorney what happened to me, does this mean that the case is under way and I can't back out?*

Answer: No. A civil case does not begin until you and your attorney file a *complaint* in court against your perpetrator, and the decision of whether or not to file a *complaint* belongs to you. Once an attorney has agreed to represent you, he or she will help you assess the strengths and weaknesses of your case, and then you can decide whether or not to file a *complaint*.

Question: *Can I back out once a complaint is filed?*

Answer: Sometimes. If you have filed a *complaint* against your perpetrator and he or she has not filed any *counterclaims* against you, in most cases you can get the case dismissed (ended), as most perpetrators are only too happy to see claims against them disappear. You may have to pay your attorney for the time spent representing you, however. If a *counterclaim* has been filed against you, though, it is just as if another suit has been filed, which means that you must defend against this *counterclaim*.

Question: *In general, what are the chances that I can get a settlement before trial?*

Answer: Probably good. The vast majority of all cases settle before going to *trial*. If the law in your *jurisdiction* is in your favor (most notably the *statute of limitations*), the chances of your case settling before *trial* are good, especially because of the type of *claims* you are making. No one wants the stigma of being labeled a child molester. On the other hand, failing to prepare for *trial* in anticipation of receiving a *settlement* check is a surefire prelude to disaster at *trial*.

Question: *What might be contained in a settlement agreement?*

Answer: A *settlement agreement* usually sets out the money *damages* that the perpetrator agrees to pay you and how and when payment will occur. It usually contains a statement that the perpetrator does not admit any *liability* (responsibility), even though the settlement implies that the perpetrator must have done something to you or else he or she would not be paying you.

Settlement agreements often contain *gag provisions* (statements requiring the confidentiality of certain things agreed to) regarding the amount of recovery you receive and possibly who abused you. This type of provision may not be acceptable to you.

Question: *Who decides whether or not I settle?*

Answer: You do. You have the deciding vote. Only you can determine if an offer made by your perpetrator gives you enough of the things you were seeking from filing suit (money, the right to speak about your abuse, etc.). Most likely, a *settlement agree-*

ment will not contain an admission of *liability* or guilt and you will not get a public confrontation or condemnation of your abuser, so you must determine if you are willing to give up these possible outcomes of a *trial.*

Question: *At some point in my case will I have to tell everything about my story?*

Answer: Yes. To ensure the best chance of monetary recovery from your abuser, you should tell your attorney everything about your abuse, even before you file suit. Also, if your case goes beyond the initial stages, which many do, you will undoubtedly have to recount many of the most intimate details of your story under very adversarial conditions, either at *trial*, in a *deposition*, or both.

Question: *Will news of my lawsuit be in the local newspaper or the local news?*

Answer: Probably. Because most documents filed in a lawsuit, including the initial *complaint*, are considered public records, their contents can be seen by anyone. Depending on how closely the local media follow filings of *complaints*, in most places the chances are good that the facts involved in your lawsuit will become public knowledge.

Question: *How long will my case take?*

Answer: Probably longer than one year. The length of your lawsuit depends on if it settles early or goes to *trial* and also on how backed up the court's calendar is in your *jurisdiction*. In general, if your case doesn't settle early, in most *jurisdictions* you should expect the suit to last at least a year, probably two, and possibly longer.

Question: *Will my brothers, sisters, or nonoffending parent have to testify?*

Answer: Probably yes. If any of your siblings or your nonoffending parent can be found before *trial*, both your attorney and your abuser's attorney will undoubtedly want to question them about your and your siblings' childhoods. The attorneys will question them first during their *depositions*, and then later at *trial*.

Question: *Will my therapist have to testify?*

Answer: Yes. Both your personal therapist and any other psychological *experts* you and your attorney hire to prove your claims will be questioned during *trial* and possibly during *depositions*.

Question: *Will my abuser be present when I testify?*

Answer: Probably. In some states, it is possible to have abusers banned from *depositions* of survivors, but this is not the usual rule. At *trial*, it is extremely doubtful that you will be able to testify without your abuser being present.

Question: *What will happen when I go to see an attorney for the first time?*

Answer: A first visit to an attorney should be a testing period for both the client and the attorney. The attorney will be asking for sufficient details about your case to see if it has legal merit and, in the vast majority of cases, about your abuser to determine if suing your abuser will be financially worthwhile (assuming that you will win). For you, as a client, the first visit should be used to determine if you feel comfortable with the attorney, both with his or her legal knowledge and with how you feel emotionally about him or her. Remember that you are a consumer of legal knowledge and should be treated as a valued customer.

Question: *Will I need to pay the attorney for my first visit?*

Answer: Maybe. Many attorneys do not charge for an initial consultation. Some do. When you call to make the first appointment, ask what the policy is about payment for the first visit. As a consumer of legal services, you have a right to an answer to questions like this. It might be wise to look for an attorney who does not charge for the first meeting, as there is no guarantee you will feel comfortable with the first attorney you see. Don't let an initial fee alone keep you from interviewing a highly recommended attorney, however.

Question: *How much will suing my abuser cost me?*

Answer: Suing anyone in *civil* court in a major suit, which includes child sexual abuse suits, costs thousands of dollars in attorney time, *expert* witness time, and court expenses. The total cost depends on the length of the case, but a *trial* of any length will likely cost tens of thousands of dollars. If you can find an attorney who will take your case on a *contingency fee* basis, however, you will not have to pay fees for the attorney's services unless you recover money from your abuser. In any event, you will have to pay some expenses, like court costs (*e.g.*, filing fees and *deposition* costs).

Question: *Will my attorney tell anyone else my story?*

Answer: No. Your attorney cannot ethically tell anyone else the details of your story, with the exception of other members of his or her law firm. Your right to silence is known as a *privilege*. If your attorney does tell anyone these *privileged* details, you can sue your attorney. If you are uncomfortable with anyone else hearing these details, ask your attorney to set up a confidential file in his or her office to be seen only by him or her and limited support staff.

Question: *What should I do if I don't understand what my attorney is telling me?*

Answer: Ask questions. Don't be afraid to say that you don't understand. You are paying your attorney to represent you and care for your legal needs. If he or she will not describe what is happening, or what may happen, in intelligible language, look for another attorney. As a child sexual abuse survivor, the last thing you need is someone else in a position of power who should be protecting you telling you gibberish or acting superior.

Question: *If I have little or no money, is it still possible for me to sue my abuser?*

Answer: Possibly. Many attorneys will not take cases without being assured of regular monthly payments. Many other attorneys, however, will represent survivors based on a *contingency fee arrangement*, which means that the attorney takes the case and represents the survivor in return for a percentage of any money recovered from the abuser or his or her insurance company. Attorneys who take these cases on *contingency*, however, almost always require that the abuser have a large sum of money or other assets that can be recovered, and they generally take only strong cases.

Question: *If my abuser has little or no money, will I be able to sue him or her?*

Answer: Maybe. It will probably be difficult to find an attorney to take your case on a contingency fee basis. You'll have more chance of finding an attorney if you have enough money to pay your attorney's fees or are lucky enough to gain access to a free or low-cost legal clinic.

Question: *If the law in my state says that my abuser can't be prosecuted and put in jail for his or her actions, can I still file a civil case for monetary damages against my abuser?*

Answer: Generally, yes. If your abuser is prosecuted in *criminal* court and found guilty of a sex crime against you, you will have a much better chance of proving the case against your abuser in *civil* court, because a *criminal* conviction proves most of the *elements* of your civil case. Your *civil* action for monetary *damages*, however, does not depend on a *criminal* conviction, or even on whether or not *criminal* charges can be brought against your abuser.

Question: *Can I sue my abuser if he or she is in jail?*

Answer: Yes. Your abuser is not immune from *civil* suits just because he or she is in jail. Also, your abuser will not have the right to appointed counsel because it is not a *criminal* case.

Question: *If I have more than one perpetrator, must I sue all of them?*

Answer: No. You have the right to choose who you are going to sue, but your perpetrator may be able to add other abusers as *defendants* in the case, or defend by saying that you were abused by one of the others and not by him or her.

Question: *My perpetrator is dead. Can I sue the people who inherited the perpetrator's money?*

Answer: Probably not. When someone dies, people with *claims* against the deceased have a very short time period to file a *claim* against the estate of the deceased (generally within four months). After that period passes and money has been given to inheritors, your *claims* may not be allowed. Even if you file a *claim* within four months, you may not be able to recover anything because of court rules such as the *dead person's statute*.

Appendix A

Glossary

Affidavit
written statement of facts made under oath by a person

Affirmative defense
defense to a claim that, if proved, excuses a defendant's actions

Allegations
statements made in a complaint that have not yet been proven in court

Alleged
claimed; not yet proven; see *allegations*

Amicus *brief*
a document filled with legal arguments, and referring to legal authorities (cases, statutes, or persuasive articles) (a *brief*), dealing with a particular issue, filed by someone who is not a party to the lawsuit, but is interested in the case's outcome (*amicus*–a friend [of the court])

Answer
legal response to a complaint in which the defendant admits, denies, or denies because of lack of information all allegations made by the plaintiff; may also include affirmative defenses or counterclaims

Appellate court
court that reviews trial court decisions for legal errors (does not generally decide facts); also called a higher court

Assault
acts intended to cause harmful or offensive contact or the apprehension of such imminent contact to another person or a third person, that cause such contact or apprehension to another person

Attach
seize property under a writ

Battery
intentionally harmful or offensive contact caused by one person to another

Beneficiary
person whom another person intends to receive payment should some named event happen

Beyond a reasonable doubt
standard of proof that requires a fact-finder (judge or jury) to find that there can be no reasonable doubt that something happened; usually a criminal standard

Case law
law created by various courts, state and federal, based on the facts of individual cases, that makes, overrules or extends rules of law; published in volumes known as *legal reporters*; derived from English *common law*

Cause of action
a right to bring a legal action because of some injury that was caused by another party; also known as a *claim* or *claim for relief*

Challenge
right used by an attorney to excuse a juror from hearing a case; either *for cause*, when a juror shows legal bias toward the other side (each party has an unlimited number), or *peremptory*, when one party doesn't like a juror for some reason that doesn't amount to a legal bias (each party has a limited number)

Civil
concerning private rights and remedies

Compensatory damages
amount of money that most closely approximates the value of, or cost of repairing, the actual injuries or losses suffered by a person

Complaint
document that normally starts the legal process in a civil case; plaintiff files this document, which states the wrongful or negligent actions the defendant has committed and the injuries—financial, physical, and psychological—that have resulted, and asks for some compensation or other remedy

Consent
willingness for conduct to occur, given either expressly or impliedly

Consortium
companionship of husband and wife, including affection, aid, and sexual relations

Contingency fee arrangement
payment schedule in which a plaintiff pays his or her attorney for non-court costs only after the defendant pays following a settlement or judgment; usually a percentage of the total amount recovered from the defendant; typical percentages are 25% for settlement before trial, 33.3% for settlement during or after trial, and 40% for settlement after an appeal following trial; percentages vary by area and law firm

Contract
agreement to do or not do something, in return for an agreement to do or not do something else; can be written or oral

Corroborative
tending to support a claimed fact

Count
group of paragraphs in a complaint that together state a complete legal claim; also known as a claim for relief

Counterclaim
generally, a claim made by a defendant against a plaintiff

Criminal
concerning public rights and penalties

Cross examination
questioning by an attorney opposed to the party who presents a witness for direct examination; follows direct examination

Damages
approximate amount of money necessary to compensate a person wrongfully injured by another

Dead person's statute
rule of evidence that prevents testimony by the surviving party about a controversy if the other party to the controversy is deceased

Decision
written ruling by a court that states which party has prevailed on the questions put before the court by the parties; usually includes explanations for the rulings

Defamation
statement that harms the reputation of another, when the statement is known, or should be known, to be false; verbal defamation is generally known as *slander*, and written defamation is generally known as *libel*

Defendant
a person against whom a lawsuit is filed; the party who is defending in the legal action

Delayed discovery rule
extension of the beginning of the statute of limitations to when the damage from a tortious act is discovered or, alternatively, to when the relationship between the tortious act and the damage is realized

Demand letter

letter sent by a plaintiff's attorney to a defendant or defendant's attorney that demands that the defendant pay or do something the plaintiff wants

Deposition

oral questioning, under oath, by one party's attorney of another party or other witness, generally well in advance of trial, to determine the facts as the witness remembers them; similar to trial questioning, except that the questioning can be broader than what is allowed at trial; participants include attorneys for all parties, a witness (to be questioned), and a court reporter

Dictum

a statement by a judge in an appellate court decision that shows how the judge thinks a particular issue should be decided, but which has no current or future legal effect on anyone (*precedential* value)

Direct examination

initial questioning of a trial witness

Disability

legal handicap, caused by either age or infirmity, that is a justifiable reason for not suing another person for a wrong; *e.g.,* minors are considered to be under a disability

Discoverable

information capable of being found through the process of discovery

Discovered

information found through the process of discovery

Discovery

the formal legal process of learning what the other party has or knows that will have a bearing on the case; also, the techniques allowed under the law to find this information, such as interrogatories, depositions, requests for production of documents, and requests for admission

Duress

illegal pressuring of a person to do something that they wouldn't normally do

Elements

parts of a legal cause of action that must be proven by the plaintiff

Emancipated

no longer living under parents' or guardians' control

Equitable

remedy based on fairness, rather than under traditional rules of law; derived from the old Chancery courts in England, which had only these powers, and no legal jurisdiction

Execution

carrying a court judgment into effect, usually by seizing and/or selling the debtor's property

Exempt

legally not subject to execution

Expert

a person hired because of his or her special skill, training, or experience to give guidance to an attorney and/or testify at trial

Fact-finder

person or group of people who decide what the facts are in a particular case; depending on the case and court, either a judge or a jury

False imprisonment

intentional confining by one person of another who is aware of or is harmed by the confinement, within boundaries fixed by the confiner

Fiduciary

person legally entrusted with a duty of caring for the interests of another

Forensic

pertaining to or used in legal proceedings; *e.g.*, a *forensic* psychiatrist would evaluate someone for litigation purposes

Fraud

false representation intended to deceive another and cheat him or her of legal rights or property

Gag order

court demand that attorneys and witnesses in a case not discuss the facts of the case with anyone

Gag provision
a statement in a settlement agreement in which the parties agree to keep certain information confidential; in a child sexual abuse case, this information usually includes the fact that abuse occurred, the name of the abuser, and the amount of the settlement

Garnishment
executing against a judgment debtor's wages or salary

Hearing
oral legal argument before a judge; less formal than a full trial

Hearsay
the repeating in court of a statement made out of court, for the purpose of proving the statement true

Impeachment
demonstration of prior, inconsistent statements; demonstrates witness' lack of credibility

Incest
the imposition of sexually inappropriate acts, or acts with sexual overtones, by—or any use of a minor child to meet the sexual or sexual/emotional needs of—one or more persons who derive authority through ongoing emotional bonding with that child; see E. Blume, *Secret Survivors: Uncovering Incest and Its Aftereffects in Women* (1990)

Incompetent
without the legally required qualification or capacity

Injunction
court order commanding a party not to do something

Intentional infliction of emotional distress
outrageous conduct that one person hopes will, and does, cause severe emotional distress in another

Intentional tort
wrong committed through the act of a person desiring to cause injury

Interrogatory
a question asked by one party, through his or her attorney, of another party, through his or her attorney, that relates in some way to the issues involved in a civil lawsuit; it must be answered under oath (usually administered by a notary public); generally several questions are asked in one set of interrogatories

Judgment
court's final ruling in a case; usually accompanied by an order from the court demanding payment of a sum of money by one party to another

Jurisdiction
a legally recognized area governed by a specific set of laws (*e.g.*, Missouri, the Western District of Washington); also, authority to hear and decide a case

Jury instructions
explanations of the applicable law given by the judge to the jury; attorneys for both sides to a lawsuit usually give desired jury instructions to the judge, who decides which to use

Legislation
laws, ordinances, and regulations drafted and enacted by elected officials on the state, local, and federal levels

Liability
party's responsibility to another to pay an obligation or debt, generally monetary; assessed in a civil case by a judge or jury; compare *guilt* (assessment of responsibility for wrongdoing by a judge or jury in a criminal case)

Litigant
a participant in a lawsuit; a party

Minor
person younger than the age of majority (generally 16–21 years)

Motion
a written or oral request of a court to take some action

Motion for summary judgment
request asking a judge to rule in the party's favor based on evidence

Motion to dismiss for failure to state a claim
request asking a judge to rule that a claim is legally insufficient based solely on what was claimed

Negligence
wrong committed when a person injures another through acts that a reasonable person should know would lead to a foreseeable chance of harm

Negligent hire
hiring someone a reasonably prudent person would have foreseen would harm someone (usually because of the employee's background)

Negligent infliction of emotional distress
conduct that a reasonable person should have known would cause severe emotional distress in another

Negligent supervision
failure to provide sufficient supervision of an employee

Opening statement
speech to the court in which attorney tells the facts he or she intends to present during the trial (through witnesses and documents), and how those facts should lead to a decision for his or her client

Opposition
legal argument against the arguments supporting a motion

Parent-child immunity
legal protection of a parent from a suit by a child for negligent, reckless, or intentional acts committed by the parent

Personal jurisdiction
court's power to hear a controversy involving a person

Plaintiff
a person who files a lawsuit against someone else; the party who is initiating the legal action

Prayer for relief
statement in the complaint of what the plaintiff seeks in the case from the defendant, such as money damages

Preponderance of the evidence
amount of evidence necessary to persuade a judge or jury it is more likely than not that what one party claims is true; *greater than a 50% likelihood*

Privilege
a peculiar advantage, exemption, or immunity; an immunity from testifying about conversations between specified people

Pro bono
legal work provided free of charge; literally, *for the (public) good* (short for *pro bono publico*)

Pro se
representing yourself in legal proceedings rather than having an attorney represent you

Process server
person empowered by a court to deliver court papers to a person, generally a defendant

Proper venue
correct court in which to file a suit

Prospective
applying only after a certain time

Punitive damages
amount of money added to actual losses and injuries to punish the defendant and deter others from committing similar egregious actions

Rape shield statute
law in some jurisdictions that protects rape survivors from being questioned about their sexual experience before the rape incident

Recross examination
questioning by an attorney on issues addressed in redirect examination

Redirect examination
questioning by an attorney on issues addressed in cross examination

Relevant
testimony or documents that are considered legally important and appropriate to be seen or read in a particular case; having a bearing on the case

Reply
legal argument in response to an opposition to a motion

Request for production of documents
formal, written document prepared by an attorney which requests specific documents possessed by another party

Respond
make arguments, either legal or factual, to the contrary

Retainer
a prepayment of fees to an attorney estimated by the attorney to be the cost of preliminary legal work on the case; attorneys often require additional prepayments as the initial retainer is depleted

Retroactive
applying to events in the past as well as to future events

Served
given a legal document (in a legally binding way)

Settlement agreement
contract by parties settling a lawsuit without a trial that states the parties' agreement about money to be paid and other important matters

Settlement
resolution of a pending legal dispute without trial

Statute
law enacted by the legislature that demands, regulates, or prohibits some act

Statute of limitations
the time within which a particular legal claim must be filed in a particular jurisdiction

Statute of ultimate repose
law setting an absolute time limit after which an action cannot be filed; *e.g.*, a state may allow a medical malpractice claim to be filed at any time up to 3 years after the discovery of the injury, but in no event later than 10 years after the surgery occurred

Statutory rape
sexual intercourse with a minor (generally a female) under a certain age (generally 16 years)

Subpoena
court order demanding that a person appear before a court or at a deposition

Subpoena duces tecum
court order demanding that a person appear before a court or at a deposition with named documents

Summons
demand to appear before a court

Tolling
stopping of the running of the statute of limitations until a later time or occurrence

Tort
wrong committed either intentionally or negligently by one person against another that leads to damages and is recognized under common law; *e.g.*, battery, negligence, intentional infliction of emotional distress

Trial
a public determination of one person's liability to another person (in a civil action), or guilt (in a criminal action) for a wrong committed

Trial court
court in which evidence is presented by the parties to a judge or jury; also called a *lower court*

Undue influence
improper inducement or persuasion that takes advantage of or overpowers a person and causes the person to do something he or she would not ordinarily do

Vicarious liability
indirect legal responsibility for the acts of another; also known as *respondeat superior*

Voir dire
questioning of potential jurors by attorneys

Writ
court order commanding a party to do something

Appendix B

Sources

Attorneys

The following attorneys either have represented incest or sexual abuse survivors in civil suits against their abusers or are interested in representing survivors in such cases. Attorneys licensed to practice in more than one state are listed in each state licensed. The information was provided by the attorneys listed, and the attorneys have not paid to be included in this listing.

Because this information is supplied by each attorney or law firm and we, the authors and publisher of this book, have no personal knowledge of any of these attorneys (including the quality of their services), we do not warrant the quality of the legal services they may provide and are not responsible for any act or failure to act by them on your behalf. This does not mean we know that any of these attorneys will provide poor services; rather, it means that we are unaware of any lack of quality in their work. It is because of our unfamiliarity with their work and relationships with other survivors that we cannot guarantee that the attorneys listed below will provide good quality legal representation.

Please remember that any relationship you enter into with an attorney should begin only after you interview the attorney and make your own choice.

Addresses and phone numbers may be inaccurate due to the passage of time since the data were collected.

Alabama

Mr. Rick Drummond
Crime Victims Law Center
453 S. Hull St.
Montgomery, AL 36104
Phone: (205) 269-0556
Fax: (205) 269-0556
Also bar member in: No other states
Experience with CSA cases? Yes

Arkansas

Ms. Leslie B. McWilliams
See Tennessee

California

Ms. Gloria Allred
Allred, Maroko, Goldberg and Ribakoff
6380 Wilshire Blvd., Suite 1404
Los Angeles, CA 90048
Phone: (213) 653-6530
Fax: (213) 653-1660
Also bar member in: No other states
Experience with CSA cases? Yes

Ms. Justine Durrell
Law Offices of Mahmoud Abouzeid, Jr.
1700 California St., Suite 440
San Francisco, CA 94109
Phone: (415) 673-0377
Fax: Not listed
Also bar member in: No other states
Experience with CSA cases? Yes

Ms. Julia J. Hubbard
Williams, Kelly, Romanski, Polveari & Skelton
1775 Woodside Road
Redwood City, CA 94061
Phone: (415) 364-9110
Fax: (415) 366-8995
Also bar member in: No other states
Experience with CSA cases? Yes

Mr. Dana Scruggs
Brown & Scruggs
340 Soquel Ave., Suite 205
Santa Cruz, CA 95062
Phone: (408) 429-1434
Fax: (408) 458-1165
Also bar member in: No other states
Experience with CSA cases? Yes

Ms. Pauline Tesler
Tesler & Sandmann
16 Buena Vista
Mill Valley, CA 94941
Phone: (415) 383-5600
Fax: Not listed
Also bar member in: Washington
Experience with CSA cases? Yes

Colorado

Ms. Joyce Seelen
Holland, Seelen & Pagliuca
1700 Lincoln, Suite 2530
Denver, CO 80203
Phone: (303) 832-7700
Fax: (303) 832-2127
Also bar member in: No other states
Experience with CSA cases? Yes

Connecticut

Ms. Phyllis Gelman
See New York

District of Columbia

Ms. Sharon Goley
Meyer, Faller, Weisman & Rosenberg, PC
4400 Jenifer St., NW, Suite 380
Washington, DC 20015
Phone: (202) 362-1100
Fax: (202) 362-9818
Also bar member in: Maryland, Virginia
Experience with CSA cases? Yes

Ms. Dorothy Flores
See Texas

Mr. Keith Rosenberg
Meyer, Faller, Weisman & Rosenberg, PC
4400 Jenifer St., NW, Suite 380
Washington, DC 20015
Phone: (202) 362-1100
Fax: (202) 362-9818
Also bar member in: Maryland, Virginia
Experience with CSA cases? Yes

Florida

Ms. Leslie B. McWilliams
See Tennessee

Illinois

Ms. Julie Kunce Field
See Michigan

Mr. Neil H. Good
1655 N. Arlington Heights Road, #202E
Arlington Heights, IL 60004
Phone: (708) 577-4476
Fax: (708) 577-4696
Also bar member in: No other states
Experience with CSA cases? Yes

Maryland

Ms. Sharon Goley
See District of Columbia

Mr. Keith Rosenberg
See District of Columbia

Massachusetts

Ms. Colleen C. Currie
78 Main Street
Northampton, MA 01060
Phone: (413) 586-2905
Fax: (413) 584-6605
Also bar member in: No other states
Experience with CSA cases? No

Ms. Julie Kunce Field
See Michigan

Michigan

Ms. Diane L. Bernick
Bernick & 0mer, PC
2400 Lake Lansing Road, Suite F
Lansing, MI 48912
Phone: (517) 371-5361
Fax: (517) 371-1211
Also bar member in: No other states
Experience with CSA cases? Yes

Ms. Julie Kunce Field
Women and The Law Clinic
University Of Michigan Law School
801 Monroe Street
Ann Arbor, MI 48109-1215
Phone: (313) 763-4319
Fax: Not listed
Also bar member in: Massachusetts, Illinois
Experience with CSA cases? No

Ms. Sally Claire Fink
Josephson and Fink
300 North Fifth Ave., Suite 220
Ann Arbor, MI 48104
Phone: (313) 994-1221
Fax: (313) 994-1201
Also bar member in: No other states
Experience with CSA cases? Yes

Ms. Elaine Frost
Elaine Frost, P.C.
15224 E. Jefferson #207
Grosse Pointe Park, MI 48230
Phone: (313) 823-1830
Fax: (313) 823-0936
Also bar member in: No other states
Experience with CSA cases? Yes

Ms. Jean Ledwith King
277 E. Liberty Plaza
Ann Arbor, MI 48104
Phone: (313) 662-1334
Fax: (313) 662-8733
Also bar member in: No other states
Experience with CSA cases? Yes

Mr. Keldon K. Scott
Bernick & 0mer, PC
2400 Lake Lansing Road, Suite F
Lansing, MI 48912
Phone: (517) 371-5361
Fax: (517) 371-1211
Also bar member in: No other states
Experience with CSA cases? Yes

Mr. Clark Shanahan
P.O. Box 187
Owosso, MI 48867
Phone: (517) 723-5203
Fax: Not listed
Also bar member in: No other states
Experience with CSA cases? Yes

Minnesota

Mr. Jeffrey R. Anderson
Reinhardt and Anderson
E-1400 First National Bank Building
332 Minnesota Street
St. Paul, MN 55101
Phone: (612) 227-9990
Fax: (612) 297-6543
Also bar member in: Wisconsin
Experience with CSA cases? Yes

Mr. Mark Douglass
Suite 500
701 Fourth Avenue South
Minneapolis, MN 55415-1631
Phone: (612) 338-6625
Fax: Not listed
Also bar member in: No other states
Experience with CSA cases? Yes

Ms. Lisa Drill
See Wisconsin

Mr. James W. Kerr
McDonald and Kerr
701 Fourth Avenue So.
Suite 500
Minneapolis, MN 55415
Phone: (612) 337-9565
Fax: (612) 338-0218
Also bar member in: No other states
Experience with CSA cases? Yes

Mr. Michael W. McDonald
McDonald and Kerr
701 Fourth Avenue So.
Suite 500
Minneapolis, MN 55415
Phone: (612) 337-9565
Fax: (612) 338-0218
Also bar member in: No other states
Experience with CSA cases? Yes

Mr. Gregg Meyers
See South Carolina

Montana

Ms. Virginia A. Bryan
Wright, Tolliver & Guthals, P.C.
10 N. 27th Street, Box 1977
Billings, MT 59103
Phone: (406) 245-3071
Fax: (406) 245-3074
Also bar member in: No other states
Experience with CSA cases? Yes

Nebraska

Ms. Susan Koenig-Cramer
300 Keeline Building
319 South 17th St.
Omaha, NE 68102
Phone: (402) 346-1132
Fax: Not listed
Also bar member in: No other states
Experience with CSA cases? Yes

New Hampshire

Ms. Janine Gawryl
Richards, Gawryl, and MacAllister
65 Temple St.
Nashua, NH 03060
Phone: (603) 882-3344
Fax: (603) 886-8880
Also bar member in: No other states
Experience with CSA cases? Yes

New Jersey

Ms. Doris J. Dabrowski
See Pennsylvania

Ms. Phyllis Gelman
See New York

New York

Ms. Stephanie Brand
80-1 Long Beach Road
Saint James, NY 11780
Phone: (516) 862-6141
Fax: (516) 862-6142
Also bar member in: No other states
Experience with CSA cases? Yes

Ms. Phyllis Gelman
Law Office Of Phyllis Gelman
211 West 106th St., Suite 11A
New York, NY 10025
Phone: (212) 749-5736
Fax: Not listed
Also bar member in: Connecticut, New Jersey
Experience with CSA cases? Yes

Ms. Susan Keiser
Keiser & Keiser
PO Box 350
Main Street
Livingston Manor, NY 12758
Phone: (914) 439-5550
Fax: (914) 439-5554
Also bar member in: No other states
Experience with CSA cases? Yes

Ms. Debra R. Schoenberg
358 Broadway
Saratoga Springs, NY 12866
Phone: (518) 584-3447
Fax: (518) 584-3735
Also bar member in: No other states
Experience with CSA cases? No

North Carolina

Ms. Ellen R. Gelbin
Elliot, Pishko, Gelbin & Morgan, P.A.
P.O. Box 20545
Winston-Salem, NC 27120-0545
Phone: (919) 724-2828
Fax: (919) 724-3335
Also bar member in: No other states
Experience with CSA cases? Yes

Ohio

Ms. Beverly Farlow
Artz, Dewhirst, & Farlow
533 S. 3rd Street
Columbus, OH 43215
Phone: (614) 221-0944
Fax: (614) 221-2340
Also bar member in: No other states
Experience with CSA cases? Yes

Oregon

Mr. William A. Barton
214 SW Coast Highway
P.O. Box 870
Newport, OR 97365-0067
Phone: (503) 265-5377
Fax: (503) 265-5614
Also bar member in: No other states
Experience with CSA cases? Yes

Mr. Malcolm Corrigall
Ormsbee and Corrigall
P.O. Box 1178, 936 Central
Coos Bay, OR 97420
Phone: (503) 269-1123
Fax: (503) 269-1126
Also bar member in: No other states
Experience with CSA cases? Yes

Mr. Roger Hennagin
P.O. Box 1568
Lake Oswego, OR 97035
Phone: (503) 624-0917
Fax: (503) 636-6745
Also bar member in: No other states
Experience with CSA cases? Yes

Mr. James Huegli
1515 S.W. 5th Ave.
Suite 1021
Portland, OR 97201
Phone: (503) 274-0232
Fax: (503) 274-0236
Also bar member in: No other states
Experience with CSA cases? No

Mr. Mickey Morey
Morey & Otey
Benjamin Franklin Plaza
One SW Columbia, Suite 1475
Portland, OR 97258
Phone: (503) 226-3415
Fax: (503) 226-4976
Also bar member in: Washington
Experience with CSA cases? Yes

Ms. Jill Otey
Morey & Otey
Benjamin Franklin Plaza
One SW Columbia, Suite 1475
Portland, OR 97258
Phone: (503) 226-3415
Fax: (503) 226-4976
Also bar member in: No other states
Experience with CSA cases? Yes

Pennsylvania

Ms. Doris J. Dabrowski
1411 Walnut St., #200
Philadelphia, PA 19102
Phone: (215) 972-8229
Fax: Not listed
Also bar member in: New Jersey
Experience with CSA cases? Yes

Ms. Anne C. Tiracchia
43 North Seventh St.
Stroudsburg, PA 18360
Phone: (717) 424-2550
Fax: (717) 424-5075
Also bar member in: No other states
Experience with CSA cases? No

South Carolina

Mr. Gregg Meyers
Wise & Cole, P.A.
151 Meeting Street
P.O. Drawer O
Charleston, SC 29402
Phone: (803) 727-2200
Fax: (803) 727-2238
Also bar member in: Minnesota
Experience with CSA cases? Yes

Tennessee

Ms. Susan Mackenzie
Ross & Mackenzie
100 North Main-Suite 3310
Memphis, TN 38103
Phone: (901) 525-0417
Fax: Not listed
Also bar member in: No other states
Experience with CSA cases? Yes

Ms. Leslie B. McWilliams
Suite 8304 6400 Bldg
Chattanooga, TN 37411
Phone: (615) 894-0802
Fax: (615) 894-0803
Also bar member in: Florida, Arkansas
Experience with CSA cases? No

Ms. Kelly Stark
McLean & Stark
44 N. Second Street, Suite 600
Memphis, TN 38103
Phone: (901) 521-9996
Fax: (901) 521-9999
Also bar member in: No other states
Experience with CSA cases? Yes

Texas

Ms. Dorothy Flores
Johnson, Curney & Fields
800 Spectrum Building
613 NW Loop 410
San Antonio, TX 78216
Phone: (512) 377-1990
Fax: (512) 377-1065
Also bar member in: District of Columbia
Experience with CSA cases? No

Utah

Mr. Ross C. Anderson
Anderson and Watkins
700 Valley Tower
50 West Broadway
Salt Lake City, UT 84101-2006
Phone: (801) 534-1700
Fax: (801) 364-7697
Also bar member in: No other states
Experience with CSA cases? Yes

Virginia

Ms. Sylvia Clute
Sylvia Clute and Associates
1301 N. Hamilton St., Suite 200
Richmond, VA 23230-3945
Phone: (804) 355-2155
Fax: Not listed
Also bar member in: No other states
Experience with CSA cases? Yes

Ms. Sharon Goley
See District of Columbia

Mr. Keith Rosenberg
See District of Columbia

Washington

Mr. David J. Balint
De Funis & Balint, P.S.
800 United Airlines Building
2033 Sixth Ave.
Seattle, WA 98121-2523
Phone: (206) 728-7799
Fax: Not listed
Also bar member in: No other states
Experience with CSA cases? Yes

Mr. Robert K. Dawson
Pence & Dawson
506 Second Avenue, Suite 300
Seattle, WA 98104
Phone: (206) 624-5000
Fax: (206) 382-1105
Also bar member in: No other states
Experience with CSA cases? Yes

Ms. Yvonne Huggins-McLean
Schroeter, Goldmark & Bender
500 Central Building
810 3rd Ave.
Seattle, WA 98104
Phone: (206) 622-8000
Fax: (206) 682-2305
Also bar member in: WI
Experience with CSA cases? Yes

Ms. Barbara Jo Levy
Sindell and Levy, Inc. PS
614 1st Ave., Suite 300
Seattle, WA 98104
Phone: (206) 622-9050
Fax: (206) 622-1698
Also bar member in: No other states
Experience with CSA cases? Yes

Mr. Mickey Morey
See Oregon

Mr. Mark Panitch
P.O. Box 61841
Vancouver, WA 98666
Phone: (206) 699-2261
Fax: Not listed
Also bar member in: No other states
Experience with CSA cases? Yes

Ms. Roberta Riley
Keller Wohrback
1201 3rd Ave., Suite 3200
Seattle, WA 98101
Phone: (206) 623-1900
Fax: (206) 623-3384
Also bar member in: Washington
Experience with CSA cases? Yes

Ms. Pauline Tesler
See California

Wisconsin

Mr. Jeffrey R. Anderson
See Minnesota

Mr. Lee Atterbury
Atterbury, Riley, Luebke, & Pretto, S.C.
411 W. Main St.
Madison, WI 53703
Phone: (608) 257-4715
Fax: (608) 257-1727
Also bar member in: No other states
Experience with CSA cases? Yes

Ms. Lisa Drill
Doar, Drill and Skow
103 N. Knowles Ave.
Richmond, WI 54017-0069
Phone: (715) 246-2211
Fax: (715) 246-5781
Also bar member in: Minnesota
Experience with CSA cases? Yes

Mr. Robert Pledl
Courtney, Pledl & Molter, S.C.
633 W. Wisconsin Ave., Suite 509
Milwaukee, WI 53203
Phone: (414) 224-6070
Fax: (414) 224-0811
Also bar member in: No other states
Experience with CSA cases? Yes

Appendix C

Statutes and Decisions

***Disclaimer:* These laws are subject to statutory change and court interpretation. The authors are not providing legal advice. Readers should consult competent professionals for analyses of individual cases.**

Statutes of Limitations—Delayed Discovery

At the time of writing, 14 states had legislatively amended their statutes of limitations to grant "delayed discovery"–type periods within which adult survivors of childhood sexual abuse can sue their abusers. These states, citations to and wording of their respective statutes of limitations, and the cases to which the new statutes of limitations apply are listed below.

State Statutory Citation Application	Statutory Language
Alaska Alaska Statutes §§ 09.10.060, 09.10.140, 09.55.650 Applies to all actions commenced on or after February 2, 1990, regardless of when the cause of action may have arisen.	09.10.060(c)—A person who was the victim of sexual abuse may not maintain an action for recovery of damages against the perpetrator of the act or acts of sexual abuse based on the perpetrator's intentional conduct for an injury or condition suffered as a result of the sexual abuse unless commenced within three years. 09.10.140(b)—An action based on a claim of sexual abuse under AS 09.55.650 may be brought more than three years after the plaintiff reaches the age of majority if it is brought under the following circumstances:

Table continued on next page

State Statutory Citation Application	Statutory Language
Alaska (Continued)	(1) if the claim asserts that the defendant committed one act of sexual abuse on the plaintiff, the plaintiff shall commence the action within three years after the plaintiff discovered or through use of reasonable diligence should have discovered that the act caused the injury or condition; (2) if the claim asserts that the defendant committed more than one act of sexual abuse on the plaintiff, the plaintiff shall commence the action within three years after the plaintiff discovered or through use of reasonable diligence should have discovered the effect of the injury or condition attributable to the series of acts; a claim based on an assertion of more than one act of sexual abuse is not limited to plaintiff's first discovery of the relationship between any one of those acts and the injury or condition, but may be based on plaintiff's discovery of the effect of the series of acts. 09.55.650(a)—A person who, as a minor under 16 years of age, was the victim of sexual abuse may maintain an action for recovery of damages against the perpetrator of the act or acts of sexual abuse based on the perpetrator's intentional conduct for an injury or condition suffered as a result of the sexual abuse. (b) If the defendant committed more than one act of sexual abuse on the plaintiff, the plaintiff is not required to prove which specific act caused the injury.

Table continued on next page

State Statutory Citation Application	Statutory Language
California^ California [Civil Procedure] Code § 340.1 Applies to any action commenced on or after January 1, 1991	340.1(a)—In any civil action for recovery of damages suffered as a result of childhood sexual abuse, the time for commencement of the action shall be within eight years of the date the plaintiff attains the age of majority or within three years of the date the plaintiff discovers or reasonably should have discovered that psychological injury or illness occurring after the age of majority was caused by the sexual abuse, whichever occurs later.
Illinois* Illinois Annotated Statutes, Code of Civil Procedure § 13-202.2 Effective January 1, 1991. Applies to actions pending on the effective date, as well as to actions commenced on or after that date.	§ 13-202.2. (a) In this Section: "Childhood sexual abuse" means an act of sexual abuse that occurs when the person abused is under 18 years of age. "Sexual abuse" includes but is not limited to sexual conduct and sexual penetration as defined in Section 12-12 of the Criminal Code of 1961. (b) An action for damages for personal injury based on childhood sexual abuse must be commenced within 2 years of the date the person abused discovers or through the use of reasonable diligence should discover that the act of childhood sexual abuse occurred and that the injury was caused by the childhood sexual abuse, but in no event may an action for personal injury based on childhood sexual abuse be commenced more than 12 years after the date on which the person abused attains the age of 18 years.

Table continued on next page

^ California also requires any survivor 26 years old or older to file a "certificate of merit," which is a statement by the survivor's attorney and therapist that they are familiar with the case, and based on their knowledge of the facts, there is a reasonable basis to believe that the survivor had been subjected to childhood sexual abuse, thus giving reasonable and meritorious cause to file the suit. *See* Cal. Code of Civ. Proc., § 340.1 (d)–(j) (1991).

* Note that this statute also includes an ultimate time limit on when suits can be filed—a *statute of ultimate repose*—in its language.

State Statutory Citation Application	Statutory Language
Illinois (Continued)	(c) If the injury is caused by 2 or more acts of childhood sexual abuse that are part of a continuing series of acts of childhood sexual abuse by the same abuser, then the discovery period under subsection (b) shall be computed from the date the person abused discovers or through the use of reasonable diligence should discover (i) that the last act of childhood sexual abuse in the continuing series occurred and (ii) that the injury was caused by any act of childhood sexual abuse in the continuing series. (d) The limitation periods under subsection (b) do not begin to run before the person abused attains the age of 18 years; and, if at the time theperson abused attains the age of 18 years he or she is under other legal disability, the limitation periods under subsection (b) do not begin to run until the removal of the disability.
Iowa Iowa Code Annotated § 614.8A Applies to all actions filed on or after the effective date of the Act (1990).	§ 614.8A—An action for damages for injury suffered as a result of sexual abuse which occurred when the injured person was a child, but not discovered until after the injured person is of the age of majority, shall be brought within four years from the time of discovery by the injured party of both the injury and the causal relationship between the injury and the sexual abuse.
Maine Maine Revised Statutes Annotated tit. 14 § 752-C	752-C—Actions based upon sexual intercourse or a sexual act, as defined in Title 17-A, chapter 11, with a person under the age of majority shall be commenced within 6 years after the cause of action accrues, or within 3 years of the time the person discovers or reasonably should have discovered the harm, whichever occurs later.

Table continued on next page

State Statutory Citation Application	Statutory Language
Minnesota Minnesota Statutes Annotated § 541.073 Applies to actions pending on or commenced after May 20, 1989. (Amendments that allow actions based on both intentional torts and negligent torts to be brought "within 6 years" [in Subdivision 2.] were signed into law on May 29, 1991. Previously, actions based on negligence had to be brought "within two years.")	Subdivision 1. Definition. As used in this section, "sexual abuse" means conduct described in sections 609.342 to 609.345. Subdivision 2. Limitations Period. (a) An action for damages based on personal injury caused by sexual abuse must be commenced within six years of the time the plaintiff knew or had reason to know that the injury was caused by the sexual abuse. (b) The plaintiff need not establish which act in a continuous series of sexual abuse acts by the defendant caused the injury. (c) The knowledge of a parent or guardian may not be imputed to a minor. (c) This section does not affect the suspension of the statute of limitations during a period of disability under section 541.15. Subdivision 3. Applicability. This section applies to an action for damages commenced against a person who caused the plaintiff's personal injury either by (1) committing sexual abuse against the plaintiff, or (2) negligently permitting sexual abuse against the plaintiff to occur.

Table continued on next page

State Statutory Citation Application	Statutory Language
Missouri Missouri Statutes Annotated § 537.046 Applies to any action commenced on or after August 28, 1990, including any actions barred by earlier applicable limitations periods.	537.046.2.—In any civil action for recovery of damages suffered as a result of childhood sexual abuse, the time for commencement of the action shall be within five years of the date the plaintiff attains the age of eighteen or within three years of the date the plaintiff discovers or reasonably should have discovered that the injury or illness was caused by child sexual abuse, whichever later occurs.
Montana Montana Code Annotated § 27-2-216 Applies to all causes of action commenced on or after October 1, 1989, regardless of when the cause of action arose.	27-2-216—(1) An action based on intentional conduct brought by a person for recovery of damages for injury suffered as a result of childhood sexual abuse must be commenced not later than: (a) 3 years after the act of childhood sexual abuse that is alleged to have caused the injury; or (b) 3 years after the plaintiff discovers or reasonably should have discovered that the injury was caused by the act of childhood sexual abuse. (2) It is not necessary for a plaintiff to establish which act, in a series of acts of childhood sexual abuse, caused the injury that is the subject of the suit. The plaintiff may compute the period referred to in subsection (1)(a) from the date of the last act by the same perpetrator. (3) As used in this section, "childhood sexual abuse" means any act committed against a plaintiff who was less than 18 years of age at the time the act occurred and that would have been a violation of 45-5-502, 45-5-503, 45-5-504, 45-5-505, 45-5-507, 45-5-625, or prior similar laws in effect at the time the act occurred.

Table continued on next page

State Statutory Citation Application	Statutory Language
Nevada Revised Statutes Annotated § 11.215 Applies to all actions filed on or after, pending on, or barred by limitations periods applicable before, October 1, 1991.	1. An action to recover damages for an injury to a person arising from the sexual abuse of the plaintiff which occurred when the plaintiff was less than 18 years of age must be commenced within 3 years after the plaintiff: (a) reaches 18 years of age; or (b) discovers or reasonably should have discovered that his injury was caused by the sexual abuse, whichever occurs later. 2. As used in this section, "sexual abuse" has the meaning ascribed to it in NRS 432B.100.
Oregon* Oregon Revised Statutes § 12.117 Applies to all actions commenced on or after October 3, 1989, including any action that would have been barred by application of any period of lmitations prior to October 3, 1989.	12.117(1)—Notwithstanding ORS 12.110, 12.115 or 12.160, an action based on conduct that constitutes child abuse or conduct knowingly allowing, permitting or encouraging child abuse accruing while the person who is entitled to bring the action is within 18 years of age shall be commenced not more than six years after that person attains 18 years of age, or if the injured person has not discovered the injury or the causal connection between the injury and the child abuse, nor in the exercise of reasonable care should have discovered the injury or the causal connection between the injury and the child abuse, not more than three years from the date the injured person discovers or in the exercise of reasonable care should have discovered the injury or the causal connection between the child abuse and the injury, whichever period is longer. However, in no event may an action based on conduct that constitutes child abuse or conduct knowingly allowing, permitting or encouraging child abuse accruing while the person who is entitled to bring the action is within 18 years of age be commenced after that person attains 40 years of age.

Table continued on next page

* Note that this statute also includes an ultimate time limit on when suits can be filed—a *statute of ultimate repose*—in its language.

State Statutory Citation Application	Statutory Language
South Dakota South Dakota Codified Laws §§ 26-10-25, 26-10-26, 26-10-27, 26-10-28, 26-10-29	26-10-25. Any civil action based on intentional conduct brought by any person for recovery of damages for injury suffered as a result of childhood sexual abuse shall be commenced within three years of the act alleged to have caused the injury or condition, or three years of the time the victim discovered or reasonably should have discovered that the injury or condition was caused by the act, whichever period expires later. 26-10-26. The victim need not establish which act in a series of continuing sexual abuse or exploitation incidents caused the injury complained of, but may compute the date of discovery from the date of discovery of the last act by the same perpetrator which is part of a common course of conduct of sexual abuse or exploitation. 26-10-27. The knowledge of a custodial parent or guardian may not be imputed to a person under the age of eighteen years for the purposes of §§ 26-10-25 to 26-10-29, inclusive. 26-10-28. For the purposes of §§ 26-10-25 to 26-10-29, inclusive, a child is any person under the age of eighteen years. 26-10-29. As used in §§ 26-10-25 to 26-10-29, inclusive, childhood sexual abuse is any act committed by the defendant against the complainant who was less than eighteen years of age at the time of the act and which act would have been a violation of chapter 22-22 or prior laws of similar effect at the time the act was committed which act would have constituted a felony.

Table continued on next page

State Statutory Citation Application	Statutory Language
Vermont Vermont Statutes Annotated Title 12 §§522, 560 § 522(a) applies to all causes of action commenced on or after July 1, 1990, as long as either the act of sexual abuse or the discovery that the injury or condition was caused by the act of sexual abuse occurred on or after July 1, 1984. § 560 applies to all causes of action commenced on or after July 1, 1990.	522(a)—A civil action brought by any person for recovery of damages for injury suffered as a result of childhood sexual abuse shall be commenced within six years of the act alleged to have caused the injury or condition, or six years of the time the victim discovered that the injury or condition was caused by that act, whichever period expires later. The victim need not establish which act in a series of continuing sexual abuse or exploitation incidents caused the injury. 522(c)—As used in this section, "childhood sexual abuse" means any act committed by the defendant against a complainant who was less than 18 years of age at the time of the act and which act would have constituted a violation of a statute prohibiting lewd and lascivious conduct, lewd or lascivious conduct with a child, sexual assault or aggravated sexual assault in effect at the time the act was committed. 560—When a person entitled to bring an action for damages as a result of childhood sexual abuse is unable to commence the action as a direct result of the damages caused by the sexual abuse, the period during which the person is incapacitated shall not be taken as a part of the time limited for commencement of the action.

Table continued on next page

State Statutory Citation Application	Statutory Language
Virginia* Code of Virginia Annotated § 8.01-249 Applies to all actions filed on or after July 1, 1991, without regard to when the act upon which the claim is based occurred, provided that no such claim which accrued prior to July 1, 1991, shall be barred by application of those provisions if it is filed within one year of the effective date of the act.	6. In actions for injury to the person, whatever the theory of recovery, resulting from sexual abuse occurring during the infancy or incompetency of the person, when the fact of the injury and its causal connection to the sexual abuse is first communicated to the person by a licensed physician, psychologist, or clinical psychologist. However, no such action may be brought more than ten years after the later of (i) the last act by the same perpetrator which was part of a common scheme or plan of abuse or (ii) removal of the disability of infancy or incompetency. As used in this subdivision, "sexual abuse" means sexual abuse as defined in subdivision 6 of § 18.2-67.10 and acts constituting rape, sodomy, inanimate object sexual penetration or sexual battery as defined in Article 7 (§ 18.2-61 et seq.) of Chapter 4 of Title 18.2.

Table continued on next page

* Note that this statute also includes an ultimate time limit on when suits can be filed—a *statute of ultimate repose*—in its language.

State Statutory Citation Application	Statutory Language
Washington Washington Revised Code Annotated § 4.16.340 Applies to all causes of action commenced on or after May 11, 1989, regardless of when the cause of action may have arisen.	4.16.340—(1) All claims or causes of action based on intentional conduct brought by any person for recovery of damages for injury suffered as a result of childhood sexual abuse shall be commenced within three years of the act alleged to have caused the injury or condition, or three years of the time the victim discovered or reasonably should have discovered that the injury or condition was caused by said act, whichever period expires later: Provided, That the time limit for commencement of an action under this section is tolled for a child until the child reaches the age of eighteen years. (2) The victim need not establish which act in a series of continuing sexual abuse or exploitation incidents caused the injury complained of, but may compute the date of discovery from the date of discovery of the last act by the same perpetrator which is part of a common scheme or plan of sexual abuse or exploitation.

Statutes of Limitations—Minority Plus Period of Years

Three states have legislatively revised the traditional statutes of limitations by adding a period of years to the end of childhood within which a survivor can sue. These states, citations to their applicable statutes, the cases to which the new statutes of limitations apply, and the statutory language, are as follows.

State Statutory Citation Application	Statutory Language
Colorado Colorado Revised Statutes §§ 13-80-103.7, 13-81-101 (3) Applies to all actions for which the applicable statute of limitations in effect prior to July 1, 1990, has not run on July 1, 1990.	13-80-103.7—(1) Notwithstanding any other statute of limitations specified in this article, or any other provision of law that can be construed to reduce the statutory period set forth in this section, any civil action based on a sexual assault or a sexual offense against a child shall be commenced within six years after a disability has been removed for a person under disability, as such term is defined in section 13-81-101 (3), or within six years after a cause of action accrues, whichever occurs later, and not thereafter. 13-81-101 (3)—"Person under disability" means any person who is a minor under eighteen years of age, a mental incompetent, or a person under other legal disability and who does not have a legal guardian.
Connecticut Connecticut General Statutes Annotated § 52-577d. Effective June 9, 1986.	52-577d.—Notwithstanding the provisions of section 52-577, no action to recover damages for personal injury to a minor, including emotional distress, caused by sexual abuse, sexual exploitation or sexual assault may be brought by such person later than two years from the date such person attains the age of majority, except that no such action may be brought more than seven years from the date of the act complained of.
Idaho Idaho Code § 6-1704 Applies to causes of action that accrued on or after July 1, 1989.	6-1704—Notwithstanding any limitation contained in chapter 2, title 5, Idaho Code, an action under the provisions of this chapter must be commenced within five (5) years from the date that an aggrieved child reaches the age of eighteen (18) years.

Statutes of Limitations—Cases—Extension Granted

Six other states have revised the traditional statutes of limitations through court decision. These states, the cases that revised the old rules, and short descriptions of the rulings are as follows.

State Case Citation	Case Ruling
Massachusetts	
Unnamed Plaintiff v. Unnamed Defendant, Suffolk County Superior Court, number confidential, June 21, 1988. Reported in 31 ATLA L. Rep. 389 (Nov. 1988)	in father-daughter incest case, holding that discovery rule applies in incestuous abuse case
Michigan	
Meiers-Post v. Schafer, 170 Mich. App. 174, 427 N.W. 2d 606 (1988)	in teacher molestation case, holding that the statute of limitations is tolled under the insanity clause if the plaintiff repressed the memories and if the plaintiff's testimony is corroborated
Nicolette v. Carey, 751 F.Supp. 695 (D.C.W.D. Mich. 1990)	in father-daughter incest case, holding that the statute of limitations is tolled under the insanity clause if the plaintiff repressed the memories

Table continued on next page

State Case Citation	Case Ruling
New Hampshire	
McLean v. Gaudet, 1990 U.S.Dist. LEXIS 19054 (October 25, 1990)	in father-daughter incest case, holding that New Hampshire's general delayed discovery rule applied to incest cases
New Jersey	
Jones v. Jones, 242 N.J. Super. 195, 576 A.2d 316, cert. denied, 122 N.J. 418, 585 A.2d 413 (1990)	in sexual abuse case, holding that mental trauma resulting from a pattern of incestuous abuse may constitute insanity and toll the statute of limitations
North Dakota	
Osland v. Osland, 442 N.W.2d 907 (N.D. 1989)	in father-daughter incest case, holding that statute of limitations tolled until plaintiff knows, or with reasonable diligence should know, that a potential claim exists
Wisconsin	
Hammer v. Hammer, 142 Wis. 2d 257, 418 N.W.2d 23 (1987), reh'g denied, 144 Wis. 2d 953, 428 N.W.2d 552 (1988)	in father-daughter incest case, holding that accrual of cause of action for incestuous abuse does not begin until the plaintiff discovers, or in the exercise of reasonable diligence should have discovered, the fact and cause of the injury

Statutes of Limitations—Cases—Extension Denied

Courts in five other states have ruled against extending the statute of limitations in childhood sexual abuse cases.

State Case Citation	Case Ruling
Florida	
Lindabury v. Lindabury, 552 So. 2d 1117 (Fla. App. 1989), cause dismd 560 So.2d 233 (1990)	in father-daughter incest case, holding that statute of limitations had expired under strict mechanical application of statute of limitations with no discussion of tolling (strong dissent discusses post-traumatic stress disorder, repression of memories, and tolling of statute of limitations)
Indiana	
Hildebrand v. Hildebrand, 736 F.Suppl. 1512 (S.D. Ind. 1990)	in father-daughter incest case, holding that discovery rule was not applicable in suit for intentional infliction of emotional distress caused by physical and sexual abuse or for negligent failure to exercise reasonable care
New York	
Smith v. Smith, 830 F.2d 11 (2d Cir. 1987)	applying New York law in father-daughter incest case, holding that statute of limitations was not tolled based on insanity, though medical and psychological experts indicated that incestuous abuse was repressed through post-traumatic disorder and plaintiff was disabled from instituting litigation which might stimulate a traumatic recall of the childhood events

Table continued on next page

State Case Citation	Case Ruling
Pennsylvania	
Baily v. Lewis, 763 F.Supp. 802 (D.C.E.D. Pa. 1991)	applying Pennsylvania law in adult-friend sexual abuse case, holding that the statute of limitations for sexual abuse of a minor was not tolled during the period of repression of memories or tolled through the perpetrator's fradulent concealment of the abuse
Utah	
Whatcott v. Whatcott, 790 P.2d 578 (Utah App. 1990).	applying Utah law in father-son incest case, holding that the son's psychological blocking mechanisms of denial, dissociation, repression, and feelings of guilt did not constitute mental incompetence to toll the statute of limitations

Index

Defined terms are indicated by a bold number. Figures are indicated by an italicized number.

A

Responses

If you are a survivor, a survivor's attorney, or a survivor's therapist, are otherwise supportive of a survivor who has sued his or her perpetrator, or have information about child sexual abuse cases that may be helpful to others in future editions of this book, and would like to share your story, tips, information, or other comments about this book, your case, others' cases, or the legal process in general, we'd be honored to have you write to us at:

Kim and Joe Crnich

If you wo … this book, please ind … s or phone number a…

Order…

…ing from:

…nd send in …leted)

Name:

Company

Address:

City:

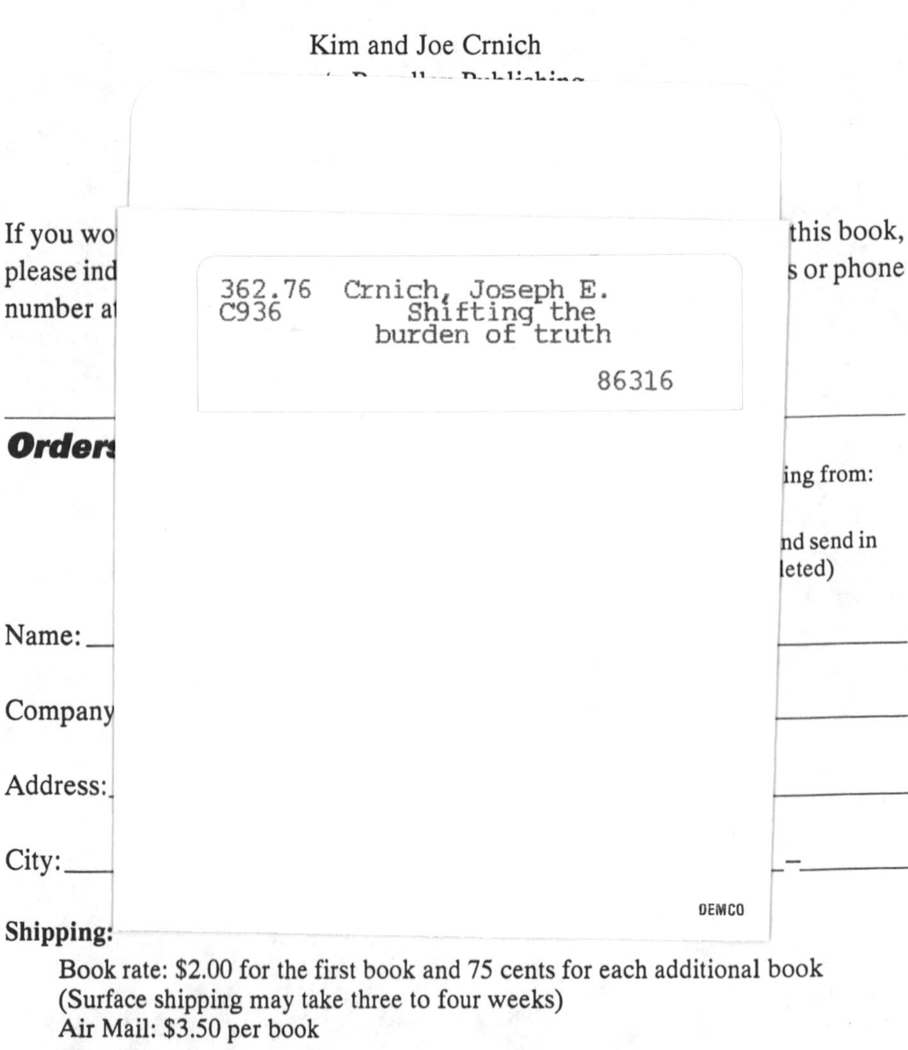

Shipping:

Book rate: $2.00 for the first book and 75 cents for each additional book
(Surface shipping may take three to four weeks)
Air Mail: $3.50 per book

Payment: ☐ Check ☐ Money Order